The Light of Faith

How Pope Francis' Teachings Guide Us
Through Modern Life

Daryl Lim

ABSOLUTE AUTHOR PUBLISHING HOUSE

Publisher: Absolute Author Publishing House
Editor: Dr. Melissa Caudle

Scripture References: Unless otherwise noted, all biblical quotations are taken from the New American Bible, NIV, or CCC. Used with permission.

Hardback ISBN: 979-8-89401-069-4
Paperback ISBN: 979-8-89401-070-0

ABOUT THE BOOK

In a world filled with uncertainty, division, and personal struggles, many seek deeper meaning and direction. Inspired by Pope Francis's profound and compassionate teachings, this book presents a unique perspective on his homilies—not through an academic or theological lens but through the eyes of a layperson striving to live out the Gospel in everyday life.

This book is not just an analysis of Pope Francis' words; it is a journey. Through themes of forgiveness, regret, humility, faith, family, and service, it explores how the Pope's messages can illuminate the struggles, hopes, and joys of modern life. Each chapter delves into a core human experience, reflecting on how Pope Francis' wisdom can guide us through challenges such as anxiety, betrayal, ambition, and the search for meaning.

From the idols of success to the power of humility, from the wounds of betrayal to the freedom found in forgiveness, each chapter provides deep reflection, practical application, and a call to action. Through engaging examples, relatable insights, and thought-provoking questions, readers are invited to take these teachings beyond the pages—to reflect, grow, and transform their lives.

At its heart, this book is about rediscovering the simple yet radical truth of the Gospel: God is present in our littleness, our struggles, and our everyday encounters. Pope Francis calls us to open our hearts, embrace faith with courage, and choose love over fear.

Whether you are a lifelong Catholic, a seeker of faith, or someone longing for spiritual renewal, this book offers a compelling guide to living with purpose, compassion, and trust in God's plan. The journey doesn't end with understanding—it begins with transformation.

Are you ready to walk this path of faith, hope, and renewal?

Table of Contents

Introduction

Pope Francis' Homilies Through the Eyes of the Everyday Catholic

Every Sunday, in churches around the world, Catholics gather to celebrate the Mass—the central act of worship in our faith. At the heart of this sacred liturgy is the homily, a moment of deep reflection in which the priest, guided by the Holy Spirit, interprets the Word of God and applies it to the lives of the faithful.

It is a time of clarity and instruction, a moment in which Scripture is broken open—not merely as a historical or theological text but as a living message that speaks directly to the challenges, joys, and struggles of modern life.

For Catholics, the homily is not just another part of the Mass—it is its climax, the moment when God's voice is made present through the words of His minister. And when that minister is the pope himself—the Vicar of

Christ, entrusted with shepherding the universal Church—his words take on even greater significance. Pope Francis, known for his pastoral heart, deep humility, and ability to speak to the realities of everyday life, has delivered some of the most powerful and thought-provoking homilies of our time. His words cut through complexity, reaching the essence of faith—how we live, how we love, how we serve, and how we remain close to God in an ever-changing world.

Yet despite their power, Pope Francis's homilies are often understudied, underappreciated, or buried beneath layers of theological analysis that can feel distant from ordinary Catholics' lived experiences.

While scholarly commentaries have value, they tend to emphasize doctrinal precision, historical context, and deep theological constructs—elements that, while important, may not always resonate with the daily struggles of the average believer.

This book seeks to offer something different—a way for everyday Catholics to engage with the pope's homilies in a manner that speaks directly to their lives, concerns, and faith journeys. It is not a theological textbook, nor is it an academic analysis of papal teaching. Instead, it is a conversation—one that weaves together the voices of ordained clergy and the perspective of a lay Catholic, seeking to illuminate the pope's words and their relevance in today's world.

Why the Importance of a Lay Perspective on the Book's Structure

Scholars, theologians, or clergy author most books analyzing papal homilies—those deeply immersed in the intellectual and doctrinal traditions of the Church. While their insights are invaluable, they often presume a level of theological knowledge that not all Catholics possess. Many ordinary believers, though deeply faithful, may find such analyses dense, inaccessible, or removed from their lived experience.

This book seeks to bridge that gap. It is structured to blend theological expertise with lay interpretation, uniting the voices of ordained priests with my reflections as a lay Catholic. This structure is intentional, providing both an informed understanding of the homily and a practical application that resonates with the daily lives of ordinary Catholics.

By including theological insights from clergy, this book ensures that each homily is understood within the broader tradition of the Church. These insights offer historical background, biblical context, and doctrinal clarifications, helping readers grasp the depth of the pope's words while remaining faithful to Church teaching. However, theology alone is not enough. The spiritual life is not merely an intellectual pursuit—it must be lived, experienced, and wrestled with in the messiness of daily existence. This is where the lay perspective becomes essential.

As a layperson, I approach homilies from the perspective of someone living in the world—outside the priesthood or religious life—while navigating the challenges of work, family, relationships, and faith in a secular culture. My reflections explore what the pope's words mean for those not formally trained in theology yet deeply committed to growing in faith. What does homily mean for a working professional striving to balance career ambitions with spiritual commitments? How does it speak to a parent raising children in a world where faith is increasingly challenged? What hope does it offer to those grappling with doubt, uncertainty, or spiritual dryness? These are the kinds of questions that theological texts do not always address but that every believer encounters at some point in their journey.

The final section of each chapter, dedicated to lessons and reflection questions, is written entirely from a lay perspective. It distills the insights of the homily into practical lessons that can be applied to daily life. These sections are designed to challenge, inspire, and encourage deeper personal reflection. Rather than presenting abstract theological concepts, these sections invite readers to reflect on their own experiences and consider how the pope's words can shape their actions, attitudes, and spiritual growth.

Why Focus on the Homily?

Homily is not just another speech. It is more than a moral lesson or an academic exegesis of Scripture—it is a moment in which God speaks to His people through the Church. In Catholic theology, the homily is understood as a continuation of Christ's teaching ministry, a direct encounter with the Word of God as it applies to our present-day struggles.

Pope Francis has repeatedly emphasized the importance of the homily, stating that it should be brief, avoid abstraction, and instead touch the heart—moving people to live out their faith. His homilies are accessible, practical, and deeply rooted in the everyday challenges people face, making them a rich source of wisdom for those seeking spiritual guidance.

Many Catholics hear these homilies during papal Masses or through Church news, but they are often overlooked or not deeply reflected upon. Yet, if we truly believe that God speaks through His ministers, then the pope's words in his homilies are worth listening to, contemplating, and applying to our lives.

This book exists to help Catholics do just that—to slow down, reflect, and engage with the Pope's words in a way that feels both relevant and personal.

What Makes This Book Different?

While many books analyze papal teaching, few focus specifically on homilies—and even fewer present them through both clerical and lay perspectives. The uniqueness of this book lies in its approach, balancing theological insight with practical, real-world application.

This book is grounded in lived experience rather than abstract theological analysis. It brings Pope Francis' words into the real, everyday concerns of Catholics—marriage, work, suffering, hope, relationships, faith struggles, and personal growth. It ensures that readers not only gain a deeper understanding of each homily's meaning but also find a relatable, down-to-earth application from someone outside the world of clergy and academia.

It also emphasizes personal engagement, as the reflection questions and lessons are designed not just to inform but to transform—to challenge, inspire, and nurture spiritual growth. This book highlights the homily as the heart of Catholic worship, recognizing that while many Catholic books focus on doctrine, catechesis, or papal encyclicals, the homily is a living, breathing expression of faith that deserves deeper reflection.

An Invitation to Listen, Reflect, and Grow

Suppose we, as Catholics, truly believe that God speaks through the Church. In that case, if we believe that the Holy Spirit moves through His ministers, especially in the homilies of the pope, the Vicar of Christ on earth—then we must also believe that these words are meant to be heard, understood, and lived.

This book is an invitation—an invitation to listen more closely to God's voice in Pope Francis' homilies, to reflect not just with the mind but with the heart, and to live out these teachings in ways that make a real difference in daily life.

By exploring these homilies through both theological insight and lay reflection, we open the door to deeper engagement—not just with the words of Pope Francis but with the voice of God speaking through him. May this book serve as a guide for those seeking a clearer, more personal way to understand the Church's teachings. May it inspire all who read it to live their faith with greater clarity, conviction, and love.

Chapter 1

Faith in the Storm: Trusting God in Life's Difficult Moments

Saint Peter's Square - Sunday, 20 June 2021

The Homily

Pope Francis' homily on the calming of the storm in Mark's Gospel (*Mk 4:35-41*) offers a profound reflection on faith, fear, and God's presence in life's most challenging moments. He presents the scene of Jesus and His disciples in the boat as a metaphor for the human experience—where peaceful waters can suddenly turn into violent storms, leaving us feeling powerless and uncertain. The disciples' terror as waves crash against their boat mirrors the emotions people experience in times of crisis—fear, doubt, and a sense of abandonment. Their desperate plea, "Teacher, do you not care if we perish?" has echoed throughout history and continues to be voiced by those enduring suffering, loss, and hardship.

The Pope highlights how Jesus, though present in the boat, is asleep—a profoundly symbolic image. In times of trial, many believers feel as though God is distant or unresponsive, questioning why He remains silent amid their struggles. Pope Francis, however, urges his listeners to see Jesus' silence not as neglect but as an invitation to deeper faith. Faith is not merely believing in God's existence; it is engaging with Him, calling out to Him, and placing Him at the center of life's struggles. Pope Francis explains that God permits moments of uncertainty not to abandon His people but to awaken them—to draw them closer and encourage them to trust beyond what they can immediately see.

A central theme of the homily is the power of crying out to God. Pope Francis emphasizes that prayer is not always composed or formal—sometimes, it is a desperate plea for help. Just as the disciples urgently called out to Jesus in their fear, believers today should never hesitate to cry out to God in their struggles. Pope Francis draws a parallel between the disciples' cry for help and the desperate pleas of refugees and those who suffer injustice—reminding us that God hears the raw, urgent prayers of the afflicted. He explains that faith begins when we acknowledge our dependence on Him, recognizing that we cannot navigate the storms of life alone.

The turning point in the Gospel passage comes when Jesus, awakened by the disciples' plea, calms the storm with a word. Then, He turns to them and asks, "Why are you afraid? Have you no faith?" Pope Francis explains that this question is not just for the disciples—it is for all of us. Fear is a natural response to uncertainty, but when it takes control, it blinds us to God's presence. The disciples focused more on the storm than on the fact that Jesus was with them. Pope Francis explains that this is what often happens in life—we become so consumed by our anxieties, worries, and struggles that we lose sight of God's nearness.

Faith does not remove life's difficulties, but it transforms how we endure them. Pope Francis challenges us to reflect on our focus: do we fixate on our problems, or do we turn our gaze to Christ? Do they let fear dictate their actions, or do they turn to God for strength? Many keep Jesus at a distance, calling on Him only when all else fails. Yet, true faith is not a last resort—it is a daily reliance on God, a constant turning to Him in every moment, not just in times of crisis.

Pope Francis then presents Mary as the ultimate model of trust in God. Throughout her life, she faced uncertainty and suffering—moments that could have led to fear. From the Annunciation to the crucifixion of her Son, she had every reason to be overwhelmed. Yet, her faith never wavered, and she did not demand explanations from God but surrendered to His will, trusting that He was always in control. Her example reminds us that true faith is not about understanding every step but about trusting—even when the path is unclear.

As he concludes, Pope Francis extends an invitation to all believers to move from fear to faith, from uncertainty to trust, from panic to peace. Life's storms are inevitable, but Jesus is always in the boat. His presence does not promise the absence of trials, but it assures us that we never face them alone. The Pope urges his listeners to turn their gaze from their problems to Christ's presence, to cry out in prayer with trust, and to surrender themselves fully to God's care.

The message is clear: fear may arise, but faith has the power to overcome it. Jesus' question to the disciples, 'Why are you afraid?' is the same question He asks every believer today. They serve as a call to trust in God, even when He seems silent, and to recognize that no storm—no matter how fierce—can separate us from His love. Faith does not calm the waves, but it assures us that we are never alone in the storm.

Homily Analysis: Faith in the Midst of Fear

The Storm as a Metaphor for Life's Struggles

Pope Francis' homily on Jesus calming the storm offers a profound and relatable reflection on the struggles of human life. The storm described in the Gospel of Mark is not merely a historical event but a powerful symbol of the chaos, suffering, and uncertainty that people encounter in their own lives. The image of the disciples in a boat, battered by violent waves and gripped by fear for their lives, mirrors the emotions that arise when people feel overwhelmed by circumstances beyond their control.

The Pope expands this metaphor beyond physical storms, applying it to a wide range of personal crises— loss of love, shattered dreams, anxiety, illness, financial hardship, and emotional exhaustion. He captures the universal human experience of questioning God's presence in times of suffering, emphasizing how hardship often leads people to cry out, "Why do You remain silent and do nothing for me?" This honest acknowledgment of despair makes the homily especially relevant to modern listeners, as it not only validates their struggles but also offers a deeper spiritual perspective on how to endure them.

By framing the storm as a reflection of human challenges, Pope Francis invites his listeners to see their struggles mirrored in the Gospel. His message is clear: storms are inevitable, but how we respond to them determines whether we grow in faith or succumb to fear.

The Paradox of Jesus' Silence: A Test of Faith

One of the most striking themes in the homily is the paradox of Jesus' presence and His apparent inaction. In the Gospel account, Jesus is physically in the boat with His disciples, yet He remains asleep even as the storm grows more violent. This situation is both puzzling and deeply unsettling. The Pope emphasizes how this moment challenges the disciples—and, by extension, all believers—to reflect on how they react when they perceive God as silent or distant.

The natural human tendency is to assume that silence signifies absence. When faced with suffering, doubt, or hardship, many believers feel abandoned, as though God is uninterested or uninvolved in their pain. Why does God seem inactive when we need Him most? This is the very question the disciples ask in their fear: "Teacher, do You not care if we perish?"

Pope Francis suggests that Jesus' silence is not neglect but an invitation. He explains that moments of divine silence are tests of faith—opportunities to deepen one's trust in God rather than relying solely on human strength. Faith, he emphasizes, is not merely a belief in God's existence but an active seeking of Him—crying out to Him and allowing Him to take control.

The disciples' mistake was not their fear but their failure to recognize that Jesus was with them all along. This powerful insight shifts the focus from external struggles (the storm) to an internal transformation—from faith over fear. The Pope encourages believers to view Jesus' apparent inaction as an opportunity to grow in trust rather than as a reason to doubt His presence.

Furthermore, Pope Francis challenges the misconception that faith eliminates difficulties. Instead, he presents faith as a means of enduring hardship with trust in God's presence. The storm was real, and the waves were threatening, yet Jesus remained with the disciples. His silence was not a sign of abandonment but a call for them to awaken to faith rather than relying on their fears.

The Power of Crying Out to God: The Role of Prayer

A crucial element in the homily is Pope Francis' emphasis on crying out to God. He makes it clear that prayer is not always meant to be quiet or composed— sometimes, it is a desperate plea for help. The disciples did not approach Jesus calmly; they woke Him urgently, crying out for salvation.

The Pope draws a powerful parallel between the disciples' cries and the cries of refugees, the poor, and those suffering from injustice. He reminds listeners that the world is full of people who are metaphorically—and literally—drowning—those who have lost everything, who live in fear, and who call out for help. This connection broadens the homily's message, showing that suffering is not just a personal experience but a shared reality across humanity.

By encouraging believers to cry out to God, Pope Francis dismantles the notion that prayer must always be controlled or structured. Many hesitate to pray in moments of deep distress, feeling they must maintain composure. However, the Pope challenges this idea, affirming that God welcomes honest, desperate, and unfiltered prayers.

The call to cry out also challenges a passive approach to faith. Many treat prayer as a last resort, turning to God only when all else has failed. Pope Francis urges believers to reverse this mindset—faith should be an active, daily dependence on God, not merely an emergency response. Crying out to God should not be a sign of weakness but a declaration of trust—a recognition that He alone can provide true peace.

Fear vs. Faith: The Central Conflict

Jesus' response to the disciples—"Why are you afraid? Have you no faith?" forms the central conflict of the homily. Pope Francis explains that fear itself is not the problem; rather, the issue arises when fear takes control and overshadows faith.

The disciples' fear is understandable; the storm is real, and they are at risk of drowning. However, their mistake was allowing fear to consume them to the point that they forgot who was in the boat with them. The Pope presents this as a universal human struggle: people often focus more on their problems than on God's power.

Many today are overwhelmed by fear of failure, fear of suffering, fear of the unknown. These fears grow when people try to control everything themselves rather than placing their trust in God. The Pope warns against allowing fear to dictate one's emotions, decisions, and faith. Instead, he encourages believers to shift their focus—away from the storm and toward Jesus.

This message is especially relevant in today's world, where anxiety, uncertainty, and instability dominate many lives. Economic struggles, health concerns, and global crises make the future seem daunting. The Pope's homily reminds us that faith does not remove difficulties but transforms how we face them. Fear diminishes as faith grows, and faith grows when one keeps one's eyes on Christ rather than the storm.

Mary as the Model of Trust in God

As he concludes, Pope Francis presents Mary as the ultimate model of faith and trust. Throughout her life, she faced many storms—from the uncertainty of the Annunciation to the suffering of witnessing her Son's crucifixion. Yet she never wavered in her trust in God. She did not demand explanations or try to take control; she surrendered completely to His will.

Mary's faith was not about understanding everything but trusting in God's goodness even in darkness. This is the same faith that Jesus called His disciples to embrace. Her example serves as a challenge for all believers—to trust even when the path is unclear, to surrender fear, and to believe that God is always working, even when He seems silent.

Daryl Lim

An Invitation to Deeper Faith

Pope Francis' homily is ultimately a call to deeper, more active faith. The storms of life are inevitable, but Jesus is always in the boat. His presence does not mean there will be no hardships, but it does mean that believers do not have to face them alone.

The Pope challenges his listeners to examine their fears and ask whether those fears have replaced their faith. His message is clear: faith and fear cannot both dominate the heart at the same time. One must give way to the other.

By urging believers to cry out to God, trust in His presence, and shift their focus from their fears to Christ, Pope Francis offers a path to true peace. His final reminder is that no storm—no matter how powerful—can separate us from God's love. Faith does not eliminate the waves, but it ensures that we never face them alone.

Jesus' words to the disciples—"Why are you afraid?"—are a personal question for every believer today. They serve as an invitation to let go of fear, embrace trust, and find rest in the unwavering presence of God. No matter how fierce the storm, Christ remains in the boat—and that is enough.

Finding Peace in Life's Storms: Lessons in Overcoming Fear, Anxiety, and Uncertainty

Life is filled with unexpected challenges—crises, overwhelming responsibilities, and moments of doubt that leave people feeling lost. Whether facing financial struggles, illness, broken relationships, or global uncertainty, life's storms have the power to shake even the strongest individuals. These moments of fear and anxiety often create a sense of helplessness, leaving one feeling alone and without direction. However, peace is not found in the absence of struggles but in the ability to remain steady through them. The true test is not whether storms will come—they always do—but whether one will face them with fear or with faith.

Modern society places immense pressure on individuals to maintain control over every aspect of life. People are expected to plan their careers perfectly, manage relationships flawlessly, and achieve financial stability without setbacks. Yet, reality does not work this way. Life is unpredictable, and no amount of preparation can prevent every hardship. The relentless pursuit of control often leads to stress, anxiety, and, in many cases, burnout. Instead of resisting life's inevitable uncertainties, one must cultivate trust in oneself, in others, and, most importantly, in a higher purpose that provides guidance even when the path forward is unclear.

The Burden of Fear and Anxiety in a Fast-Paced World

One of the greatest struggles today is the overwhelming anxiety of living in a fast-paced, high-pressure society. People are constantly bombarded with messages about success, how to achieve more, earn more, and become more.

Social media amplifies the fear of falling behind, creating the illusion that everyone else has life figured out. This fosters a cycle of comparison and dissatisfaction, making individuals feel as though they are never doing enough or are failing simply because their journey does not match the carefully curated images of success they see online.

The pressure to achieve can make every setback feel like a personal failure. Losing a job, struggling in a relationship, or facing financial difficulties can trigger deep feelings of insecurity and self-doubt. Fear creeps in, whispering that these struggles mean one is not good enough, not capable, or somehow destined to fail. The reality, however, is that setbacks are not signs of failure but opportunities for growth. Every crisis holds a lesson, every disappointment offers a new perspective, and every delay can lead to something greater when approached with the right mindset.

For example, losing a job may initially feel like a failure, leaving a person feeling lost. However, that same experience could open the door to a better opportunity, a career shift more aligned with their passions, or even the chance to build something of their own. The key is not to let fear dictate one's response but to trust that even setbacks can serve a greater purpose.

Trusting in the Unknown: Learning to Let Go

Fear thrives on uncertainty, yet the truth is that life itself is uncertain. No one can predict the future, and the attempt to control every aspect of it only leads to frustration. Many live in constant worry about what could go wrong—financial insecurity, health concerns, the future of their children, or the possibility of failure. While planning and preparation are important, an obsession with control often leads to unnecessary stress.

A person facing financial worries may become consumed by anxiety—constantly calculating expenses, fearing the worst, and struggling to feel secure. While financial responsibility is important, fear-driven decisions often lead to missed opportunities and an inability to enjoy the present moment. The reality is that true security does not come from hoarding resources or micromanaging every financial detail—it comes from trusting that, no matter what happens, one can adapt, learn, and move forward.

Letting go does not mean being reckless. It means recognizing that control is an illusion and that true stability does not come from having all the answers.

Still, from trusting that, even in uncertainty, things will eventually fall into place.

Resilience in the Face of Personal and Professional Setbacks

Life is full of unexpected events—relationships break down, businesses fail, loved ones pass away, and personal ambitions sometimes unfold differently than planned. In these moments, it is easy to feel abandoned or question whether life has meaning. Some people fall into despair, allowing their struggles to define them, while others find strength in adversity, using setbacks as stepping stones for growth.

For instance, consider someone who goes through a painful breakup or divorce. The immediate reaction is often heartbreak, disappointment, and self-doubt. It can be tempting to believe that happiness is out of reach or that the pain will never fade. However, those who embrace healing and trust that life still has more to offer often rediscover love—not just in romantic relationships but in deeper self-understanding, meaningful friendships, and personal growth.

Similarly, an entrepreneur who dedicates years of effort to a business that ultimately fails may see it as a sign that they were never meant to succeed. Yet, many of today's most successful individuals experienced failure before building something great. The difference between those who rise and those who remain stuck is their willingness to learn from failure rather than be defined by it.

Challenges are not punishments; they are opportunities for growth. Every storm has the potential to reveal strength, resilience, and the capacity to overcome. The key is to view difficulties not as insurmountable obstacles but as moments to cultivate greater trust—both in oneself and in the journey ahead.

Finding Peace Amidst the Noise: The Importance of Stillness

In a world overwhelmed by constant noise—emails, social media updates, financial worries, and societal expectations—finding peace has become increasingly difficult. Many have grown so accustomed to busyness that they fear silence, equating productivity with worth. However, true peace is not found in doing more but in knowing when to pause.

Stillness is not inactivity; it is the intentional creation of space for clarity. It allows individuals to reflect, gain perspective, and listen to their hearts' deeper callings. Cultivating moments of stillness is essential to maintaining inner peace, whether through meditation, prayer, or simply stepping away from distractions.

Consider a person overwhelmed by stress at work. Instead of pushing through exhaustion, stepping back—whether by taking a walk, practicing deep breathing, or pausing for quiet reflection—can make all the difference. Often, the best solutions do not emerge in moments of frantic problem-solving but in stillness, when the mind is free to process without pressure.

Embracing the Journey Instead of Fearing the Storm

Fear convinces people that they must have all the answers before acting. It keeps them stuck, afraid to take risks or make decisions. However, life is not about having absolute certainty—it is about moving forward despite the unknown.

A person who dreams of changing careers but hesitates out of fear of failure may spend years in dissatisfaction, waiting for the "right time" that never comes. Yet those who leap—despite their fears—often discover that what once seemed terrifying was merely the first step toward something greater.

The storms of life will come, but they do not have to steal one's peace. The choice remains: to live in fear or to trust that, even in chaos, a path forward exists. Letting go of the need for absolute control, embracing stillness amid uncertainty, and choosing faith over fear are the steps toward lasting peace.

The real question is not "Will the storm come?" but rather "How will I choose to face it?"

Reflection Questions for Modern Life: Finding Peace in Chaos

1. What are the biggest "storms" in my life right now?

Everyone encounters challenges that shake their sense of stability—whether financial struggles, health concerns, career setbacks, relationship difficulties, or personal doubts. Take a moment to reflect:

- What are the major sources of stress in your life?
- Do you feel overwhelmed?
- Are you trying to face them alone?

Acknowledging your storms is the first step toward learning to trust God through them.

2. How do I usually respond to fear and uncertainty?

When difficulties arise, how do you respond— with panic, avoidance, or a need for excessive control? Do you try to handle everything on your own, or do you turn to God?

The disciples were terrified in the storm, even though Jesus was with them. Take a moment to reflect on how you typically handle stress. Do you allow fear to dictate your actions, or do you place your trust in Him?

3. Do I truly believe that God is present in my struggles, even when I cannot feel Him?

One of the greatest challenges of faith is trusting in God's presence when He seems silent. Have there been times in your life when you felt abandoned, only to realize later that He was guiding you all along?

How can you deepen your trust, knowing that even when Jesus appears to be "asleep," He is still in control?

4. What areas of my life am I struggling to surrender to God?

It's easy to trust God when life is going smoothly, but true faith is tested in times of uncertainty. Are there specific areas—your career, health, relationships, or finances—where you struggle to surrender control? What would it look like to fully place those concerns in God's hands?

5. How can I shift my focus from my problems to God's power?

Fear grows when we focus on our problems instead of God's power to lead us through them. What practical steps can you take to shift your focus from fear to faith?

Could strengthening your prayer life, spending more time in Scripture, or surrounding yourself with a faith-filled community help you trust God more fully?

6. Do I call out to God in prayer only in moments of crisis, or do I seek Him daily?

Prayer should not be a last resort but a daily habit that sustains you in both good times and bad. Do you turn to God only in times of need, or do you cultivate a continuous relationship with Him? Reflect on how you can make prayer a consistent part of your daily life.

7. In what ways do I allow fear and anxiety to control my decisions?

Fear has a way of shaping our choices; it can keep us from taking risks, hold us back from meaningful relationships, or drive us to act out of self-preservation rather than faith. Have you ever decided based on fear instead of trust? How might your life change if faith, rather than fear, guided your actions?

8. How do I respond to the suffering of others?

Pope Francis highlights the cries of refugees and the marginalized as a powerful reminder that fear and suffering are not isolated experiences. Do you acknowledge the struggles of those around you, or do your storms consume you? How can you become a source of peace and support for those in distress?

9. What small step can I take today to grow in faith and trust?

Faith isn't built overnight; it grows through daily choices. Whether it's spending a few extra minutes in prayer, surrendering a specific worry to God, or choosing gratitude over anxiety, what is one small step you can take today to deepen your trust in Him?

10. How would my life look different if I fully trusted in God's presence and plan?

Imagine how your life would change if you truly believed that God was with you in every storm. Would you worry less? Would you take bolder steps of faith? Would you experience greater peace? Take a moment to reflect on how embracing a deeper trust in God could transform the way you face challenges.

These questions invite you to engage with Pope Francis' message in a personal and meaningful way. They challenge you to confront your fears, deepen your faith, and take intentional steps toward trusting God more fully amid life's uncertainties. Take time to sit with these reflections and allow them to lead you toward greater peace and confidence in His presence.

Chapter 2

Rising Beyond the Tomb – A Call to New Life

Piazza Martiri (Carpi) - Fifth Sunday of Lent, 2 April 2017

The Homily

Pope Francis' homily on the raising of Lazarus offers a powerful reflection on suffering, despair, and Christ's transformative call to new life. He highlights the profound contrast between human grief and divine hope, emphasizing that while suffering is an inevitable part of life, it does not have the final word. Through the story of Lazarus, Pope Francis highlights God's closeness to human suffering, the necessity of faith in moments of despair, and the call to step out of personal tombs of fear, regret, and sin.

At the heart of the homily is the image of the sealed tomb—a place of finality, grief, and apparent defeat. When Jesus arrives, He is met with deep sorrow from Mary, Martha, and the gathered mourners. Even Jesus Himself is moved by the weight of human suffering— He weeps, showing that God does not remain indifferent to pain but fully enters into it. Yet, despite sharing in their sorrow, Jesus does not allow Himself to be overcome by grief. Jesus does not resign Himself to the reality of death; instead, He moves toward the tomb with purpose and authority, demonstrating that God's power is greater than human despair. His response to Lazarus' death reveals that while God does not eliminate suffering from the world, He transforms it from within, leading those who trust in Him toward life, healing, and renewal.

A central theme in the homily is the clash between two perspectives—one of hopeless resignation to death and suffering and the other of faith in Christ's life-giving power. The mourners represent those overwhelmed by grief, unable to see beyond their loss. They believe that nothing more can be done—death is final, and the tomb is sealed. In contrast, Jesus embodies a radical new reality of hope—one that does not erase suffering but transcends it. He does not merely offer comfort—He declares, "I am the Resurrection and the Life," revealing that belief in Him leads not only to eternal life but also to a transformed way of living in the present. This new life is no longer bound by fear, sorrow, or despair but is open to the infinite possibilities of God's love and power.

Pope Francis then shifts the reflection from the Gospel event to a deeply personal examination of the "tombs" within each person's heart. He explains that everyone carries hidden places of grief, sin, regret, and fear— areas where something inside them has "died." It could be a lingering wound from the past, a resentment that refuses to fade, a sin that weighs heavily on the conscience, or a deep regret that feels impossible to move beyond. These "inner tombs" become places of entrapment, where people remain stuck—dwelling in sorrow or self-pity instead of allowing Christ to enter and bring healing. The Pope warns against the temptation to remain in self-pity and despair, urging believers to reject the false belief that their wounds cannot be healed or that their past defines them. Rather than shutting themselves off from Christ, he encourages each person to invite Jesus into these dark places—just as He entered Lazarus' tomb—and to listen for His call to new life.

The words of Jesus—"Come out!"—are not only for Lazarus but for everyone who feels trapped in personal suffering. Christ's command is a call to step beyond fear, let go of guilt and despair, and embrace the possibility of transformation. Many people, the Pope explains, bind themselves in the "bandages" of anxiety, doubt, and regret, keeping themselves from moving forward. Yet, faith in Christ calls them to unwrap these burdens, trusting that He has the power to bring light where there was once only darkness. The Pope reassures believers that while suffering and challenges will always exist, true stability is found in Christ—not in worldly security or the absence of hardship. This stability is rooted in the assurance that Jesus walks with them, turning their suffering into trust and their fear into peace.

The homily concludes with a striking call to action: just as Jesus commanded the stone to be removed from Lazarus' tomb, believers must remove the barriers that separate them from God. Pride, sin, resentment, and worldly distractions become obstacles that hinder Christ's full presence in their hearts. Removing these "stones" requires courage and faith, but it is the only path to truly experiencing the renewal Christ offers. The Pope urges believers to let go of anything that hinders them from embracing the fullness of life Christ promises—whether it be unhealthy attachments, bitterness, or self-imposed isolation.

The homily's final mission is one of witness. Those freed by Christ are called to share His life-giving message with a world thirsting for hope. Just as Lazarus' resurrection became a sign to those who witnessed it, every believer is meant to be a living testimony of Christ's power to transform, restore, and renew. This is not just about preaching or teaching but about becoming bearers of hope—lifting others from despair, sharing God's love, and demonstrating that life does not end in darkness but always moves toward resurrection.

Pope Francis concludes by emphasizing that Jesus' invitation—"Come out!"—is just as relevant today as it was at Lazarus' tomb. Christ does not want people to live in fear or remain paralyzed by the past; He calls them into the light, into healing, and into a life renewed by love and grace. The challenge is whether one will remain in a tomb of sadness and regret or step forward into the freedom Christ offers.

The Pope reminds believers that Jesus still speaks the same words today that He spoke at Lazarus' tomb: "Do not be afraid." This is an invitation to trust in Christ's power, remove the barriers that keep them from Him, and step into the fullness of life that only He can give.

Homily Analysis: From Darkness to Light

Pope Francis' homily on the raising of Lazarus is a profound reflection on God's power over death, the reality of human suffering, and the invitation to spiritual resurrection. He presents the miracle as more than just a moment in Jesus' ministry—it is a sign of Christ's ultimate victory over sin and death, a foreshadowing of His resurrection, and an invitation for every person to experience transformation. The homily urges a deeper understanding of how faith and trust in Christ overcome despair, how God's love reaches into even the darkest corners of human experience, and how each believer is called to step out of their personal "tombs" and embrace new life.

The Power of God Over Death and Despair

At the heart of this homily is the clash between death and divine authority. The scene at Lazarus' tomb is filled with hopelessness and grief. His family and friends have accepted the finality of his death, their sorrow overwhelming. Even Jesus Himself is described as deeply moved and troubled—an expression that reflects not only His compassion but also His awareness of the tragic consequences of sin and mortality in the human condition. The shortest yet most powerful verse in the Gospel—"Jesus wept" (*John 11:35*)—is a striking reminder that God is not distant from human suffering but fully enters into it.

Despite His sorrow, Jesus does not allow despair to take hold of Him. While those around Him mourn in resignation, He steps forward with unshaken faith in the Father's power to bring life from death. Then, He issues a command that changes everything: "Take away the stone" (*John 11:39*). This moment directly challenges the human perception of finality. While the people see an immovable obstacle, Jesus sees the possibility of resurrection. This powerful contrast reinforces the theme that faith in Christ does not ignore suffering but transforms it.

Pope Francis emphasizes that God does not erase pain from human life but enters into it, making it His own and transforming it from within. This is why, instead of shielding Himself from sorrow, Jesus chooses to share in human grief—but He does not stop there. He moves beyond lamentation to action, demonstrating that the true response to suffering is not to remain trapped in it but to trust in God's power to bring forth life even from the most hopeless situations.

Jesus as the Resurrection and the Life

A central theological message of the homily is Jesus' self-identification as "the Resurrection and the Life" (*John 11:25*). Unlike the prophets before Him, who called upon God's power to perform miracles, Jesus speaks as one who possesses divine authority over life and death itself. His words reveal that faith in Him does not merely provide temporary relief but offers eternal life—a reality that transcends both physical death and spiritual decay.

The raising of Lazarus, then, is not merely about restoring a man to life—it is a sign pointing to a greater reality. Unlike Lazarus, who was raised only to die again eventually, Jesus will soon rise from the dead in a way that definitively conquers death forever. Pope Francis underscores that this miracle foreshadows Christ's Passion, Death, and Resurrection. While Lazarus walks out of the tomb only to face death again someday, Jesus will rise never to die again, opening the way for all who believe in Him to share in eternal life.

The Symbolism of the Tomb and the Stone

The imagery of the tomb and the stone that seals it carries deep spiritual significance. The tomb represents not just physical death but also everything that imprisons the human soul—sin, despair, fear, guilt, and unresolved pain. The heavy stone represents the barrier that separates humanity from divine life—a reminder of the burdens people carry and the obstacles that prevent them from fully experiencing the freedom Christ offers.

Jesus' command to remove the stone is an act of divine authority over everything that binds and limits human existence. It is a moment of invitation—a call to trust that something greater is at work, even when it cannot yet be seen. The hesitation of those around Him, particularly Martha's concern that the body may already be decomposing, reflects the natural human resistance to faith. People often cling to their burdens, believing them to be permanent—just as Martha assumes that Lazarus' death cannot be undone. But Jesus challenges this mindset, showing that no situation is beyond God's power to restore and redeem.

When Jesus calls Lazarus to "Come out!" (*John 11:43*), it is more than a command to a dead man—it is a call to everyone trapped in darkness, inviting them into the fullness of life. The burial cloths that bind Lazarus mirror the spiritual entanglements that restrict human freedom—whether sin, fear, resentment, or doubt. Jesus does not merely restore Lazarus to life; He also commands that he be unbound, showing that resurrection is not just about existing but about truly living in freedom.

Faith as the Precondition for Resurrection

Pope Francis highlights a key message: faith must come before a miracle. Before calling Lazarus out of the tomb, Jesus prays to the Father, thanking Him in advance for hearing His prayer. This is a profound act of trust—Jesus acknowledges God's power before the visible sign of resurrection appears. It reveals that true faith does not wait for proof; it believes in God's power even when all seems lost.

The homily subtly emphasizes that faith is not about understanding every detail but about trusting that God is at work, even in uncertainty. Just as Martha and the others are asked to remove the stone before witnessing the miracle, believers are often called to step out in faith before seeing the results. This requires courage, surrender, and a willingness to let go of human limitations to make room for divine possibilities.

Jesus' Invitation to New Life

A key takeaway from the homily is that Jesus' call to resurrection extends beyond Lazarus—it is an invitation to all. Pope Francis presents the raising of Lazarus as both a miraculous event and a deeply personal call for every believer. The command "Come out!" is directed to anyone trapped in spiritual stagnation, grief, guilt, or hopelessness.

Too often, people remain in their metaphorical tombs, weighed down by past mistakes, fears, or a reluctance to embrace change. Pope Francis challenges believers to identify the personal "stones" that hinder them from experiencing Christ's power—whether bitterness, an unwillingness to forgive, or resistance to trusting in God's plan.

By calling Lazarus out of the tomb, Jesus reveals that no situation is beyond redemption, no person is too lost, and no suffering is beyond his transformative power. The homily ultimately presents resurrection not merely as a historical event but as an ongoing reality—one that every person is invited to experience.

Resurrection as a Continual Reality

Pope Francis concludes his reflection by emphasizing that God's victory over death is not merely something to be celebrated but something to be lived. The resurrection is not just a distant hope, it is a present and ongoing reality that reshapes how believers face suffering, sin, and life's challenges.

The homily calls people to remove the barriers that hinder their encounter with Christ, step forward in faith even amid uncertainty, and trust that Jesus' power surpasses all human limitations. In doing so, believers do not merely witness resurrection—they participate in it, becoming living testimonies of God's triumph over death and despair.

Ultimately, the Pope's message is one of hope, transformation, and the assurance that Christ's voice continues to call, inviting all to step into the newness of life. The challenge remains: will one stay bound by the past, or will one move forward in faith, embracing the fullness of resurrection?

From Darkness to Light: Breaking Free from Regret, Guilt, and Fear in Modern Life

Regret, guilt, and fear are among the most paralyzing emotions a person can experience. They weigh down the heart, distort perspective, and trap individuals in a cycle of self-condemnation and hesitation. Many people spend years—even decades—dwelling on past mistakes, reliving painful memories, or fearing the future, unable to embrace the present fully. The weight of unhealed wounds, unresolved failures, and self-doubt can feel like a tomb—an internal prison where the spirit feels lifeless, trapped in stagnation.

Yet, the truth remains: no failure is final, no mistake defines a person, and no sin is beyond redemption. Growth, renewal, and healing are always possible. Moving beyond regret, guilt, and fear does not mean erasing the past or ignoring one's mistakes—it means allowing them to become steppingstones rather than stumbling blocks. It is about transformation—learning from the past without being trapped by it, making amends where possible, and stepping forward with courage, even when the future is uncertain. No matter how hopeless a situation may seem, there is always a way forward—always the possibility of a new l

The Burden of Regret and the Power of Perspective

Regret is a natural human emotion, arising when we look back and realize things could have been different.

It can stem from small, everyday choices—words left unspoken, missed opportunities, or neglected relationships. But it can also be tied to life-altering moments—choosing the wrong path, making a decision that caused pain, or failing to act when it mattered most.

One powerful example is the regret that lingers over relationships left unresolved. A son who never mended his strained bond with his father may carry deep sorrow after his father's passing, wishing he had spoken the words left unsaid. A woman who once dreamed of traveling the world but postponed it indefinitely for the sake of her career may later look back with regret at all the years that slipped by without fulfilling that dream. In both cases, the regret arises from missed opportunities, but it doesn't have to remain permanent. That son can choose to honor his father's memory by mending relationships with other family members. Similarly, the woman can still pursue new experiences, even if on a smaller scale, finding fulfillment in ways that align with her current life.

Regret, however, is not inherently negative. It serves as a sign that a person cares that they recognize where they could have done better. The danger lies not in the regret itself but in how one responds to it. Some allow regret to shape them positively, learning from their past and making changes, while others let it trap them in self-blame and paralysis. Others, however, remain stuck, unable to forgive themselves, endlessly replaying their mistakes. They live in a constant state of 'What if?'—what if they had made a different choice, acted sooner, or been braver?

Dwelling on 'what ifs' doesn't change the past—it only steals the present. The past cannot be rewritten, but the future remains unwritten. Someone who regrets not pursuing a passion or career path can still find ways to weave that passion into their life today. *Someone who regrets neglecting a friendship can choose to reach out and rebuild that relationship now. The question is not, 'What could I have done differently?' but rather, 'What can I do today to move forward?*

Guilt: When to Let Go, When to Make Amends

Guilt is often tied to actions—wrong decisions, hurtful words, or moments of weakness where one fails to live up to one's values. Unlike regret, which revolves around missed opportunities, guilt focuses on harm done—whether to others or oneself. It can be overwhelming, especially when someone feels they have deeply hurt those they love or failed to be the person they wanted to be.

For example, a father who worked long hours during his children's childhood may carry deep guilt for not being present enough, feeling as though he can never make up for lost time. Or someone who betrayed a close friend may feel haunted by the pain they caused, even if years have passed. In both cases, guilt can be crippling, leading to self-condemnation instead of growth.

Not all guilt is harmful. There is a distinction between constructive guilt, which fosters growth, and destructive guilt, which breeds self-condemnation. Constructive guilt serves as a sign of moral awareness—it compels a person to take responsibility for their actions, apologize, and seek change. Destructive guilt, however, keeps a person trapped in shame, convincing them that they are unworthy of forgiveness or that their mistakes define who they are.

The only way forward from guilt is through accountability and acceptance. If a person has hurt someone, they must ask themselves: Can I make amends? If so, they should take the necessary steps—whether through an apology, an act of restitution, or a commitment to change. But what if reconciliation is not possible? What if the person they hurt is no longer in their life, or if the situation cannot be undone? In such cases, the only path forward is to acknowledge the mistake, learn from it, and let it go.

A teacher who unfairly dismissed a struggling student years ago cannot go back in time to change that moment. However, they can choose to be more patient and encouraging with the students they teach today. A person who regrets how they treated a deceased loved one can honor their memory by being more loving toward others. The past cannot be changed, but the future remains within reach.

Fear: The Invisible Chain That Keeps People Stuck

Fear is perhaps the most insidious of these burdens because it is future oriented. While regret and guilt keep people anchored to the past, fear prevents them from stepping into the future. Fear of failure, fear of judgment, fear of the unknown—these anxieties stop people from taking risks, embracing opportunities, and living fully.

A talented musician who never shares their music out of fear of criticism will never experience the joy of self-expression. A person who dreams of starting a business but is afraid of financial instability may spend their life in a career they dislike. In these cases, fear becomes a silent jailer, preventing people from finding fulfillment.

Overcoming fear does not mean ignoring risk or acting recklessly. It means taking small but meaningful steps forward. A person afraid of public speaking can start by speaking up in smaller settings. Someone afraid of starting a new career can begin with side projects before making a full transition. The key is movement—even the smallest step forward weakens fear's grip.

Stepping Out of the Tomb: A Daily Commitment to Renewal

Breaking free from regret, guilt, and fear is not a one-time event—it is a daily choice. Each day, people have the opportunity to remain in their "tombs"—dwelling on past mistakes, carrying burdens of guilt, or avoiding the future in fear—or to step forward into renewal.

Choosing renewal means making peace with the past—not by erasing it, but by allowing it to shape a better future. It means embracing imperfection and recognizing that everyone makes mistakes but that mistakes do not define one's worth. It means living with intention, focusing not on what was lost but on what can still be gained.

One of the most powerful ways to break free from regret is to focus on the present. Instead of asking, *What did I do wrong? Ask, What can I do right today? Instead of saying, I wish I had done things differently, say, I will do things differently now.* The past does not determine the future but the choices we make today.

A Call to Courage and Hope

The invitation to move beyond regret, guilt, and fear is not just about personal freedom—it's about becoming a source of hope for others. When people choose to let go of past burdens and embrace new life, they become examples to those around them. They show that failure does not have the final word, that redemption is always possible, and that transformation is real.

The challenge, then, is whether one will remain bound by past sorrow or step forward into the light of renewal. Each person has the power to choose how they respond to their past—whether they stay trapped in regret or walk forward into hope.

The tomb, no matter how dark, is not the end. There is always a way forward. The question is: Will you take it?

Reflection Questions for Modern Life: Breaking Free from Regret, Guilt, and Fear

In today's fast-paced world, many people carry the burdens of regret, guilt, and fear, often unaware of how deeply these emotions shape their decisions, limit their growth, and hold them back from experiencing true peace. Some dwell on past mistakes, unable to forgive themselves. Others live with an overwhelming sense of guilt, believing they are beyond redemption. Many remain trapped in fear—fear of failure, rejection, or the unknown—allowing it to dictate their choices. These questions are designed to help examine the weight of these emotions, challenge the thoughts that sustain them, and inspire action toward healing, renewal, and a deeper sense of purpose.

1. **Am I allowing past mistakes to define my future?**

Many people carry their failures with them as if they are permanent labels—believing that one mistake, one wrong decision, or one painful experience defines who they are. This belief often leads to self-sabotage, causing individuals to avoid opportunities, relationships, or new challenges because they feel unworthy or incapable.

Consider this: If a friend made the same mistake as you, would you define them solely by that moment, or would you recognize their ability to grow and change? If you believe in second chances for others, why not for yourself? True growth begins when you acknowledge your past, learn from it, and move forward with renewed purpose.

2. Have I made peace with the regrets I cannot change?

Regret often arises from things left undone—words left unsaid, dreams unpursued, relationships that faded. While some regrets can be resolved, others cannot. The challenge, then, is not to erase the past but to reframe it.

Ask yourself: Can I find meaning in my past disappointments? Did they teach me something valuable? If I cannot go back and change what happened, how can I live differently today because of it? Rather than being weighed down by the past, shift your focus to what you can do now. Each day is an opportunity to choose differently.

3. Do I take responsibility for my mistakes, or do I avoid them?

Guilt, when handled correctly, can be a guide—it teaches accountability and moral responsibility. However, when ignored or denied, it festers, leading to self-resentment or blame toward others.

Reflect on how you handle guilt. Do you acknowledge your mistakes and make amends where possible, or do you avoid confronting them? If there is someone you have wronged, have you taken the step to apologize? If reconciliation is not possible, have you found a way to atone by doing good elsewhere? Growth is not about pretending mistakes never happen; it's about learning from them and choosing to act differently.

4. Do I extend to myself the same compassion I offer to others?

People often find it easier to forgive others than to forgive themselves. They offer words of encouragement, patience, and grace to friends in need but remain harsh and unforgiving toward their struggles.

Imagine speaking to yourself the way you would to a loved one in pain. Would you tell them they are worthless because of one mistake? Would you insist that they will never change? If not, then why hold yourself to such a harsh standard? Self-forgiveness is not about excusing wrong actions; it is about allowing yourself to heal and recognizing that your worth is not defined by your lowest moments.

5. What fears are preventing me from taking action?

Fear manifests in many forms—fear of failure, fear of judgment, fear of uncertainty. Often, it is not the actual obstacles that hold people back but the stories they tell themselves about those obstacles.

Think about the dreams, decisions, or changes you have avoided. Are you afraid of failing? Of what others might think? Of stepping into the unknown? Fear loses its power when faced directly. Instead of asking, *What if I fail? Ask, What if I succeed?* What if this experience helps me grow? Taking even small steps forward diminishes the hold that fear has on your life.

6. Have I let past hurts shape my ability to trust and love?

Many people carry deep wounds from betrayal, rejection, or disappointment, allowing these painful experiences to harden their hearts. As a result, they struggle to trust, open themselves to love, or embrace vulnerability again.

Consider whether past pain is preventing you from forming meaningful relationships. Do you push people away out of fear of being hurt again? Do past betrayals cause you to assume the worst in others? Healing doesn't mean ignoring or denying your pain—it means choosing not to let past wounds dictate your present and future. Love and trust require risk, but without them, true connection remains out of reach.

7. Do I dwell more on problems, or do I actively seek solutions?

It's easy to get trapped in cycles of complaining, fixating on everything that has gone wrong. But dwelling on problems doesn't create change—only action does.

Reflect on how you respond to challenges. Do you replay problems in your mind endlessly, or do you actively seek ways to move forward? When faced with hardship, do you focus on what you've lost, or do you search for what you can still build? Even in the most difficult circumstances, there is always something within your control—the choice to seek solutions rather than remain stuck in despair.

8. Do I fear change, even when I know it is necessary?

People often resist change, even when they are unhappy where they are. The familiar—no matter how painful—can feel safer than the unknown.

Ask yourself: Am I holding onto something—a job, a relationship, or a way of thinking—simply because it's comfortable, even though it no longer serves me? What might happen if I let go and trusted that something better awaits? Change is frightening, but it is also the gateway to growth, renewal, and transformation.

9. What would I do if I truly believed I was capable?

Self-doubt is one of the greatest barriers to success and fulfillment. Many people don't fail because they lack ability but because they never try.

Imagine failure wasn't an option—what would you pursue? What risk would you take? What goal would you chase? The difference between those who achieve and those who remain stuck isn't intelligence, talent, or luck—it's the willingness to try, to fail, and to keep going despite obstacles. If you knew success was possible, would you still hesitate?

10. How do I want to be remembered?

At the end of life, most people don't regret the things they tried and failed at, and they regret the chances they never took, the love they withheld, and the time they lost to fear and doubt.

Ask yourself: If my life ended tomorrow, would I be satisfied with how I lived today? Am I living in alignment with my deepest values? Am I prioritizing what truly matters? Regret doesn't come from living boldly—it comes from living passively. The time to embrace life is now.

Regret, guilt, and fear aren't signs of failure—they're invitations to change. They reveal what matters most, where healing is needed, and what steps must be taken to live a fuller, more meaningful life. Your past does not define you, and your future is not out of reach. The choice is always before you: remain stuck in regret, guilt, and fear, or step forward—however uncertainly—into the life you're meant to live.

The only question that remains is: Will you take that step?

Chapter 3

The Price of Betrayal: Choosing Integrity Over Self-Interest

The Chapel of The Domus Sanctae Marthae - Wednesday, 8 April 2020

The Homily

Pope Francis' homily on Holy Wednesday, also known as "Spy Wednesday," powerfully reflects on Judas Iscariot's betrayal of Jesus. The story of Judas selling Jesus for thirty pieces of silver is more than just an ancient biblical event—it is a stark reminder of humanity's tendency to choose self-interest over loyalty. The Pope draws a connection between Judas' betrayal and the modern-day realities of human exploitation, greed, and the relentless pursuit of wealth at the expense of others.

Judas' betrayal is not just a historical event—it is a recurring pattern that continues today. Pope Francis highlights the suffering of those exploited for profit, from human trafficking victims to workers denied fair wages. He warns that Judas' spirit lives on in those who profit from the suffering of others—criminal organizations, corrupt business leaders, and anyone who exploits others for personal gain. As he puts it, the betrayal of Jesus continues in every act of injustice where people are treated as commodities rather than human beings.

One of the most striking aspects of the homily is the Pope's reflection on money as a false god. He reminds us of Jesus' words: "You cannot serve both God and money." Judas' downfall began with his love of wealth, leading him from small acts of dishonesty to ultimate betrayal. When unchecked, the desire for wealth can consume a person, leading them to justify any action in its pursuit. The Pope makes it clear that many today still make the same choice as Judas—not by directly betraying Jesus, but by prioritizing profit, power, and self-interest over morality, justice, and love.

Judas' story also serves as a warning about the consequences of choosing wealth over righteousness. Pope Francis reminds us that the devil is a deceiver—promising everything yet leading only to despair. After realizing the horror of his actions, Judas returns to the religious leaders in anguish. But instead of receiving forgiveness, he is met with indifference: "What is that to us? See to it yourself." The Pope explains that this is how the devil operates—he entices, tempts, and promises, only to abandon his victims in their darkest hour.

Yet despite the gravity of Judas' actions, Pope Francis highlights that Jesus never directly calls him a traitor. Even in the moment of betrayal, Jesus addresses Judas as a "friend." This small but profound detail reflects the limitless mercy of Christ. The Pope does not speculate on Judas' eternal fate but instead invites us to reflect on the mystery of his final moments. Did he have a chance for redemption? Did he fully grasp the weight of his actions before taking his own life? Rather than offering answers, the Pope leaves these questions open, emphasizing that Jesus' love and mercy are beyond human comprehension.

The homily concludes with a challenge to every believer: "Judas, where are you?" This question is not meant for Judas alone—it is directed at each of us. The Pope reminds us that a "little Judas" exists within us all—the temptation to betray, to compromise our values for personal gain, to choose self-interest over love. Every person faces moments of decision—to act with integrity or to choose what is easiest and most profitable. The betrayal of Jesus is not just a past event but a present reality whenever greed, dishonesty, and self-interest take precedence over justice, mercy, and faithfulness.

Pope Francis urges us to look inward and ask: Where is the Judas in me? In what ways do I let greed, selfishness, or ambition shape my choices? Do I prioritize money and security over faith and justice? Do I ignore or contribute to the suffering of others for my convenience? These are difficult but necessary questions—ones that demand reflection and self-examination.

The homily serves as both a warning and an invitation—to recognize the dangers of greed and betrayal while remembering that Jesus' love and mercy remain ever-present, even in the darkest moments of human failure. The choice remains: Will we serve God or money? Will we remain loyal or betray? In answering these questions, we shape the path of our discipleship.

Homily Analysis: The Temptation of Betrayal

The Timeless Reality of Betrayal

Betrayal is a deep human experience—one that transcends time and culture. The story of Judas Iscariot selling Jesus for thirty pieces of silver is among history's most infamous acts of treachery. Yet, as Pope Francis' homily reveals, this betrayal is not confined to the past. Every generation witnesses its manifestations of betrayal—acts of self-interest that place personal gain above loyalty, integrity, and love.

Pope Francis reminds us that Judas' betrayal is not an isolated incident but a reflection of humanity's ongoing struggle with greed, power, and misplaced priorities. While circumstances have changed, the temptation remains the same—choosing self-interest over righteousness, convenience over responsibility, and wealth over morality. Judas' story is more than a cautionary tale; it is a mirror reflecting the ethical and moral dilemmas we face daily.

The Worship of Money: A Modern-Day Idolatry

One of the strongest themes in Pope Francis' homily is the warning against money as a false god. Judas' downfall was not a mere lapse in judgment but the result of his deep-rooted attachment to wealth. The Gospel of John reveals that Judas had already been stealing from the money bag long before he betrayed Jesus. His gradual descent into dishonesty illustrates how unchecked greed can consume the heart and distort moral reasoning.

The Pope extends this lesson to the modern world, where financial success is often idolized. Many, consciously or unconsciously, prioritize profit over principles. Corporations exploit workers for greater earnings, politicians accept bribes to serve their interests, and individuals justify small dishonesties in the pursuit of financial security. This reflects the same spiritual disorder that led Judas to betray Jesus—the prioritization of wealth over values, status over sincerity, and self-interest over faith.

Pope Francis reminds us that the worship of money extends beyond material wealth; it embodies power and control. When individuals become servants of money, they risk enslavement—endlessly chasing financial gain at the cost of their conscience. The Pope echoes Jesus' words: "You cannot serve both God and money," urging believers to reflect on their relationship with wealth and ensure it does not become the driving force in their lives.

The Gradual Descent into Betrayal

Judas did not become a traitor overnight. His betrayal was the result of gradual moral compromises that distanced him from Jesus. It began with small thefts from the money bag, each justified in his mind, leading him further down the path of deception. Over time, his attachment to wealth hardened his heart, making him blind to the deeper values of faith, love, and discipleship.

Pope Francis uses this example to illustrate that betrayal is not sudden—it is a gradual process. Few people intend to be dishonest or exploit others, but they begin with small compromises. A business leader, for instance, might justify an unethical decision as simply "good business," setting a dangerous precedent. A politician might accept a small bribe, convincing themselves it is a necessary trade-off for power. A worker might cut small ethical corners, believing the harm is negligible. Yet, these minor compromises add up over time, shaping character and eroding moral strength.

The Pope warns that without vigilance, anyone can fall into betrayal. Judas' story serves as a stark reminder that even small ethical lapses can lead to devastating consequences. By staying mindful of their choices and honest about their motivations, individuals can safeguard themselves from a similar path of self-destruction.

Betrayal in the Modern World: The Exploitation of Others

While Judas' betrayal was personal, Pope Francis broadened the discussion to include institutional and systemic betrayal. Even today, people are still being "sold" for financial gain—through human trafficking, exploitative labor, and corruption. The Pope emphasizes that betrayal extends beyond individual actions; it is also embedded in systems that prioritize profit over human dignity.

The Pope highlights examples like human trafficking, where women and children are sold into slavery, and corporate exploitation, where workers are deprived of fair wages and humane working conditions. He calls attention to the neglect of the elderly, where some abandon their aging parents in nursing homes, choosing convenience over familial duty. These modern forms of betrayal reveal that Judas' spirit remains alive today—not only in individuals but in societies that allow such injustices to persist.

- The homily challenges listeners to reflect:
- How do we contribute to these betrayals?
- Do we ignore injustice?
- Do we prioritize personal comfort over the well-being of others?

Betrayal is not always dramatic, it can be subtle, unfolding through indifference, complacency, or silence in the face of wrongdoing.

The Devil's Empty Promises: Deception and Despair

One of the most chilling aspects of Judas' story is his final descent into despair. Overcome with the horror of his betrayal, he returns the money to the religious leaders, seeking some form of absolution. Instead, he is met with cold indifference: "What is that to us? Look to it yourself."

Pope Francis highlights a crucial truth: the devil is a deceiver who abandons his followers in their moment of need. Judas was lured by the false promise of security that money offered, yet in the end, it left him with nothing. The Pope warns that sin never fulfills its promises. Those who chase fulfillment through power, wealth, or status ultimately find themselves empty, abandoned, and consumed by regret.

This is a profound lesson for modern times. Many chase wealth, influence, or material possessions, believing these will bring happiness. Yet, upon attaining them, they often feel unfulfilled, anxious, or spiritually lost. The world promises satisfaction through ambition and material success, but in reality, these things often leave people feeling more isolated and broken.

Jesus' Response: Mercy in the Face of Betrayal

Despite Judas' treachery, Jesus never directly calls him a traitor. Even as Judas betrays Him with a kiss, Jesus addresses him as "Friend." This moment powerfully reveals the depth of Christ's mercy and love, even in the face of betrayal.

Pope Francis invites listeners to reflect on God's infinite capacity for forgiveness. Unlike Judas, who surrendered to despair, believers have the opportunity to repent and seek redemption. The homily serves as a powerful reminder that no sin is greater than God's mercy. Even in failure, even in selfish choices, there is always a way back to God.

The Judas Within: A Call to Self-Examination

Pope Francis concludes his homily with a thought-provoking question: "Judas, where are you?" This is not merely a historical inquiry but a deeply personal one. He reminds listeners that every person can betray— whether through greed, dishonesty, or neglecting their responsibilities to others.

He urges believers to examine their hearts: Do they prioritize wealth over morality? Do they contribute to systems of exploitation? Do they make small compromises that chip away at their integrity?

Judas' betrayal was not inevitable, and neither is anyone's moral failure. The Pope calls for vigilance, self-awareness, and a steadfast commitment to choosing faithfulness over self-interest.

A Choice Between Two Masters

The core lesson of the homily is the choice between serving God or serving money. Judas attempted to do both, but in the end, he lost everything. Pope Francis warns that this same choice confronts every person every day. It is not always dramatic or obvious—it happens in small decisions, in everyday interactions, in the way people treat others.

The Pope's message is clear: following Christ requires a deliberate choice to reject greed, self-interest, and the temptation to betray others for personal gain. Only by confronting the Judas within and choosing repentance over despair can believers remain faithful to Christ.

Betrayal, Greed, and Redemption: Living the Lessons of Judas in Modern Life

Betrayal is not merely a historical event or a dramatic turning point in a person's life; it is a constant temptation woven into the fabric of modern society.

While people may not literally sell someone for thirty pieces of silver, they betray others—and themselves—through dishonesty, selfish ambition, and moral compromise. In a world consumed by profit, status, and personal success, betrayal takes many forms. It appears in corrupt business practices, broken relationships, political deception, and the exploitation of the vulnerable. The challenge today is to recognize these betrayals and choose integrity, love, and justice over convenience and personal gain.

Betrayal in the Workplace: When Profit Comes Before People

One of the most widespread forms of betrayal today is found in the corporate world, where companies prioritize profit over workers' dignity and ethical responsibility. Employees are laid off in mass numbers to boost shareholder profits, while workers in developing countries endure low wages and unsafe conditions. Companies cut corners on safety regulations to save money, even at the cost of human lives. In many industries, this has become an accepted norm, where maximizing revenue takes precedence over ethical responsibility.

A striking example of this betrayal is the fashion industry, where fast fashion brands have been exposed for relying on child labor and sweatshops to produce cheap clothing. Consumers, whether aware or unaware, sustain this system by prioritizing affordability over ethical responsibility. Many people recognize that workers in impoverished countries are being exploited, yet the allure of low prices often outweighs the commitment to human dignity.

The healthcare industry offers another alarming example. In some countries, medical care is treated as a business rather than a fundamental human right. Life-saving treatments and medications remain out of reach for those who cannot afford them, resulting in unnecessary suffering and preventable deaths. Hospitals that prioritize profit over patient well-being betray the very essence of medicine. Likewise, pharmaceutical companies have been exposed for inflating drug prices, placing shareholder profits above saving lives.

Betrayal in the corporate world is not limited to CEOs and large corporations; it is deeply embedded in everyday workplace culture. Many employees engage in dishonest practices—manipulating data, cutting ethical corners, or ruthlessly competing for promotions at the expense of their colleagues. Small acts of dishonesty are often dismissed as "just business," but collectively, they foster a workplace culture that prioritizes success over integrity.

The real question for modern individuals is this: Are we willing to compromise our values for financial security? Do we ignore unethical practices at work simply because they benefit us? Integrity in the workplace is a daily choice, yet many fail to see how small betrayals gradually erode their moral compass, leading to even greater compromises over time.

Betrayal in Personal Relationships: When Convenience Trumps Commitment

Beyond corporate and financial betrayals, Judas' story also reflects the betrayals within personal relationships. Modern culture often prioritizes self-fulfillment over-commitment, resulting in broken relationships, abandoned friendships, and neglected family bonds. The emphasis on individual happiness and instant gratification has made loyalty seem like a burden rather than a virtue.

Many marriages fail when one or both partners prioritize personal desires over their commitment to each other. Rather than working through challenges together, they walk away when difficulties arise. Social media and dating apps have fostered a culture of disposability, where relationships are easily abandoned in pursuit of the "next best thing" instead of deepening the bonds that already exist.

Friendships, too, fall victim to modern betrayal. Many people walk away when maintaining a relationship becomes inconvenient. Lifelong friends are cast aside when one person climbs the social or professional ladder and no longer sees value in the bond. Others betray friendships by exposing private information for personal gain, engaging in gossip, or prioritizing status over genuine connection.

Family relationships are not immune to betrayal. One of the most heartbreaking examples is society's treatment of the elderly. Many parents who dedicated their lives to raising their children are placed in nursing homes and forgotten. While some elderly individuals genuinely require professional care, many are abandoned simply because they are seen as burdens. Modern society often prioritizes productivity over human connection, casting aside those who are no longer deemed "useful."

The questions we must ask ourselves are:

- Are we loyal to those who have been loyal to us?
- Do we prioritize relationships, even when they demand effort and patience?

True love and friendship are not proven in moments of ease but in times of hardship. Betrayal is not always a grand act of treachery—sometimes, it is simply the choice to walk away when someone needs us most.

Betrayal in Society: When the Vulnerable Are Exploited

Societal betrayal happens when those in power exploit those without it. Governments, corporations, and institutions often fail the very people they are meant to serve, prioritizing wealth and influence over justice and human dignity.

One of the most appalling examples of societal betrayal is human trafficking, one of the world's most lucrative illegal industries. Women and children are forced into labor and sex slavery, often in plain sight, yet efforts to combat this crime remain inadequate. Many corporations and industries profit from cheap labor linked to trafficking, making the problem even more difficult to dismantle.

Corruption in politics is another widespread form of betrayal. Politicians who campaign on promises of change often prioritize their interests once in power. Corrupt governments fail to protect their citizens, allowing crime, poverty, and injustice to thrive. Leaders who accept bribes, manipulate public trust, and create policies that favor the wealthy while harming the poor are the modern-day betrayers of society.

The legal system also commits betrayal when justice is accessible only to those who can afford it. The wealthy often evade accountability, while the poor face harsher penalties for lesser offenses. A system that fails to uphold equal treatment under the law has betrayed the very principles of justice.

The greatest challenge is recognizing that societal betrayal is not only the fault of leaders and corporations. Every individual has a responsibility to reject complicity in systems that exploit others.

- Do we support businesses that exploit workers?
- Do we vote for politicians based on personal gain rather than the common good?

- Do we speak out against injustice, or do we remain silent because it is more convenient?

The Slippery Slope of Small Betrayals

Betrayal rarely occurs in a single dramatic moment. More often, it begins with small compromises—choosing dishonesty over integrity in seemingly minor ways, telling small lies, or making decisions based on fear rather than truth. Over time, these small betrayals accumulate, shaping a person's character and making greater betrayals easier to justify.

An executive who embezzles millions may have started with small acts of financial dishonesty. A politician who abuses power may have first justified accepting minor favors. A spouse who commits adultery may have begun with seemingly harmless emotional compromises. The greatest betrayals in history often began with choices that once seemed insignificant.

The challenge is to recognize the small betrayals in our own lives and stop them before they escalate into something unmanageable.

- Daily decisions shape integrity.
- Are we honest in our financial dealings?
- Do we keep our promises, even when it's inconvenient?
- Do we uphold integrity in both our public and private lives?

Choosing Redemption Over Betrayal

While betrayal is a reality in the modern world, redemption is always possible. Everyone experiences moments of failure—times when self-interest takes precedence over integrity. What truly matters is whether we acknowledge these failures and choose to make amends.

Choosing integrity means doing what is right, even when no one is watching. It means standing up for justice, even when it comes at a personal cost. It means staying loyal in relationships, even when sacrifice is required. Most importantly, it means choosing love, honesty, and truth in a world that often rewards the opposite.

Every day, we face choices that shape who we become. The question is simple: Will we take the easy path of betrayal, or will we choose integrity, justice, and love? The choice is ours—and it must be made every day.

Reflection Questions for Modern Life: The Thirty Pieces of Silver

1. What is my "thirty pieces of silver"?

Judas betrayed Jesus for money, choosing wealth over loyalty. Similarly, in modern life, we may not exchange someone for literal silver, but we often compromise our values in pursuit of financial success, comfort, or social status. Have I ever sacrificed my values, relationships, or integrity for financial gain or personal ambition? Have I placed money above people in my decision-making? Take a moment to reflect on how material desires may have influenced your choices and consider ways to realign your priorities with integrity and faithfulness.

2. In what ways do I put self-interest above relationships?

Judas' betrayal was not just about money; it was also a choice of self-interest over his relationship with Jesus. Similarly, in today's world, personal ambition, pride, and self-preservation often lead people to neglect or even betray their relationships with family, friends, and colleagues. Do I place my career above my family? Have I ever prioritized personal convenience over loyalty? Do I neglect those who rely on me because I am too focused on my own goals? Reflect on how you can nurture your relationships by being more present, faithful, and selfless in your commitments.

3. Have I ever betrayed someone emotionally through dishonesty, gossip, or neglect?

Betrayal is not always a grand act of treachery—it often occurs in subtle ways we fail to recognize. Spreading gossip, breaking confidences, or neglecting a friend in their time of need are all forms of betrayal. Have I ever broken someone's trust? Have I spoken negatively about someone behind their back? Have I neglected a friendship or family bond simply because it was inconvenient? Take time to reflect on how you can restore trust and become a more faithful and reliable presence in the lives of those around you.

4. Am I complicit in systems of exploitation?

The Pope's homily highlights modern forms of human trafficking and economic injustice. Today, many industries profit from cheap labor, unethical business practices, and exploitation. As consumers, we may knowingly or unknowingly support these systems by prioritizing convenience over justice. Do I purchase products from companies that exploit workers? Do I stay silent about workplace injustices because speaking out feels risky? Am I complicit in a culture that prioritizes profit over human dignity? Reflect on how you can make ethical choices as both a consumer and a professional, ensuring that you do not contribute to systems that undermine human dignity.

5. Do I compromise my values in small ways, thinking it does not matter?

Judas did not become a traitor overnight; his downfall began with small compromises—stealing from the common purse, deceiving others, and allowing greed to take root. Likewise, have I ever justified small lies or unethical actions, convincing myself they were harmless? Have I rationalized dishonest behavior in business, relationships, or personal life? Reflect on how small moral compromises can gradually erode integrity and commit to upholding your values, even in seemingly insignificant situations.

6. How do I respond when I realize I've made a mistake? Do I seek forgiveness or give in to guilt?

Judas' greatest mistake was not his betrayal but his despair—he believed he was beyond redemption. In contrast, Peter also betrayed Jesus but sought forgiveness and was restored. When I fail, do I allow guilt and shame to consume me, or do I seek forgiveness and healing? Do I believe that God's mercy is greater than my failures? Reflect on how you can embrace a spirit of repentance and recognize that no mistake is beyond God's redemption.

7. Do I let fear dictate my choices?

Fear often leads to betrayal, driving people to act out of self-preservation rather than truth. In today's world, the fear of financial insecurity, rejection, or failure can pressure individuals to compromise their values, making choices they might otherwise resist. Do I make choices based on fear rather than faith? Do I hesitate to stand up for what is right because I fear the consequences? Take a moment to reflect on how fear may be influencing your decisions and consider ways to cultivate the courage needed to remain steadfast in your beliefs and integrity.

8. How do I treat the vulnerable in my life?

Pope Francis highlights the betrayal of the elderly, the exploited, and the forgotten. In many societies, the weak and voiceless are often cast aside for the sake of convenience. Do I take the time to care for my aging parents, support my neighbors, or extend help to those in need? Do I engage with the marginalized in my community, or do I ignore them because their struggles don't directly affect me? How can I be more compassionate and proactive in defending and caring for the most vulnerable?

9. Have I allowed ambition, power, or pride to lead me away from God?

Judas sought wealth and influence, believing they would bring him security. Today, many idolize success, fame, or power, often at the cost of their spiritual well-being. Do I measure my worth by achievements rather than my relationship with God? Does pride keep me from admitting my mistakes or seeking forgiveness? Where is my heart truly focused, and how can I realign my life with faith and humility?

10. How can I choose love, integrity, and faithfulness over betrayal?

Ultimately, the homily presents a choice: to follow the path of Judas, which leads to despair, or the path of redemption, which leads to life. Each day, we are confronted with decisions—to embrace truth or deception, loyalty or betrayal, integrity or compromise, self-interest or love. What choices am I making in my daily life? Am I actively striving to be a person of faith, love, and trustworthiness? Reflect on how you can choose faithfulness in the small, daily decisions that shape your character and define your future.

Each of these questions invites a deeper examination of how we live, how we treat others, and how we remain faithful to our values. The story of Judas is more than just a historical account—it reflects the temptations and struggles we all face. Yet, unlike Judas, we are called to choose hope over despair, integrity over compromise, and love over betrayal.

Take time to reflect on these questions with honesty. Journal your responses, pray over them, and consider concrete actions you can take to live a life of faithfulness, justice, and love. The choice is always before us. Will we follow Judas into despair, or will we follow Christ into redemption?

Chapter 4

The Danger of Indignation and the Simplicity of God

Chapel Of The Domus Sanctae Marthae - Monday, 16 March 2020

The Homily

In this homily, Pope Francis reflects on the theme of indignation—a natural human reaction that, if left unchecked, can lead to contempt, rejection, and even violence. Drawing from two biblical passages, he illustrates how both the people of Nazareth and Naaman, the Syrian commander, became indignant when faced with the simplicity of God's ways. This reaction, he suggests, stems from a spiritual **blindness** that refuses to accept God's presence in ordinary, humble realities.

The Gospel passage from Luke recounts how the people of Nazareth first listened to Jesus with admiration but quickly turned against Him upon realizing He was 'the carpenter's son.' Their reaction was not based on Jesus' words or deeds but on their inability to accept that someone so familiar, so ordinary, could be a messenger of God. They expected grandeur, wisdom shaped by elite education, and miracles that aligned with their vision of divine power. Instead, they saw someone from their town, someone whose simplicity offended their pride.

This indignation quickly escalated to violence. What started as doubt and scorn soon turned into an attempt to kill Jesus. Unable to reconcile their preconceived notions with reality, the crowd sought to eliminate the source of their discomfort. Pope Francis suggests that this pattern is not unique to the people of Nazareth but is a recurring human tendency—one that persists today when people reject truth, wisdom, or holiness simply because it comes in an unexpected or unassuming form.

A similar pattern emerges in the *Old Testament* story of Naaman, a respected Syrian commander afflicted with leprosy. When the prophet Elisha instructs him to bathe seven times in the Jordan River for healing, Naaman responds with anger and disdain. He expected something more dramatic—a prophetic ritual, an impressive display of divine intervention. Instead, he was given a simple command.

Like the people of Nazareth, Naaman could not accept that God's power could be revealed in something so ordinary. He judged the command through worldly expectations—that important matters must be extraordinary and that divine power must manifest in visibly impressive ways. His indignation blinded him to the possibility that healing could come through something as humble as the waters of the Jordan.

Unlike the people of Nazareth, Naaman eventually overcomes his pride. Persuaded by his servants, he chooses to follow Elisha's instructions and is healed. This contrast between the two stories highlights two possible paths: one of humility that leads to transformation and one of pride that leads to destruction.

At the core of both stories is a refusal to accept that God acts through simplicity. The people of Nazareth could not recognize God in someone they had known since childhood, just as Naaman could not see divine power in the waters of an ordinary river. In both cases, indignation arose because God did not conform to human expectations.

Pope Francis warns that this reaction is not confined to biblical times. Many today still struggle with the idea that holiness can be found in the ordinary, that true wisdom can come from simple people, and that God's presence is not limited to impressive religious displays. There is a temptation to believe that divine action must be grand, intellectual, or visibly miraculous to be real.

This spiritual elitism blinds people to the everyday workings of grace.

This rejection of simplicity often leads to violence—whether physical or verbal. The people of Nazareth turned their indignation into an attempt to kill Jesus. Naaman, in his initial anger, nearly rejected his only chance for healing. In modern life, indignation still manifests in ways that harm others—through mockery, exclusion, and even outright hostility toward those who challenge deeply held biases.

Pope Francis connects this theme to a broader human tendency—the need to feel superior. Some seek reasons to be indignant as a way of asserting their importance. By looking down on others and ridiculing what they perceive as 'less sophisticated' or 'too simple,' they elevate themselves. This prideful indignation, however, is ultimately a sign of spiritual emptiness.

He offers a modern example—a man who, during a quarantine, reacted with violence and racial contempt when a police officer stopped him from leaving a restricted area. The reaction was not merely about frustration but about a deep sense of entitlement, a belief that certain rules should not apply to him. This moment of indignation turned into an act of verbal and physical violence, mirroring the same pattern seen in the biblical stories.

The Pope references what theologians call 'The scandal of the Pharisees'—a resistance to the idea that God can work through the humble, the poor, and the ordinary. Many struggle with the notion that holiness can exist in a quiet, unseen way. Some believe that God must work only through the brilliant, the powerful, or the highly educated. This mindset is a dangerous form of spiritual arrogance, one that blinds people to the reality of God's presence in their midst.

Pope Francis suggests that true faith is the ability to recognize God in simplicity—in the daily routines of life, in the quiet perseverance of good people, and in the unremarkable moments where grace is at work. Those who insist that God must act in extraordinary ways often fail to see His presence altogether.

The homily ends with an invitation to self-examination. Are we, like the people of Nazareth, rejecting wisdom because it comes from an unexpected source? Are we like Naaman, resisting grace because it seems too simple? Or can we, like Naaman in the end, humble ourselves enough to recognize God in the ordinary?

Pope Francis reminds us that indignation is a temptation that must be resisted. It is not just an emotion but a doorway to pride, blindness, and even violence. When confronted with something unexpected, especially in matters of faith, the challenge is to remain open rather than dismissive humble rather than arrogant.

God continues to reveal Himself in simple, everyday ways. The question is whether we are willing to recognize Him there—or whether, like the people of Nazareth, we will allow our pride to drive Him away.

Homily Analysis: The Spiritual Danger of Indignation and the Rejection of Simplicity

Pope Francis' homily explores the subtle yet destructive nature of indignation, particularly when it stems from a rejection of God's simplicity. Drawing from two biblical narratives—Jesus' rejection in Nazareth and Naaman's initial refusal to obey Elisha—the homily highlights how indignation can blind people to the presence of the divine, turning admiration into contempt and, in extreme cases, leading to violence.

The Pope's reflection is not merely an observation of past events but a deeper exploration of how spiritual pride and rigid expectations can prevent individuals from recognizing God's work.

At its core, this homily examines the spiritual condition that fuels indignation: a refusal to accept that God operates through ordinary means. Those who expect divine action to be grand, extraordinary, or tailored to human expectations often struggle to recognize it when it appears in simple, humble, or familiar forms. This theological insight challenges the belief that faith must always be accompanied by spectacle, emphasizing instead that God's presence is most often revealed through the unnoticed, the ordinary, and the unassuming.

Indignation as a Barrier to Faith

Indignation, as presented in the homily, is not merely an emotional reaction; it is a spiritual disposition that arises when individuals encounter something that contradicts their assumptions about how God should act. Both the people of Nazareth and Naaman are described as being offended by the idea that God's power could be mediated through simple, unexpected channels.

This reaction is significant because it reveals a fundamental resistance to faith itself. Faith requires trust in something beyond human reasoning and expectations. However, indignation arises when human reasoning clashes with divine simplicity. Those who insist that God must act in a certain way—through the powerful, the spectacular, the extraordinary— become scandalized by His choice to work through the humble, the ordinary, and the small.

In both biblical examples, indignation closes the heart. The people of Nazareth, who initially admired Jesus' words, quickly dismissed Him when they realized He was merely 'the carpenter's son.' Similarly, Naaman, a man seeking healing, became angry when Elisha's command did not align with his expectations of grandeur. Their offense was not intellectual but deeply personal—they could not accept that the divine could manifest in a way so far removed from their ideals.

This suggests that indignation is not simply about rejecting a person or a message but about rejecting the humility of God Himself. The refusal to accept that God can work through ordinary means is, in essence, a rejection of the very nature of divine wisdom, which does not conform to human standards of greatness.

The Hidden Connection Between Indignation and Violence

One of the most striking themes in the homily is the connection between indignation and violence. Pope Francis illustrates how what begins as a reaction of contempt can escalate into something far more destructive. The people of Nazareth, initially merely doubtful of Jesus, quickly turned their skepticism into aggression, driving Him out of the synagogue and attempting to kill Him. Naaman's indignation, though less extreme, manifested in an immediate act of rejection—he turned away from the possibility of healing simply because it did not align with his preconceived notions.

This progression is not coincidental. Indignation is a symptom of wounded pride, and wounded pride often seeks to reassert itself through force—whether through words, actions, or, as seen in Nazareth, outright violence. When confronted with something that challenges their understanding, people often react not with reflection but with aggression, as if eliminating the source of discomfort will resolve their inner conflict.

This insight has profound theological implications. It suggests that the rejection of divine simplicity is not a passive act but an active resistance to grace. The rejection of Jesus in Nazareth was not merely disbelief—it was an attempt to silence and remove that which could not be controlled. Similarly, Naaman's initial reaction was not just doubt but a complete unwillingness to engage with a divine action that did not align with his expectations.

This spiritual truth echoes throughout religious history. The prophets were often persecuted not because they lacked truth but because their truth was too simple, too direct, and too challenging. Jesus Himself was rejected not because His words lacked wisdom but because they threatened the structures of human pride and control. The violence that indignation produces is ultimately an attempt to resist the vulnerability required to accept God's ways.

The Rejection of Simplicity as a Theological Crisis

Underlying the theme of indignation is a deeper theological issue—the human tendency to associate God with grandeur rather than humility. This is one of the most enduring struggles in religious thought: the expectation that God must act in ways that align with human concepts of power, wisdom, and spectacle.

The people of Nazareth rejected Jesus because He was too familiar. They believed the Messiah should be someone extraordinary, someone who conformed to the image of divine power they had constructed in their minds. Similarly, Naaman rejected Elisha's command because it seemed too ordinary. He assumed that a prophet should heal in a visibly miraculous way, not through something as simple as washing in a river.

Both cases reveal the danger of placing human conditions on divine action. When people expect God to conform to their image, they risk missing His presence altogether. The rejection of Jesus in Nazareth was not because He lacked wisdom or authority but because His wisdom and authority did not come in the form people expected. Naaman almost lost his chance at healing because the divine instruction did not meet his standards of significance.

This theological crisis—the inability to recognize God in simplicity—lies at the heart of the homily. Pope Francis highlights this rejection not as a mere historical event but as a persistent spiritual blindness. It is a condition that can affect anyone who insists that divine action must be extraordinary to be authentic. The truth, however, is that God works most often in hidden, humble ways—in everyday life, in ordinary people, in small acts of grace that do not seek attention.

Indignation as a Form of Spiritual Elitism

Pope Francis delves into a deeper psychological and spiritual dynamic—the tendency for indignation to arise from a desire for superiority. Those who constantly seek reasons to be outraged or offended often do so because indignation grants them a sense of importance, reinforcing their perception of moral or intellectual superiority. This is why the rejection of divine simplicity is not just a theological issue but a reflection of the human tendency to define oneself through status, knowledge, or power.

When left unchecked, indignation turns into a form of spiritual elitism. It declares, "God must operate in a way that aligns with my understanding." This mindset places the self at the center of faith, insisting that God prove Himself through signs, miracles, or displays of power rather than through the quiet, transformative presence of grace.

This was the very temptation that plagued the people of Nazareth and Naamàn—the refusal to accept that God does not operate according to human hierarchies. This same struggle recurs throughout history whenever people reject the divine simply because it arrives through the poor, the uneducated, or the unexpected.

The Call to Humility

Pope Francis' homily ultimately calls for a posture of humility. Indignation is more than just an emotional response—it is a barrier to faith, a resistance to grace, and a manifestation of spiritual pride. Those who demand that God conform to their expectations risk missing Him entirely.

The lesson from both Naamàn and the people of Nazareth is clear: God reveals Himself through simplicity, and to reject simplicity is to reject Him. The challenge, then, is to cultivate a faith that remains open, humble, and willing to recognize the divine in the ordinary. Only by letting go of the need for grandeur, control, and certainty can one truly encounter the living God.

Recognizing the Divine in Simplicity: Lessons for Modern Life

Modern life moves at an unforgiving pace, driven by an endless pursuit of achievement, recognition, and spectacle. People are conditioned to seek significance in the grand and extraordinary, believing that only the most remarkable moments define a life well lived. Yet this obsession with visible success—promotions, wealth, fame, or social admiration—often blinds them to a deeper truth: meaning, wisdom, and transformation are not always found in these pursuits but are instead woven into the fabric of the ordinary.

There is a growing resistance to simplicity, as many assume that what is small, routine, or unnoticed lacks value. Yet a father reading his child a bedtime story, a friend offering quiet support during a difficult time, or a stranger holding the door open on a busy morning—these seemingly insignificant moments shape the very essence of human connection. Yet, they are often dismissed because they do not command attention.

The Resistance to Simplicity in Modern Life

A common belief in modern society is that only what stands out is valuable. This mindset is evident in the professional world, where many measure success not by the quality of their work but by their titles and salaries. A teacher who has inspired generations of students may feel invisible next to an executive with a high-profile career. A nurse who has comforted countless patients may question whether their impact matters simply because their name is never recognized beyond the hospital walls. Yet, these individuals often shape lives in ways that those in the public eye never could.

The same resistance to simplicity exists in relationships. Many people expect love to be constant excitement, filled with extravagant gestures and passionate declarations. When love instead takes the form of daily care—cooking a meal, listening without distraction, supporting a partner through an uneventful but tiring day—it is often overlooked. A couple who remains together for fifty years does not do so because their life is filled with grand romantic gestures but because they have mastered the art of choosing each other every day—even when no one is watching.

In spirituality, there is often a deep longing for profound, mystical experiences—those rare moments when faith feels undeniably real. Many seek emotional highs in religious settings, dramatic encounters with the divine, or life-altering revelations. However, the strongest faith is not forged in rare moments but in the daily practice of quiet devotion—a silent prayer, a choice to forgive, an act of kindness expecting nothing in return.

Social media and popular culture reinforce the belief that ordinary life is not enough. Curated images of luxury vacations, career milestones, and idealized relationships create an illusion of perfection, fostering a false sense of inadequacy and making people feel as if their own lives fall short. The truth, however, is that these carefully presented moments do not reflect the depth of a meaningful life. The joy of sitting with a loved one in comfortable silence, the satisfaction of finishing a long day's work with integrity, the peace of watching the sunrise with no audience—these are the moments that build the foundation of a life well lived.

The challenge is to break free from the illusion that meaning lies elsewhere and instead embrace the beauty and depth of what is already present.

Indignation and the Need for Superiority

Another obstacle to embracing simplicity is indignation, a reaction often rooted in pride and the desire to feel superior. People tend to reject truth or wisdom when it comes from a source they perceive as unimpressive or unqualified. A seasoned lawyer may dismiss the insights of a younger colleague, assuming experience is the only marker of intelligence. A manager may overlook an entry-level employee's idea, assuming that good solutions only come from leadership. A student may dismiss their parents' advice, believing their generation better understands the world.

This same mindset plays out in everyday social interactions. A person who values intellect may look down on simple acts of kindness, believing them to be insignificant. Someone who prides themselves on being self-sufficient may reject help from others, even when struggling. This need for superiority fuels a cycle of resentment, blinding people to the truth that wisdom, goodness, and insight are not tied to status or credentials but often emerge from the most unexpected places.

A powerful example of this is found in the medical field. Some of the most valuable insights into patient care come not from doctors but from nurses and hospital aides, who spend the most time at a patient's bedside. Yet, their contributions are often overlooked because society has conditioned people to associate authority with expertise, ignoring the reality that wisdom can be found at every level.

This same principle applies to personal relationships. Many resist apologizing, believing it will weaken their position. They reject reconciliation not because they don't desire it but because their pride prevents them from embracing humility. In reality, the willingness to apologize, learn from others, and accept wisdom from unexpected sources is a true mark of strength.

The antidote to indignation is humility—a willingness to recognize that everyone has something to teach and that the most profound lessons often come from the places least expected.

Finding Meaning in the Everyday

Once people let go of the need for spectacle, superiority, and recognition, they can begin to see the extraordinary within the ordinary.

A teacher who dedicates time to struggling students may never receive widespread recognition, yet their quiet devotion can shape the future of those they teach. A cashier who greets each customer with kindness may seem insignificant in the grand scheme of things, yet their small gestures enrich the fabric of human connection. A janitor who takes pride in keeping a school clean may not receive awards, but their work creates an environment where children feel safe and valued.

In personal relationships, embracing the power of small moments reshapes how love is understood. A spouse who listens attentively—rather than half-heartedly nodding while distracted by their phone—builds trust over time. A friend who checks in regularly, even with a simple text, nurtures a connection that endures far beyond grand gestures.

Even in personal fulfillment, meaning is not found in grand achievements alone. A musician who plays not for fame but for the love of the craft experiences a joy deeper than applause. A writer who crafts stories that may never be published still finds fulfillment in the act of creation. A person who pauses to appreciate nature sits in silence and fully embraces the present moment lives a rich life—even if it goes unnoticed.

Overcoming Resistance to Simplicity

The fear of insignificance prevents many from embracing simplicity. They worry that if they do not stand out, they will be forgotten—that if their actions go unpraised, they do not matter. But this fear is an illusion. A meaningful life is not defined by its visibility but by the depth of its impact.

A grandmother who shares family stories with her grandchildren is passing down a legacy as valuable as any public achievement. A small business owner who treats their employees with dignity changes lives in ways that will never make headlines. A person who takes the time to listen, to be present, to care—even if no one notices—contributes to the world in ways that cannot be measured but are deeply felt.

In the end, the challenge is not to seek the extraordinary but to recognize the extraordinary in what is already there. Those who can do this will find that the beauty, meaning, and depth they have been searching for were never distant or unattainable; they were always present, waiting to be seen.

Reflection Questions for Modern Life: Finding Meaning in Simplicity

In a world driven by achievement, status, and visibility, people often struggle to find meaning in the ordinary, the quiet, and the unseen. Many believe that fulfillment comes from grand moments, yet the most profound aspects of life—love, wisdom, and purpose—are often found in the simple and the overlooked.

1. Do I measure success by external validation or by internal fulfillment?

Many people define success through titles, salaries, and public recognition. Social media amplifies this perception, suggesting that achievements must be visible to be valuable. However, true fulfillment often stems from the impact we have on others, the integrity of our actions, and the quiet satisfaction of meaningful work.

Reflecting on this question demands deep introspection: Am I chasing success to impress others, or am I pursuing something that genuinely fulfills me? If external validation—likes, promotions, applause—were stripped away, would I still feel accomplished? What if success were defined entirely on my terms? How would it look? More importantly, how would it feel?

2. Do I appreciate the people in my life, or do I take them for granted?

Modern life moves at a fast pace, and amid the rush of daily responsibilities, it's easy to overlook the quiet presence of those who support us. Too often, people recognize the value of loved ones only after they are gone.

This reflection challenges readers to ask themselves: Do I express gratitude to those who care for me, or do I take their presence for granted? Have I made an effort to show appreciation, to listen, and to nurture my relationships? What simple action can I take today to let someone know they matter?

3. Do I resist wisdom when it comes from unexpected places?

There is a common belief that valuable insights must come from recognized experts, highly educated individuals, or those in positions of power. Yet wisdom often emerges from unexpected sources—the quiet observer, the elder with lived experience, or the child with a fresh perspective.

This reflection prompts an important question: Am I open to learning from those I may have overlooked? Have I dismissed advice or insights simply because they didn't come from someone I considered "qualified"? What might I gain if I listened more attentively—even to those I least expect?

4. Do I prioritize presence, or am I constantly distracted?

With the rise of technology, social media, and endless entertainment, attention spans have shortened, making genuine presence increasingly rare. Many relationships don't suffer from a lack of love but rather a lack of attention.

This reflection invites individuals to examine their habits: Do I truly listen when someone speaks, or is my mind elsewhere? How often do I reach for my phone instead of fully engaging in the moment? How might my relationships transform if I offered my undivided attention more often?

5. Do I find joy in every day, or am I always waiting for something bigger?

People often postpone happiness, believing it will arrive after a promotion, a big vacation, or a certain milestone. Yet life unfolds in the present, and joy is most often found in the simple, overlooked moments.

This question invites reflection: Do I appreciate the beauty of my daily life, or am I always looking ahead to the next big thing? When was the last time I paused to enjoy something small—a conversation, a meal, a quiet moment of rest? If I could no longer chase external goals, would I still find contentment in my life?

6. Do I let pride prevent me from apologizing or admitting when I am wrong?

Indignation and pride often make it difficult for people to admit their mistakes or seek reconciliation. Many hold grudges—not because they want to, but because their ego prevents them from taking the first step toward healing.

This reflection challenges readers to examine their relationships: Is there someone I need to apologize to but haven't because of pride? Have I avoided admitting I was wrong, even when I knew I should? What would it take for me to choose humility over the need to be right?

7. Am I living according to my values, or am I following societal expectations?

The pressure to conform—to follow certain careers, lifestyles, or definitions of success—can pull people away from what they truly desire. Many wake up years later, realizing they have built a life based on expectations rather than authentic wants.

This question prompts reflection: Am I making choices that align with what truly matters to me? If I removed the pressure to impress others, would I still be on the same path? What changes—big or small—could help me live a life more authentic to my values?

8. Do I practice generosity, or do I hold tightly to what I have?

In a world that prioritizes accumulation—wealth, possessions, and status—generosity often takes a back seat. Yet some of the most content people are those who give freely—not just money, but also their time, kindness, and compassion.

This reflection invites self-examination: Do I give only when it's convenient, or do I make generosity a habit? Do I freely share knowledge, encouragement, and kindness, or do I keep them to myself? When was the last time I gave without expecting anything in return?

9. Am I open to change, or do I resist it out of fear?

Many people fear change, even when it is essential for growth. They stay in jobs they dislike, hold onto relationships that have outlived their purpose, or cling to routines that no longer serve them—all because the unknown feels more daunting than the familiar discomfort they have learned to endure.

This reflection prompts readers to consider:

- Am I clinging to something that no longer serves me out of fear of change?

- How might my life evolve if I embraced uncertainty instead of avoiding it?
- What is one small step I can take toward the transformation I need?

10. Do I practice generosity, or do I hold tightly to what I have?

How can I choose love, integrity, and faithfulness over betrayal?

What is one simple action I can take today to create a more meaningful life?

Reflection is valuable, but without action, it remains merely an intellectual exercise. Meaningful change rarely begins with dramatic decisions; instead, it unfolds through small, consistent steps.

This final question challenges readers to take one small, intentional action. It could be as simple as expressing gratitude, setting aside distractions when speaking with a loved one, extending kindness to a stranger, or taking a step toward a long-neglected dream. What is one small act I can commit to today that will bring more depth, connection, or joy into my life?

The modern world urges people to chase what is grand, loud, and visible—often at the cost of life's quieter, more meaningful moments. Yet, true fulfillment is not found in relentless striving but in presence, humility, and the ability to appreciate the beauty in the everyday.

These questions are not meant to be answered once and then forgotten. They serve as an invitation to ongoing self-reflection—a way to continually reassess what truly matters. By embracing the simple, the overlooked, and the ordinary, we discover that life does not need to be grand to be meaningful; it simply needs to be lived with intention, gratitude, and love.

Dedication

A Life of Faith and Miracles

Gladys Lim

This book is dedicated to my beloved mother, Gladys Lim—a woman of unwavering faith, boundless love, and quiet strength. More than the one who gave me life, she has been my anchor, my guiding light, and my first teacher in faith. Through both her words and the fabric of her life, she has shown me what it truly means to trust in God with absolute surrender. Her faith has never been fleeting or performative, it is the very foundation upon which she stands. Deeply rooted, it has shaped not only her own life but also the lives of everyone around her.

From my earliest memories, I have watched my mother dedicate herself to the service of God—not in grand, ostentatious ways, but through quiet, steadfast devotion, the true mark of a holy life. Whether in the kindness she extends to others, the compassion in her heart, or the countless prayers whispered in the stillness of the night, she embodies what it means to live a life centered on faith. She has taught me that faith is not merely about reciting prayers or attending Mass but about how we carry ourselves in the world—how we love, how we serve, and how we endure.

She has faced trials that would shake even the strongest souls, yet she has never wavered. Even in moments of hardship—when others might have questioned God—she stood firm, trusting that His presence was with her, even in suffering. It is through her that I have learned faith is not the absence of struggle but the courage to trust in God amid uncertainty. She has carried burdens with grace, faced difficulties with quiet resilience, and remained steadfast in her belief that God's hand is at work in every moment—both the joyous and the painful.

What makes her journey even more remarkable is that she has been blessed to witness not just one but two miracles in her lifetime. These were not mere coincidences or strokes of luck—they were divine interventions, affirmations of what she has always known: God is real, He is listening, and He is ever-present in our lives. These miracles were not just for her; they were a testament to all of us who had the privilege of witnessing her faith. They served as a powerful reminder that we do not believe in an abstract

God but in a living, active God who moves in ways beyond our understanding.

Yet the greatest miracle of all is the life she has lived— a life of sacrifice, humility, and unwavering devotion— a life that has quietly yet powerfully transformed those around her. She gave it without expecting anything in return. She has loved with a heart so full it could never be emptied. She has lived not for herself but for others, always placing her family and faith above her own needs.

Because of my mother, I have spent the past 40 years immersing myself in the teachings of the Catholic Church, drawn not only to its doctrines but also to the beauty of a faith lived with sincerity. She never imposed religion upon me; she lived it so authentically that I could not help but be drawn to it. She taught me, through her own life, that faith is not merely something we profess but something we embody. It is how we show up for others, how we extend grace, and how we trust in God even when we do not understand His ways.

This book, in many ways, reflects her influence. It was born from the seeds of faith she planted in me, nurtured by the lessons she imparted, and inspired by the unwavering trust in God she has exemplified. Because of her, I have sought to deepen my understanding of Catholicism. Because of her, I have come to appreciate the wisdom of the Church, the sacredness of the Mass, and the transformative power of God's word, and it is her example that has drawn me to the teachings of Pope Francis, whose words—much like hers—call us to a faith lived out in love, humility, and service.

As I wrote these pages, I often thought of her—of the quiet moments when she knelt in prayer, entrusting everything to God, and of the unwavering hope she carried in the face of adversity. I thought of the love she has poured into our family, into her faith and the very essence of her being. This book is as much a reflection of her as it is a testament to the wisdom of the Church.

It is a tribute to your faith, your sacrifices, and your unwavering love. I will never be able to repay all that you have given me fully, but I pray this book serves as a small token of my gratitude and testament to the legacy of faith you have built. Your faith has been my compass, and your prayers, my shield. Your love is my greatest blessing.

May God continue to bless you abundantly, just as you have blessed all of us with your presence. May He walk beside you always, just as you have always walked with Him. May this book serve as a reminder that faith, at its core, is not about grandeur or recognition but about the quiet, steadfast devotion you have lived so beautifully.

This book is for you, my mother—my heart, my hero, my greatest example of love and unwavering trust in God.

Chapter 5

Jealousy: The Struggle Between the Holy Spirit and the Spirit of Envy

The Chapel of The Domus Sanctae Marthae - Saturday, 9 May 2020

The Homily

Pope Francis' homily delves into a profound spiritual reality that has shaped the Church since its inception—the ongoing struggle between the Holy Spirit, which builds and strengthens the Church, and the forces of envy, which seek to undermine it. Drawing from the Acts of the Apostles, he highlights how early Christian communities experienced both extraordinary growth and intense opposition. The homily focuses specifically on events in Antioch, where Paul and the apostles preached with such conviction that the entire city gathered to hear them. The people's enthusiasm was undeniable—the Gospel spread rapidly, drawing new believers and deepening the faith of the early Church.

However, this great success was met with an immediate and forceful backlash from those who opposed the apostles. The religious leaders, consumed by jealousy over Paul and his companions' growing influence, incited violent opposition. Their envy was not mere resentment but an active campaign to contradict, attack, and silence the apostles. Pope Francis emphasizes that this pattern of resistance is a fundamental truth in Christian history. Every great movement of the Holy Spirit is met with an equally determined effort by the forces of evil to suppress it.

To reinforce this point, the Pope recalls several other incidents from the Acts of the Apostles where jealousy and selfish interests led to persecution. In Lystra, for instance, after Paul and Barnabas healed a crippled man, the people initially treated them as gods. However, when others came to spread doubt and misinformation, the same crowd turned against them, and Paul was stoned nearly to death. Similarly, when Paul and Silas preached in Philippi, they disrupted the business of men who profited from a slave girl's ability to tell fortunes. In retaliation, the merchants stirred up the city against them, leading to their imprisonment. Another example comes from Ephesus, where craftsmen who made idols of the goddess Artemis saw their business decline as more people converted to Christianity. Instead of embracing the truth of the Gospel, they instigated a riot to force Paul out of the city.

Through these examples, Pope Francis highlights an essential truth about the nature of evangelization: the spread of the Gospel will always be accompanied by resistance. This is not because the Gospel itself is violent or oppressive but because it disrupts power structures rooted in greed, manipulation, and control. The message of Christ challenges social systems built on exploitation, corruption, and self-interest, inevitably provoking opposition from those who benefit from them.

The Pope identifies jealousy as one of the devil's primary tools for opposing the Gospel. He recalls the words from the Book of Wisdom: "Because of the devil's envy, sin entered the world" (Wisdom 2:24). Jealousy is not merely an emotion but a destructive force that compels people to act against goodness and truth. The jealous leaders in Antioch could not tolerate the success of the apostles because it diminished their influence. Rather than rejoicing that people were discovering God's truth, they allowed their envy to fuel hostility and rejection.

This same pattern, Pope Francis notes, played a role in the Passion of Christ. The religious leaders of Jesus' time were not merely skeptical of His teachings; they were enraged by His growing influence. Their jealousy blinded them to His miracles, His wisdom, and the fulfillment of Scripture. Rather than recognizing Him as the Messiah, they conspired to have Him crucified. Their envious hearts, hardened by pride, drove them to commit the greatest injustice in history.

Even today, Pope Francis warns, jealousy continues to sow chaos in the world. It lies at the root of much of the division, hostility, and persecution faced by the Church. Whether in personal relationships, workplaces, or society at large, jealousy fuels competition, resentment, and conflict. It can drive people to tear others down instead of seeking the truth and uplifting one another.

Despite these challenges, Pope Francis reminds us that the Church has always moved forward "between the consolations of God and the persecutions of the world." Quoting St. Augustine, he emphasizes that the Church's journey has always been shaped by both divine blessings and worldly opposition—a truth that has endured from the time of the apostles to the present day. Wherever the Gospel flourishes, resistance inevitably follows. Pope Francis makes it clear that if the Church encounters no struggle, it may be a sign that something is amiss—that it has grown complacent or too comfortable with the world.

Yet, history also shows that persecution never succeeds in silencing the Gospel. It often strengthens the Church. The blood of the martyrs has always been the seed of new believers, and even in the face of immense suffering, Christianity has continued to flourish. Pope Francis assures us that the balance always tilts in favor of the Holy Spirit. The forces of evil may strike, but they can never ultimately prevail against God's truth.

The homily also serves as a warning against the temptation to use worldly power to advance the Gospel. Pope Francis recalls how the religious leaders in Antioch manipulated influential men and women to oppose the apostles. Likewise, in the case of Jesus, the high priests leveraged their authority over the Romans to ensure His crucifixion. Money and political power have often been used to silence the truth.

This, Pope Francis warns, is a dangerous trap even for believers. There is always a temptation for Christians to seek protection or influence by aligning themselves with worldly power. But history reveals that whenever the Church grows too reliant on politics, wealth, or social influence, it risks compromising its true mission. The Church's strength comes from the Holy Spirit, not from governments, financial power, or political alliances.

Pope Francis draws a parallel between the opposition faced by the apostles and the attempts to suppress the truth of Christ's resurrection. After Jesus rose from the dead, the religious leaders bribed the Roman guards to spread false reports that His body had been stolen. Even in the face of undeniable divine power, worldly authorities sought to distort the truth through bribery and deception.

Pope Francis concludes his homily with a call for vigilance. He urges Christians to remain aware of the forces that seek to weaken their faith—whether through persecution, jealousy, or the lure of worldly power. Yet, he also offers encouragement: the Holy Spirit is the Church's true source of strength, and no force of darkness can ultimately prevail against it.

He reminds us that true faith does not seek comfort or security but embraces opposition for the sake of truth. The Church will always face struggles, yet these challenges are a sign that it is faithfully living out its mission. Pope Francis urges believers to stand firm, trust in God's providence, and continue proclaiming the Gospel, confident that the Holy Spirit will always guide and strengthen them.

The key takeaway from this homily is clear: wherever the Gospel is preached, opposition will arise. Yet, as Christians, we are called to trust in the power of the Holy Spirit, resist the temptations of jealousy and worldly ambition, and remain faithful in the face of adversity. In the end, truth and love will always triumph over envy and opposition.

Homily Analysis: The Eternal Struggle Between Truth and Power

Pope Francis' homily presents a profound reflection on the persistent tension between truth and the forces that seek to suppress it. By examining the reaction of the religious leaders in Antioch, Pope Francis highlights how jealousy often lies at the root of opposition to the Gospel. Yet, this is not merely an isolated event in history—it is a recurring struggle within human nature, religious institutions, politics, and society as a whole.

Throughout history, jealousy has been one of the most insidious and destructive forces, blinding people to goodness, distorting reality, and fueling acts of suppression, persecution, and injustice. Pope Francis' homily serves as a cautionary lesson on the dangers of jealousy, the consequences of valuing power over truth, and the resilience needed to remain faithful in the face of opposition.

Jealousy as a Destructive Force in Human History

Jealousy has long been a corrupting force in human relationships, shaping the course of history in deeply damaging ways. It is often the cause of conflicts, betrayals, and divisions within families, communities, and nations. Pope Francis emphasizes that the opposition to Paul and Barnabas was driven not by reasoned debate or theological disagreement but by jealousy. The Jewish leaders saw the apostles drawing large crowds and feared losing their influence. Rather than engaging with the truth, they let envy consume them, leading to hostility and violence.

This reaction reflects a pattern seen throughout history. The persecution of early Christians was not solely about religious doctrine but also about power. Leaders feared that Christianity's rapid spread would weaken their control, so they employed whatever means necessary—propaganda, imprisonment, and even execution—to suppress it. Similarly, throughout history, political and social contexts are filled with stories of leaders, institutions, and individuals who sought to silence those they perceived as threats rather than engaging with them in dialogue.

In modern life, jealousy continues to hinder progress and suppress truth. In workplaces, envious colleagues may seek to undermine those who excel by spreading falsehoods or creating obstacles to block their success. In politics, jealousy and fear of losing influence often fuel smear campaigns and misinformation. Even in religious communities, jealousy can create internal divisions, as those in positions of authority may resist new ideas or emerging leaders out of a sense of threat.

Jealousy, as Pope Francis warns, not only harms those who are targeted but also corrupts the soul of the one who harbors it. It blinds individuals to truth and goodness, leading them down a path of bitterness and destruction. It is no coincidence that Scripture states, "Through the envy of the devil, sin entered the world" (Wisdom 2:24). Left unchecked, jealousy poisons relationships and communities, preventing the very harmony that God desires for humanity.

Opposition to the Gospel: A Pattern That Repeats Itself

One of the central insights from the homily is that the spread of the Gospel is always met with opposition. This is not merely a historical phenomenon but an ongoing reality. Pope Francis connects the persecution of Paul and Barnabas to the broader truth that wherever the Gospel flourishes, there will always be forces seeking to silence it.

In every age, Christianity has faced resistance. The early Church suffered persecution under the Roman Empire—not because its message was harmful, but because it was transformative. The Gospel challenged existing power structures, calling for justice, equality, and faithfulness to God over loyalty to imperial authority. This made it a threat to those who benefited from the status quo.

The same pattern continues today. In many parts of the world, Christians still face persecution—whether through government-imposed restrictions, social ostracization, or even violence. However, beyond physical persecution, the Gospel also encounters more subtle forms of opposition in modern society. Faith is often marginalized in the public sphere and dismissed as irrelevant or outdated. Those who uphold Christian values in business, politics, or academia may find themselves ridiculed or pressured to conform to secular ideologies.

Pope Francis reminds us that opposition to truth is inevitable, but it should not discourage believers. Instead, it should strengthen their resolve. The endurance of Christianity, despite centuries of resistance, proves that the Gospel cannot be silenced. It flourishes not through force or coercion but through its inherent power to transform hearts and societies.

The Role of Temporal Power in Suppressing Truth

Another crucial point in the homily is the role that political and economic power plays in opposing the Gospel. The religious leaders in Antioch did not act alone; they enlisted the help of influential figures—wealthy women and city leaders—to drive out Paul and Barnabas. This tactic of using power to suppress faith has been repeated throughout history.

Pope Francis highlights the danger of placing too much trust in worldly power. When religious institutions become entangled with political and economic forces, they risk losing their prophetic voice. Rather than standing for truth and justice, they may become compromised, prioritizing survival over their mission. History has shown this danger, as some Church leaders have aligned themselves with oppressive regimes, choosing silence over confrontation.

The Pope's warning remains highly relevant today. In a world where influence is often mistaken for success, religious groups may be tempted to seek political backing to secure their position. However, history has shown that when faith is used as a tool for power, it loses its integrity. The true strength of Christianity does not stem from alliances with governments or institutions but from the Holy Spirit.

Pope Francis calls on believers to trust in God's power rather than worldly structures. The Holy Spirit is the true force behind the Church's growth. Christianity is not sustained by political strategies or financial resources but by faith, perseverance, and divine grace.

The Christian Response: Resilience, Not Retaliation

A key lesson from the homily is how Christians should respond to opposition. Paul and Barnabas, despite being driven out of Antioch, did not retaliate with anger or hatred. Instead, they shook the dust from their feet and continued their mission elsewhere. This act was not one of defeat but of trust in God's plan.

Pope Francis presents this as a model for believers today. When confronted with opposition, criticism, or injustice, Christians should respond not with retaliation or resentment but with resilience and faithfulness. Just as the early Christians persevered despite persecution, modern believers must remain steadfast in their mission, trusting that God will bring good even from adversity.

This is especially relevant in today's culture, where outrage and retaliation have become the norm. Social media, for example, often turns disagreements into personal attacks. Pope Francis urges Christians to rise above this, choosing patience, humility, and perseverance over hostility.

He reminds us that true victory does not come from winning arguments or overpowering opponents but from remaining faithful to God's truth. When confronted with jealousy, opposition, or rejection, the right response is not to retaliate in anger but to live the Gospel with integrity and trust.

Trusting in the Holy Spirit Amid Struggles

The homily ultimately calls for deep trust in the Holy Spirit. No matter how strong the opposition or how persistent the forces of jealousy, the Gospel will continue to thrive. The Church has endured centuries of persecution, internal corruption, and external attacks, yet it remains steadfast. This endurance is not because of human efforts but because of God's guiding presence.

Pope Francis' message is both a warning and a reassurance. Jealousy will always be a force of destruction, and opposition to truth will never fully disappear. But those who remain faithful, who trust in the Holy Spirit rather than worldly power, will see the Gospel continue to grow. The challenge for believers today is to remain resilient, to reject jealousy in their hearts, and to place their confidence not in status or influence but in the unfailing presence of God.

The Christian life is not without struggle, but as history has shown, the struggle is always worth it. No amount of resistance can silence truth forever. The real question, as the Pope implies, is not whether opposition will come but how we choose to respond to it.

Breaking Free from Jealousy in Modern Life: Transforming Envy into Growth

Jealousy is one of the most corrosive emotions, capable of poisoning relationships, eroding self-worth, and distorting reality. It thrives on comparison, convincing people that their achievements, possessions, or happiness are inadequate simply because someone else appears to have more. Left unchecked, jealousy creates division—whether in the workplace, friendships, families, or society as a whole. It is a universal emotion, present across cultures, periods, and social structures. Yet, it can also be confronted, understood, and transformed into something constructive.

The modern world has amplified jealousy in ways previous generations never experienced. With constant exposure to curated images of success, wealth, and beauty on social media, the opportunities for comparison have multiplied. People are now bombarded with images of others excelling in areas where they feel inadequate. It is not just about material possessions—jealousy seeps into personal relationships, career progression, and even self-worth. Seeing a friend's engagement announcement, a colleague's promotion, or an influencer's seemingly perfect life can trigger resentment, fostering the false belief that another person's success diminishes one's own.

However, jealousy does not have to be destructive. Instead, it can become a catalyst for personal growth, gratitude, and faith. When approached with self-awareness, jealousy can uncover hidden insecurities and provide an opportunity to refocus on self-improvement rather than external validation. It is possible to turn envy into motivation, to shift from a mindset of scarcity to one of abundance, and to cultivate a deep trust that each person's journey unfolds in their own time.

The Power of Self-Reflection: Identifying the Root of Jealousy

Before jealousy can be overcome, it must first be understood. Often, jealousy is a symptom rather than the root issue. It may arise from fears of inadequacy, unfulfilled potential, or deep-seated insecurity. Rather than suppressing jealousy, it is more helpful to recognize it as a signal—one that highlights unresolved self-doubt or dissatisfaction.

For example, if a person feels envious when a friend achieves a career milestone, the jealousy is not necessarily about the friend's success. Jealousy may reveal a personal fear of stagnation or a longing for professional recognition. In relationships, it often arises from feelings of unworthiness rather than actual security threats. In every case, jealousy reflects more about the person experiencing it than the external situation.

By reflecting on the origins of jealousy, individuals can gain deeper insight into their own needs and aspirations. Rather than resenting others for what they have, they can reframe jealousy as a tool for self-examination, asking: *What does this emotion reveal about what I truly value? How can I redirect this energy toward self-improvement instead of comparison and resentment?*

Shifting from Comparison to Inspiration

Jealousy often stems from the habit of comparing oneself to others—a practice that is almost always misleading. People witness the successes of others but rarely see the full journey behind them—the sacrifices, struggles, and failures that shaped their path. When individuals measure their reality against someone else's highlight reel, they create an unfair and distorted perception of success.

Rather than letting comparison fuel resentment, it can be reframed as a source of inspiration. Instead of asking, *Why do they have what I don't?*, a more constructive question is, *What can I learn from their success?* Every achievement is built on effort, strategy, and persistence. Observing how others have grown can provide valuable insights into what is possible. Rather than dwelling on jealousy, a person envious of a colleague's career advancement might instead ask what skills or habits contributed to their success. Similarly, a friend's happy relationship can serve as motivation to cultivate deeper emotional connections, rather than a source of self-doubt.

By replacing envy with curiosity and appreciation, moments of jealousy can become growth opportunities. The key is to focus on progress rather than comparison—to celebrate personal milestones alongside the successes of others, recognizing that everyone's journey is unique.

Cultivating Gratitude to Combat Jealousy

Gratitude is one of the most powerful antidotes to jealousy. When people fixate on what others have, they overlook the abundance in their own lives. Shifting the focus from lack to appreciation fosters a mindset that values what is already present rather than what is missing.

Practicing gratitude does not mean ignoring aspirations or ambitions; it simply means appreciating what is already good while striving for growth. Research shows that those who cultivate gratitude regularly experience lower stress levels, greater emotional resilience, and an overall sense of well-being. Gratitude reorients the mind, making it less susceptible to comparison and more attuned to personal fulfillment.

Simple daily practices, such as keeping a gratitude journal or taking time to reflect on three things to be thankful for each day, can help break the cycle of envy. When gratitude becomes a habit, jealousy loses its grip. There is less desire to compare, less anxiety about what others have, and more contentment in the present moment.

Strengthening Faith and Trusting in the Journey

Jealousy is often fueled by impatience—the fear that success or happiness must be achieved immediately. However, faith reminds us that each person's journey unfolds in its own time. Trusting in a greater plan eases the pressure to measure success by external achievements and nurtures a deeper sense of peace.

When a person trusts that they are exactly where they need to be, jealousy begins to fade. There is no need to envy someone else's timeline when one has confidence that their path is unfolding with purpose. Faith replaces doubt with trust, transforming jealousy into patience.

This mindset does not imply complacency or a lack of ambition. Rather, it reflects an understanding that comparison is unnecessary when every journey is unique. A person who trusts in life's process feels no need to control every outcome or compete with others. Instead, they can focus on their growth, confident that what is truly meant for them will arrive in due time.

Replacing Jealousy with Generosity and Kindness

Another powerful way to counteract jealousy is through generosity. Jealousy often leads people to withdraw or become resentful, but actively choosing to celebrate others' successes and contribute to their well-being diminishes its grip. Acts of kindness foster an abundance mindset—the belief that happiness, success, and opportunity exist in limitless supply for everyone.

Celebrating a friend's success, supporting a colleague's achievements, or offering help to someone in need shifts the focus from personal lack to shared joy. Over time, this practice rewires the brain to view success as a collective experience rather than a competition. The more generosity is embraced, the less room envy has to take hold.

Choosing Freedom from Jealousy

Jealousy is a natural emotion, but it doesn't have to be a defining one. By understanding its root causes, shifting from comparison to inspiration, practicing gratitude, trusting life's timing, and replacing envy with generosity, we can break free from its grip.

True fulfillment doesn't come from having more than others but from living with purpose, peace, and appreciation. Each person follows a unique journey shaped by different blessings and challenges. When jealousy is replaced with self-awareness, gratitude, and faith, life becomes richer—not through what is acquired but through how it is experienced.

Freedom from jealousy isn't about ignoring ambition or settling for less. It's about transforming the desire for more into a force for good—one that fuels personal growth, strengthens relationships, and fosters an unshakable trust in the path ahead. The choice is always there: to be weighed down by comparison or to rise above it with faith, generosity, and joy.

Reflections on Overcoming Jealousy: A Path to Growth, Gratitude, and Fulfillment

Jealousy is a powerful emotion that, if left unchecked, can consume thoughts, erode relationships, and prevent personal and spiritual growth. Jealousy often stems from comparison, insecurity, or the fear of not measuring up. However, it also presents an opportunity—an invitation to explore deeper truths about ourselves, our desires, and our sense of self-worth. Rather than letting it control us, we can transform it into motivation, self-awareness, and gratitude.

The following reflection questions will help guide an honest exploration of jealousy's role in modern life. They are meant not to condemn but to foster self-awareness, helping to reveal hidden fears, false beliefs, and growth opportunities. As you reflect, consider journaling your thoughts or discussing them with someone you trust. True freedom from jealousy begins with self-reflection and a willingness to grow beyond its grasp.

1. What triggers my jealousy most often, and what does it reveal about me?

Jealousy is often triggered by specific situations, people, or experiences—whether it's witnessing someone else's career success, seeing a friend in a happy relationship, or noticing someone who exudes confidence or attractiveness. The key is not only to identify what sparks jealousy but to understand what it reveals about underlying insecurities.

If career-related jealousy is a recurring pattern, does it reveal feelings of stagnation or unfulfilled ambition? If jealousy arises in relationships, does it stem from a fear of abandonment or feelings of unworthiness? Recognizing these patterns shifts the focus from resentment to self-improvement.

2. Do I compare myself to others in a way that leads to dissatisfaction?

The comparison lies at the heart of jealousy. Social media, career achievements, physical appearance, and even family dynamics often become benchmarks for success. But are these comparisons truly fair? Are they grounded in reality or distorted by selective presentation?

A healthier way to reframe this question is to ask: Am I measuring myself against someone else's highlight reel while overlooking my journey? Instead of comparing, shifting toward self-awareness fosters a deeper appreciation for one's unique path.

3. How does jealousy affect my thoughts, relationships, and decisions?

Jealousy isn't just a private emotion—it shapes behavior. It can cause withdrawal, passive-aggressive actions, or even self-sabotage. Left unchecked, it breeds resentment, creates distance in relationships, and leads to self-destructive choices.

Reflect on moments when jealousy has influenced your interactions. Did it lead you to withhold support for someone's success? Did it make you question your worth? Recognizing how jealousy manifests in daily life helps prevent it from shaping behavior in unhealthy ways.

4. How do I react to others' success—do I celebrate it or feel diminished by it?

One of the most revealing tests of jealousy is how we react to someone else's success. When a friend gets a promotion, do we truly celebrate, or does it sting? When someone is praised for their talents, do we feel happy for them, or does it make us question our worth?

Shifting the mindset from their success takes something away from me to their success, and shows what's possible is a liberating practice. Learning to celebrate others without comparison fosters deeper, more authentic relationships.

5. What are three things I am deeply grateful for right now?

Gratitude is the antidote to jealousy. It shifts focus from what is lacking to what is already abundant. Rather than resenting what others have, practicing gratitude fosters a sense of contentment.

When jealousy arises, pausing to acknowledge three blessings—whether personal achievements, supportive relationships, or small daily joys—can help reframe perspective. Over time, this practice cultivates an internal sense of fulfillment that isn't dependent on external validation.

6. How can I use jealousy as motivation rather than discouragement?

Rather than viewing jealousy as purely negative, it can be transformed into motivation for self-improvement. If someone else's success sparks envy, ask: What steps can I take to achieve my own goals?

Rather than dwelling on why someone else has what you desire, focus on the practical steps you can take. Learning new skills, setting clear goals, and developing better habits can transform envy into empowerment.

7. **Do I truly believe that my path is unique, or do I feel pressured to follow someone else's timeline?**

Jealousy often stems from the false belief that life is a competition. Seeing peers achieve milestones—marriage, career growth, financial success—can create pressure. But does another person's timeline have to be your own?

Understanding that each person's journey unfolds differently allows for peace. Some people achieve success early; others find fulfillment later in life. Trusting that the right opportunities will come at the right time removes the urgency that fuels envy.

8. **Have I ever acted unfairly because of jealousy, and how can I make amends?**

Jealousy can lead to behaviors that harm relationships—whether through gossip, distancing from people, or acting out of insecurity. Recognizing past actions influenced by jealousy is an important step toward personal growth.

If jealousy has strained relationships, consider ways to repair them. Apologizing for past behaviors, reaching out to express genuine support, or simply shifting attitudes toward generosity and kindness can restore harmony.

9. How does social media influence my feelings of jealousy, and how can I set boundaries?

Social media has intensified jealousy by creating constant exposure to curated, idealized versions of life. Scrolling through images of vacations, luxury, success, or beauty can make people feel inadequate. But these platforms rarely show struggles, setbacks, or the reality behind the image.

Setting boundaries—such as limiting time on social media, following accounts that uplift rather than trigger envy, or taking digital detoxes—can help break the cycle of comparison. Being mindful of how social media affects self-perception is essential for mental well-being.

10. How can I cultivate a mindset of abundance rather than scarcity?

Jealousy thrives in a mindset of scarcity—the belief that there is a limited amount of success, happiness, or love, and if someone else has more, there is less available for you. But this is a flawed perspective.

An abundance mindset recognizes that opportunities are limitless. Someone else's success does not diminish your potential. Love, career growth, and personal fulfillment are not reserved for a select few. By trusting in life's possibilities rather than fearing what is lacking, jealousy loses its power.

Jealousy, while natural, doesn't have to dictate thoughts, actions, or emotions. Through honest reflection, a focus on personal growth, and the practice of gratitude, envy can be transformed into a force for good.

Each of these questions is a step toward self-awareness, breaking the cycle of jealousy and replacing it with confidence, contentment, and joy. The more focus shifts to personal progress rather than comparison, the more fulfilling life becomes.

True freedom isn't found in having more than others but in appreciating what is already present. As jealousy fades, a deep sense of peace remains—the confidence that every person's journey is unfolding exactly as it should.

Chapter 6

The Cry of the Forsaken: Finding God in Abandonment and Suffering

St Peter's Square - Sunday, 2 April 2023

The Homily

Pope Francis' homily reflects on one of the most agonizing moments of Christ's Passion—the cry from the cross: "My God, my God, why have you forsaken me?" (*Matthew 27:46*). This desperate plea, the only recorded words of Jesus from the cross in Matthew's Gospel, reveals the profound depth of His suffering— not only physical but also spiritual. The Pope takes us into the heart of this moment, urging us to see not only Christ's pain but also his profound act of love.

From the very start of His public ministry, Jesus faced rejection, betrayal, and opposition. He endured the physical torment of beatings, the humiliation of mockery, and the excruciating pain of crucifixion. Yet, even amid these trials, He never wavered in His connection with the Father. His trust in God remained unshaken, and He always addressed Him intimately as "Father." Yet, in this final moment of suffering, something shifts. The closeness He had always known now seems absent. Instead of calling God "Father," He cries out with the more distant plea, "My God." This shift signifies the depth of his abandonment—he is experiencing the complete weight of sin, absorbing the pain of all humanity.

Jesus' cry of abandonment is not merely an expression of His suffering; it is a moment in which He takes upon Himself the forsakenness of all who have ever felt rejected, lost, or alone. Pope Francis reminds us that this cry echoes every cry of despair throughout history—the pain of the betrayed, the sorrow of those facing injustice, and the grief of the unloved and forgotten. The desolation that so many endure—through sickness, loss, loneliness, or social exclusion—was carried by Christ on the cross. His suffering was not only physical but also profoundly emotional and spiritual as He entered into the deepest depths of human pain.

Yet, as Pope Francis emphasizes, this was not the end of the story. Jesus' abandonment was not for Himself but for us. His suffering was not meaningless; it was a radical act of love. By willingly enduring complete separation from the Father, Jesus ensured that no one would ever have to face suffering alone. He took upon

Himself every human experience of loss so that, in our moments of despair, we might find hope in Him. His cry of abandonment transforms suffering—no longer a path to destruction but a passage to redemption.

Even in His abandonment, Jesus continued to trust in God. He did not let despair overcome Him; instead, He turned to prayer. His cry—drawn from *Psalm 22*—was not a rejection of God but a profound lament that ultimately leads to hope. He knew that God would not forsake Him forever. In His final moments, He continued to love—offering forgiveness to those who crucified Him, mercy to the repentant thief, and care for His mother and disciples. Though burdened by the weight of separation from God, He still entrusted His spirit into the Father's hands. His love never wavered; His mission was fulfilled.

Pope Francis then shifts the focus from Christ's suffering to the suffering in our world today. If we truly understand Jesus' abandonment, we must also recognize the many people who experience the same forsakenness in our world. The Pope calls attention to the forgotten and the discarded—the homeless dying alone on the streets, the elderly left in nursing homes with no visitors, the refugees reduced to statistics, the prisoners rejected by society, the sick abandoned in hospitals, and the young people trapped in loneliness and despair. These are the "Christs" of today. Just as Jesus took on abandonment for us, we are now called to respond to the suffering of others with love and compassion.

The Pope's challenge is clear: we must not turn away. The cry of Jesus on the cross continues in the voices of those who are suffering today. The question is whether we will listen or whether we, like so many in the Passion narrative, will walk away in silence. True discipleship means seeing Jesus in the faces of the abandoned and responding with action. Love is not passive; it is a call to be present, to care, and to bring hope to those who feel forsaken.

The homily concludes with a call to open our hearts. In His abandonment, Jesus invites us to a deeper love— one that does not turn away from suffering but enters into it with compassion. The love of Christ, fully revealed on the cross, has the power to transform even the hardest of hearts. It is a love that does not end in death but leads to new life. When we embrace this love and extend it to the forsaken, we become true followers of the crucified and risen Lord.

Homily Analysis: The Meaning Behind Christ's Forsaken Cry

Pope Francis' homily on Christ's cry from the cross— "My God, my God, why have You forsaken Me?" (*Matthew 27:46*)—invites deep reflection on one of the most profound mysteries of the Christian faith. This moment in Jesus' Passion presents a theological paradox: the Son of God, who had always been in perfect communion with the Father, now experiences what appears to be total separation. Yet, in this very act of abandonment, the ultimate expression of divine love is revealed. Pope Francis delves into the depths of this mystery, illustrating how Jesus' suffering is not merely a past event but a living reality that continues to shape the Christian understanding of redemption, suffering, and love.

The Reality of Christ's Suffering: Physical, Emotional, and Spiritual Pain

When reflecting on the Passion of Christ, physical suffering is often the most visible and immediate aspect. The brutal scourging, the crown of thorns pressed into His head, the exhaustion of carrying the cross, and the unimaginable pain of crucifixion all paint a harrowing picture of human agony. Jesus endured what was considered the most shameful and excruciating form of execution in the Roman world.

But Pope Francis reminds us that the Passion was not only a bodily suffering—it was also a deep emotional and spiritual torment. Jesus endured the pain of betrayal, the abandonment of His disciples, and the rejection of the very people He had come to save. The same crowds that once praised Him with "Hosanna!" now cried, "Crucify Him!" The religious and political leaders condemned Him unjustly, and even His closest followers, such as Peter, denied knowing Him.

Yet, the deepest suffering of all was spiritual. This was not merely a moment of doubt or despair—it was the profound experience of separation from the Father. For the first time in eternity, Jesus, who had always lived in perfect communion with God, felt the abyss of divine absence. He did not simply suffer for humanity—He suffered as humanity. In that moment, He took upon Himself the full weight of human sin and alienation from God, embodying the total experience of forsakenness that sin brings.

Pope Francis describes this as the darkest moment of Jesus' Passion—the culmination of His sacrifice. His cry, "Why have You forsaken Me?" is not a rhetorical question but an entry into the depths of human suffering. It is a cry that echoes throughout history in the pain of every person who has ever felt abandoned, betrayed, or lost.

The Theological Meaning of Abandonment: Sin, Separation, and Redemption

One of the most striking aspects of Jesus' cry is that He does not call out to God as "Father," as He always had throughout His ministry. Instead, He uses the more distant term "God." This marks a dramatic shift—Jesus, who taught His disciples to pray "Our Father," now experiences the full consequence of human sin: separation from divine intimacy.

Pope Francis emphasizes that this abandonment is not because the Father has turned away but because Jesus is voluntarily taking upon himself the burden of sin. In Catholic theology, sin is not just a moral failing; it is a rupture in the relationship between humanity and God. Jesus, in His Passion, enters into that rupture completely. He does not merely observe human suffering from a distance—He immerses Himself in it.

This is the paradox of the cross: in the moment of greatest separation, the greatest union is accomplished. By embracing the experience of being forsaken, Jesus ensures that no human being will ever be truly abandoned. His suffering becomes redemptive because He takes upon Himself the very condition that separates humanity from God, offering in return a path to reconciliation.

This moment also demonstrates the depth of divine love. It is not a love that remains detached but one that enters fully into the human condition, even to the point of experiencing what it means to be utterly forsaken. Pope Francis highlights that this cry is not simply an expression of despair—it is a cry of solidarity. Jesus aligns Himself with every person who has ever suffered injustice, loneliness, or despair. His words become the voice of all who have ever asked, *"God, where are you?"*

Psalm 22 and the Cry of Hope in Desolation

Pope Francis highlights that Jesus' words are a direct quotation from *Psalm 22*. This psalm, though it begins with deep lament—"My God, my God, why have you forsaken me?"—ultimately moves toward hope and restoration. By choosing these words, Jesus does more than express His anguish; He places His suffering within the greater narrative of God's faithfulness.

Psalm 22 is often regarded as a Messianic Psalm, foreshadowing Christ's suffering. The psalmist cries out in anguish, describing mockery, physical pain, and abandonment—details that mirror Jesus' Passion. Yet, as the psalm progresses, it shifts toward a declaration of trust: *"You who fear the Lord, praise him! For he has not despised or abhorred the affliction of the afflicted."*

By quoting this psalm, Jesus is not merely voicing despair—he is also pointing toward ultimate redemption. Even in his darkest moment, he does not abandon his faith in the Father. His suffering is real, but it is not the end of the story. Pope Francis emphasizes that Jesus' trust in the Father remains steadfast, even when all sense of divine presence seems lost. This becomes a model for believers: in moments of personal suffering, even when God feels distant, faith calls for trust in his unseen presence and ultimate deliverance.

Christ's Love in the Midst of Abandonment

Another key point Pope Francis emphasizes is that even in his abandonment, Jesus continues to love. Despite his agony, he prays for the forgiveness of those who crucify him: "Father, forgive them, for they do not know what they are doing." He offers salvation to the repentant thief, promising him paradise, and entrusts his mother to the beloved disciple.

This is a radical form of love—one that does not retreat in the face of suffering but instead reaches out even more. It reveals that circumstances do not dictate true love; rather, it remains steadfast, unwavering even in the depths of pain.

Jesus does not meet abandonment with bitterness, nor does he curse those who betray him. Instead, he chooses mercy. This reveals the very heart of Christian discipleship: to follow Christ is to love when it is hardest, to trust when God feels distant, and to forgive even in the face of injustice.

The Transformative Power of Christ's Suffering

Pope Francis concludes his reflection by pointing to the ultimate victory of the cross. Jesus' cry of abandonment is not the final word—it is the gateway to resurrection. His suffering is not in vain; it is redemptive.

This is the essence of Christian hope. Because Jesus fully entered into suffering, it is no longer a dead end—it has become a path to new life. The resurrection reveals that abandonment is never the final word. Even in the darkest moments, God's love prevails.

Pope Francis urges believers to contemplate this mystery—not merely as a past event but as a present reality. Jesus remains present in the suffering of the world. He is found in the abandoned, the forgotten, and the rejected. To follow Christ is to recognize him in

THE LIGHT OF FAITH

those who suffer and to bring them the same love and hope he offers.

Ultimately, Jesus' cry from the cross is a call to trust, to love, and to redemption. Even in the silence of abandonment, God is at work, transforming suffering into salvation.

Turning Despair into Hope: Lessons from Christ's Cry on the Cross

The cry of abandonment from the cross—*"My God, my God, why have you forsaken me?" (Matthew 27:46)* — is not just a historical moment but a deeply human experience that continues to resonate in the modern world. Jesus' suffering mirrors the struggles of countless individuals today—those who feel abandoned, lost, or forsaken. His cry is the cry of the suffering, the forgotten, the oppressed, and the brokenhearted. Yet, within this moment of deepest despair lies a profound truth: God is never absent, even when He seems silent.

By contemplating Jesus' experience of abandonment, we are invited to reflect on our suffering and the suffering of others. How do we confront feelings of forsakenness? How can we bring hope to those who feel forgotten? What does it mean to trust in God when He seems distant? This chapter explores how we can apply the lessons of Christ's abandonment to our lives today—finding meaning in suffering, extending compassion to the forsaken, and cultivating faith even in the darkest times.

The Experience of Feeling Forsaken: When God Feels Distant

At some point in life, nearly everyone has felt abandoned—by friends, family, society, or even by God. Times of deep suffering often give rise to questions that seem to have no answers: Why did this happen to me? Where is God in my pain? Why do I feel alone? These are the very questions Jesus voiced on the cross, and they remain profoundly relevant today.

People experience this sense of abandonment in various ways. A young woman battling depression may cry out to God in prayer yet feel nothing but silence. A father struggling to provide for his family after losing his job may wonder why God has left him in financial ruin. A refugee fleeing a war-torn homeland, having lost everything, might question whether God has abandoned his people. The sense of divine absence is one of the most painful experiences a person can endure.

The story of Jesus on the cross teaches us that even when we feel abandoned, we are never truly alone. Christ entered into our suffering so that no pain would be foreign to Him. He understands the depths of human despair because He has lived it Himself. His cry from the cross assures us that even in our darkest moments, He is with us.

Rather than turning away from faith in difficult times, we are invited to embrace the mystery of trust. Faith is not about always feeling close to God but about choosing to trust Him, even when His presence seems distant. The lesson of Christ's abandonment is that God's silence is not His absence. His love remains, even when we cannot immediately perceive it.

Elie Wiesel, a Holocaust survivor and author of *Night*, describes how his faith was deeply shaken when he witnessed the suffering in concentration camps. At one point, he saw a young boy being executed and heard someone say, *"Where is God now?"* Wiesel writes that he felt as though God was hanging on the gallows with the boy. His words echo Jesus' cry from the cross. Yet, even in this profound moment of despair, Wiesel later discovered that faith could coexist with suffering. Many survivors, despite witnessing unimaginable horror, held onto faith—not because they understood God's plan, but because they refused to let evil extinguish their belief in goodness.

Finding Hope in the Midst of Suffering

One of the most powerful lessons of Jesus' cry from the cross is that suffering is not the final word. Even in His moment of abandonment, Jesus did not succumb to despair—He continued to trust in the Father. That trust ultimately led to His resurrection.

In modern life, suffering often feels meaningless, but faith reveals that it can be redemptive. When people endure pain, loss, or failure, they can either let it break them or allow it to transform them. Many of the greatest acts of heroism, compassion, and faith come from those who have suffered deeply and chosen to turn their suffering into love.

Nelson Mandela spent 27 years in prison, much of it in the harsh conditions of Robben Island. He could have let this suffering make him bitter or vengeful, but instead, he used it to cultivate patience, wisdom, and resilience. His pain shaped him into a leader capable of uniting a divided South Africa. Mandela's story proves that even the darkest suffering can be transformed into a force for good. Like Christ on the cross, he did not let suffering defeat him; instead, he allowed it to refine his character and deepen his purpose.

Rather than viewing suffering as something to escape at all costs, the Christian perspective invites us to see it as a place where God's grace works most powerfully. Jesus' Passion reveals that even in our lowest moments, God is at work, shaping us for something greater.

Recognizing the Forsaken in Society: Seeing Christ in the Abandoned

Pope Francis makes it clear that Jesus' cry of abandonment is not only about His suffering—it is also about the suffering of all who are abandoned in the world today. To follow Christ, we must be willing to see Him in the faces of the forsaken.

The modern world is filled with people who experience abandonment every day—the homeless sleeping on the streets, the elderly left in nursing homes with no visitors, the refugees fleeing war with nowhere to go, the prisoners forgotten by society, and the sick suffering in isolation. These are the "Christs" of today.

Millions of refugees around the world are forced to flee their homes due to war, persecution, or natural disasters. Many arrive in foreign lands where they are unwelcome, living in poverty, and facing discrimination.

Organizations like Doctors Without Borders and the Jesuit Refugee Service work tirelessly to provide care, yet many still feel forgotten. The question we must ask ourselves is this: Do we see these people as burdens, or do we recognize Christ in them?

Recognizing Jesus in the forsaken requires a shift in perspective. Instead of seeing the abandoned as problems to ignore, we must recognize them as human beings in whom Christ is present. This means not only acknowledging their suffering but also taking action to ease it.

Forgiving in the Face of Betrayal

One of the most extraordinary aspects of Jesus' suffering is that, even in His abandonment, He forgave.

He prayed for those who crucified Him, showing that His love was not dependent on how He was treated.

In modern life, betrayal and abandonment are all too common. Friendships fracture, marriages collapse, and people turn away from one another in moments of weakness or selfishness. It is easy to respond with resentment and bitterness, yet Jesus shows us a different way.

After being shot in 1981, Pope John Paul II visited his attacker, Mehmet Ali Ağca, in prison and forgave him. Over the years, the two even developed a friendship. This radical act of forgiveness mirrors Jesus' prayer on the cross: "Father, forgive them, for they do not know what they are doing."

Forgiveness does not mean forgetting or ignoring wrongdoing. Rather, it means choosing not to be consumed by anger. Holding onto resentment only deepens wounds, while forgiveness allows healing to begin. When we choose to forgive, we break the cycle of pain and open ourselves to the freedom Christ's love offers.

Turning the Cry of Abandonment into a Call to Action

Jesus' cry from the cross is not just something to contemplate—it is a call to action. It invites us to trust in God even when we feel forsaken, to find meaning in suffering, to recognize Christ in the abandoned, to practice forgiveness, and to live with faith even in the darkest moments.

His cry continues to echo in the voices of those who suffer, in the silence of those who feel alone, and in the prayers of those searching for meaning. But just as the cry of Jesus was not the end of His story, neither is it the end of ours. If we respond with love, trust, and faith, we can turn even the darkest moments into paths of grace and redemption.

Reflection Questions on Abandonment, Suffering, and Hope in Modern Life

The cry of abandonment that Jesus uttered on the cross is one of the most profound moments in the Gospel. It resonates deeply with human experiences of suffering, loss, and questioning. This chapter invites reflection on how Christ's Passion speaks to modern struggles and challenges, offering a path to healing, trust, and renewal. These reflections will guide you through key aspects of faith, suffering, and compassion, helping you navigate life's trials and deepen your understanding of God's presence, even in the darkest moments.

1. When Have I Felt Abandoned, and How Did I Respond?

At some point in life, everyone experiences feelings of abandonment—whether from family, friends, society, or even God. These moments often arise during times of crisis, such as the loss of a loved one, the end of a meaningful relationship, or personal failure. Reflecting on these experiences can reveal how they have shaped your faith and resilience. Did you turn inward and isolate yourself, or did you seek support? Did you find strength in faith, or did you wrestle with doubt? Acknowledging these experiences honestly can offer clarity about how abandonment has shaped your spiritual journey.

2. How Do I Respond When God Seems Silent?

There are times when prayer feels empty, and God appears distant. Many people go through periods where faith feels like an unanswered call, and life's struggles seem to persist without relief. These moments of spiritual dryness can be discouraging, but they also present an opportunity for growth. Consider how you respond when faced with divine silence. Do you persevere in faith, trusting that God is present even when He feels absent? Or do you let doubt and despair take hold? Reflecting on these patterns in your life can help you cultivate a deeper, more steadfast relationship with God, even when His presence is not immediately felt.

3. Do I Recognize the Forsaken in My Community?

The cry of abandonment that Jesus expressed on the cross is echoed today by those who are suffering and alone. The homeless, the elderly, the sick, refugees, and those battling mental illness often feel forgotten. Society frequently turns away from these individuals, viewing them as problems rather than people. Do you take the time to see the suffering in your community? Have you ever reached out to someone in need, even in a small way? Reflecting on this can help you assess whether you are living out Christ's call to serve the least among us. Even simple gestures—a kind word, a visit, or an act of generosity—can make a profound difference in someone's life.

4. In What Ways Do I Contribute to the Abandonment of Others?

While it is easy to see ourselves as victims of abandonment, it is harder to admit that we may have also abandoned others. Have you ever distanced yourself from a friend going through a difficult time because it was too emotionally draining? Have you neglected a family member in need of your support? Have you turned away from someone who asked for help? Recognizing these moments is not about self-condemnation but about acknowledging areas for growth. If we wish to follow Christ's example, we must be willing to stand beside those who feel lost and alone rather than turn away out of convenience or discomfort.

5. How Do I Process My Suffering?

Suffering is an inevitable part of life, but how you respond to it determines whether it leads to growth or despair. Do you see suffering as meaningless, or do you seek to find purpose in it? Have you allowed past pain to make you bitter, or have you used it to cultivate empathy for others? Jesus transformed His suffering into an act of redemption. Reflecting on your suffering can help you recognize where you may need healing and how your experiences can be used to support and uplift others.

6. How Do I Forgive Those Who Have Hurt or Betrayed Me?

One of the most difficult yet powerful lessons from Jesus' Passion is the act of forgiveness. Even in His suffering, He forgave those who crucified Him. In contrast, many people today hold onto grudges, allowing resentment to take root in their hearts. Is there someone in your life whom you have struggled to forgive? How has holding onto anger affected you? Are you open to the possibility of letting go, even if reconciliation is not possible? Forgiveness does not mean forgetting or condoning harm, but it is a choice that frees you from the burden of resentment.

7. What Role Does Faith Play in My Life When I Face Uncertainty?

Life is unpredictable, and challenges often arise without warning. How do you react when faced with uncertainty? Do you turn to faith as a source of strength, or do you rely solely on your ability to fix the situation? Trusting in God's plan does not mean passively waiting for things to improve, but it does mean surrendering control and believing that even amid confusion, God is working for your good.

Reflecting on this can help you develop a resilient faith, not just when times are easy but especially when they are difficult.

8. How Do I Treat the Elderly, the Sick, and the Vulnerable in My Life?

Many societies value productivity and independence, often overlooking those who can no longer contribute in traditional ways. The elderly, the sick, and those with disabilities are often pushed to the margins. Have you taken the time to care for an aging relative, visit someone who is ill, or show kindness to those who are often overlooked?

Jesus' suffering reminds us of the inherent dignity of all people, especially the most vulnerable. Reflecting on your actions can help you recognize where you might be called to offer more love and care.

9. How Can I Be a Source of Hope for Someone Who Feels Forsaken?

Jesus' cry from the cross was not just an expression of His suffering—it was also a call for His followers to respond to the pain of others. Who in your life is struggling with loneliness, depression, or hopelessness? Have you made an effort to be present for them, to listen, and to encourage them? Sometimes, even the smallest gestures—checking in on a friend, offering words of encouragement, or simply sitting with someone in pain—can bring light to a dark situation. Reflecting on this can help you become more mindful of how you can be a source of strength for those who need it most.

10. Am I Living My Life with the Awareness That Earthly Things Are Temporary?

It is easy to become consumed by the pursuit of wealth, status, and material success. But Jesus' suffering and death remind us that these things are fleeting. At the end of life, what truly matters is not how much we have accumulated but how much we have loved. Are you focusing on what is temporary at the expense of what is eternal? Are you investing in relationships, acts of kindness, and spiritual growth, or are you more preoccupied with things that will ultimately fade away? Taking time to reflect on this can help you realign your priorities with what truly matters.

These reflections challenge us to confront our own experiences of abandonment, suffering, and faith. Jesus' cry from the cross serves as a reminder that even in moments of deep despair, God is still present. It is a call to trust in His plan, to open our hearts to those who feel forsaken, and to live lives marked by compassion, forgiveness, and hope. By engaging in these reflections, we allow ourselves to grow spiritually, heal from past wounds, and become instruments of God's love in the world. His suffering was not in vain, and neither is ours if we allow it to transform us into people who reflect His grace and mercy.

Chapter 7

The Healing Power of Forgiveness: Restoring Communion and Trust

St Peter's Basilica, Altar of the Confessio - Tuesday, 1st October 2024

The Homily

Pope Francis' homily on forgiveness is a profound reflection on the Church's need for humility, reconciliation, and healing. His message goes beyond individual repentance to emphasize a collective examination of conscience—one that acknowledges the wounds caused by sin and the necessity of restoring broken relationships. By calling for a renewed spirit of humility, the Pope underscores the essential role of forgiveness in the life of the Church and the journey toward synodality.

At the core of his homily is the recognition that sin is not merely a personal failing but a rupture in relationships—with God, with others, and with creation itself. He emphasizes that the Church, while a place for the righteous and the saints, is fundamentally a home for sinners—those who acknowledge their failures and seek mercy. This honest confession of weakness is not a sign of defeat but of spiritual maturity. In contrast to those who stand in self-righteousness, the Pope encourages the faithful to imitate the humility of the publican in the Gospel, who, instead of exalting himself, pleads for mercy.

Forgiveness is not merely about wiping away sins but about healing the wounds those sins have caused. Pope Francis makes it clear that sin is relational—it harms not only the individual but also affects the entire community. Just as everything is connected in goodness, everything is also connected in brokenness. The failure of one member of the Church has repercussions that extend beyond themselves, weakening the trust and unity that binds the faithful together.

The Pope's call to reconciliation is deeply intertwined with the Church's mission of becoming a "synodal Church," a community that walks together in faith. But how can the Church credibly proclaim its mission if it does not acknowledge its failings? The ability to recognize and confess sins is the first step in the healing process. Without this, there can be no true communion. By asking for forgiveness, the Church does not weaken itself but strengthens its credibility, for only through humility can it be an authentic witness of God's love and mercy.

Using the parable of the Pharisee and the publican, Pope Francis contrasts two attitudes in approaching God: arrogance versus humility. The Pharisee, convinced of his righteousness, takes up all the space, leaving no room for grace, others, or even God. His prayer is self-congratulatory, an assertion of his superiority rather than a plea for divine mercy. His sin is not outward wickedness but spiritual pride—believing he has already earned salvation through his deeds.

On the other hand, the publican stands at a distance, fully aware of his

unworthiness. His prayer is simple but powerful: "Lord, have mercy on me, a sinner." Unlike the Pharisee, he does not list his merits nor compare himself to others. He surrenders to God's mercy, and it is this posture of humility that Jesus commends. Pope Francis invites the Church to adopt this same attitude—one of self-examination, honesty, and dependence on God's grace.

In the life of the Church, the temptation to behave like the Pharisee is ever-present. Clergy, lay leaders, and even everyday believers can fall into the trap of spiritual elitism, believing themselves to be superior to others. This mindset leads to exclusion, judgment, and a lack of empathy toward those who struggle. It also creates an environment where sins are hidden rather than confessed, where appearances matter more than true conversion. The Pope warns against this danger, urging believers to make room for the surprising grace of God instead of closing themselves off in self-sufficiency.

Pope Francis does not limit his call for repentance to individuals; he extends it to the Church as a whole. He acknowledges that the Church has made mistakes, failed in its mission, and caused harm. This recognition is especially important in light of the Church's past failures, whether in addressing abuses, mistreating marginalized communities, or failing always to embody the love and mercy it preaches.

The Pope's words serve as an invitation to restore trust. He acknowledges that wounds still bleed and that there are people who the Church's actions or inactions have hurt. Seeking forgiveness is not merely about repairing the Church's image; it is about genuinely addressing these wounds and committing them to a path of renewal. It is a reminder that holiness is not about perfection but about the willingness to rise after every fall.

The Pope's reflection on forgiveness extends beyond the Church's internal failings. He speaks to a world that is deeply divided, where conflicts are often met with vengeance rather than reconciliation. The temptation to respond to evil with more evil, to seek justice through destruction, is a recurring theme in human history. Yet, the Pope reminds us that true justice cannot be built on violence or the suffering of others. Peace can only be achieved through the courage to forgive.

The question he poses is a challenging one: "How can we pursue happiness paid for by the unhappiness of our brothers and sisters?" It calls us to rethink how conflicts—whether personal, social, or political—are resolved. Retaliation may bring temporary satisfaction, but only forgiveness leads to lasting healing. The Pope's words are a reminder that the path of mercy is not the easy path, but it is the only one that leads to true peace.

In a striking moment, Pope Francis turns to the younger generation, asking for their forgiveness as well. He acknowledges that the Church has not always been a credible witness and that it has failed at times to be the example that young people seek. This humility is essential—rather than demanding blind obedience from youth, the Pope invites dialogue, trust, and the rebuilding of relationships. It is an appeal for young people to see the Church not as an institution of rigid perfection but as a community that, though flawed, seeks constant renewal.

His reference to St. Therese of Lisieux, the patroness of missions, is particularly meaningful. Despite her young age and hidden life, St. Therese had a profound impact on the Church through her "Little Way"—a spirituality of doing small acts with great love. By invoking her intercession, the Pope emphasizes that renewal does not come from grand gestures but from daily acts of humility, kindness, and repentance.

Pope Francis concludes his homily with a heartfelt prayer, recognizing the Church's need for God's mercy. His words are not just an appeal for forgiveness but a proclamation of hope. The Church is a place for sinners, not for the perfect. It is precisely in acknowledging its weakness that the Church can be a true witness to Christ's love.

The invitation to seek and give forgiveness is not just a call for the Church but for every individual. It is an invitation to let go of pride, step beyond self-righteousness, and enter into a deeper relationship with God and with others. In a world where divisions run deep and past wounds often dictate the present, forgiveness remains the only path to true freedom and communion.

The Pope's homily is ultimately a call to transformation—a reminder that, while sin will always be a part of human existence, mercy is greater. The Church, like each of its members, is constantly in need of renewal. And this renewal begins with a humble heart, willing to say, "Lord, have mercy on me, a sinner."

Homily Analysis: The Depth of Forgiveness

Pope Francis' homily on forgiveness is a profound meditation on the nature of sin, reconciliation, and the

Church's role in the healing process. His words go beyond a simple call to repentance; they reveal the intricate connection between personal sin, communal responsibility, and the Church's credibility in fulfilling its mission. At the heart of his message is the understanding that sin is relational—it disrupts not only an individual's relationship with God but also the fabric of the faith community. Likewise, forgiveness is not just an individual act but a process of restoration that binds the Church together and reaffirms its witness to the world.

Sin as a Wound in Relationship: A Communal Reality

The homily begins by emphasizing that sin is not an isolated act but a rupture in relationships. Pope Francis frames sin as a communal reality, asserting that "no one is saved alone," and likewise, "the sin of one affects many others." This theological understanding of sin echoes traditional Catholic teaching, particularly the doctrine of the Mystical Body of Christ. Just as good works and virtues strengthen the Church, sins weaken and damage it. The Pope reminds the faithful that everything is interconnected—both in goodness and in evil—highlighting the communal responsibility each believer carries.

This perspective is deeply rooted in biblical tradition. In Scripture, sin is rarely depicted as Sin is not merely an offense between an individual and God; rather, it is often portrayed as a violation that affects the entire community. The story of Adam and Eve in Genesis illustrates how their disobedience led not only to their suffering but to the fall of all humanity. Similarly, in the *Old Testament,* the sins of Israel often led to the suffering of the entire nation. The Pope's emphasis on communal sin aligns with this biblical precedent, urging the Church to recognize the far-reaching consequences of its failures.

This understanding also carries significant moral and ethical implications. In a world that increasingly promotes individualism, where people often believe their actions affect only themselves, Pope Francis reminds the faithful that sin has social consequences. Whether it is corruption, dishonesty, abuse, or neglect of the marginalized, the effects of wrongdoing ripple outward. The homily serves as a powerful reminder that no one's moral choices exist in isolation; seeking forgiveness, therefore, is not just a private act but a vital step in restoring communal integrity.

The Pharisee and the Publican: A Lesson in Humility

Pope Francis turns to Jesus' parable of the Pharisee and the publican as a model for understanding the proper disposition toward forgiveness. The Pharisee, proud of his righteousness, approaches God with a sense of entitlement, enumerating his good deeds and positioning himself as superior to others. In contrast, the publican stands at a distance, humbly acknowledging his unworthiness and pleading for mercy.

The Pope highlights how the Pharisee's prayer is not truly directed to God; rather, it is a self-congratulatory declaration, a performance of righteousness that leaves no room for grace. His certainty in his goodness blinds him to his need for forgiveness, ultimately cutting him off from divine mercy. In contrast, the publican, by recognizing his sinfulness, opens himself to God's transforming love.

This distinction is crucial in the Pope's homily, as he warns against the danger of spiritual pride within the Church. Too often, the faithful, he suggests, can become like the Pharisees—convinced of their righteousness while blind to their shortcomings. Clergy, religious, and laypeople alike can fall into the temptation of believing they are beyond reproach, filling the Church with presumption instead of humility. This attitude is not only spiritually dangerous but also detrimental to the Church's credibility. If believers refuse to acknowledge their sins, they undermine their ability to be effective witnesses of Christ's love.

The Pope's critique goes beyond personal attitudes to address institutional behavior. He suggests that, at times, the Church has mirrored the Pharisee's posture—occupying spaces of power, issuing moral judgments on the world, while failing to recognize its own need for repentance. This warning serves as a call to ecclesial humility—an invitation for the Church to see itself not as morally superior but as a pilgrim community in constant need of God's mercy.

The Church's Need for Corporate Repentance

A significant theme in the homily is the Pope's call for the Church to seek forgiveness collectively. He acknowledges that the Church has caused wounds that continue to affect the faithful, and he insists that healing cannot begin until these wounds are confronted. This marks a departure from a purely individualistic understanding of sin and repentance; it is not just individuals who must seek forgiveness but the Church as a whole.

This emphasis on corporate repentance reflects the broader tradition of the Church's penitential history. Throughout history, the Church has publicly acknowledged its failures—whether in its treatment of indigenous peoples, its involvement in past wars, or its mishandling of abuse scandals. The Pope continues this tradition by urging the Church to recognize its shortcomings and seek reconciliation. His words emphasize that the Church's credibility hinges on its willingness to be honest about its mistakes.

The Pope's call for the Church to be a "synodal Church" is deeply connected to this theme of repentance. Synodality, in its truest sense, is not merely about governance or ecclesial structures; it is about walking together in faith. But how can the Church walk together if the divisions caused by past wounds remain unhealed? How can it authentically proclaim the Gospel if it has not confronted the sins that have tarnished its witness? True synodality requires not only dialogue but reconciliation, and reconciliation begins with the courage to seek forgiveness.

The Scandal of Mercy and the Challenge of True Forgiveness

Pope Francis touches on one of the most difficult aspects of forgiveness: the reality that mercy is often scandalous. Many struggle with the idea that those who have wronged others can be fully forgiven, especially when the wounds they cause remain. The Pope acknowledges that asking for forgiveness is not easy, nor is granting it. He recognizes that the wounds of the Church "do not stop bleeding" and that healing takes time.

This understanding is essential in Catholic theology. Forgiveness does not mean ignoring justice or pretending that wrongdoing never occurred. Rather, it means creating space for grace to transform both the wrongdoer and the victim. The Pope's reference to Isaiah's vision of the wolf and the lamb living together reminds us that true reconciliation does not erase differences or ignore pain. Still, it allows opposites to coexist in harmony.

The Pope's insistence on the Church's need for repentance also speaks to the tension between justice and mercy. While justice seeks to set things right, mercy acknowledges that no one is beyond redemption. The Catholic tradition holds both principles together, understanding that divine justice and divine mercy are not opposites but two aspects of God's love. The Pope calls the Church to embody this balance—acknowledging its failures while trusting in the boundless mercy of God.

The Connection Between Forgiveness and Mission

The Pope concludes his homily by linking forgiveness to mission. The Church cannot fulfill its role in the world if it remains burdened by unacknowledged sin. Just as individuals must confess their sins to receive grace, the Church must confess its failures to regain its credibility.

His appeal to young people is particularly striking. By asking forgiveness from the next generation, he acknowledges that many have lost trust in the Church. This humility is essential in reestablishing that trust. It is not enough to call young people back to the faith; the Church must show that it is willing to listen, to change, and to become a more faithful witness of Christ's love.

Forgiveness as the Path to Renewal

Pope Francis' homily presents forgiveness not as a passive act but as an active force of renewal. Sin disrupts relationships, but forgiveness restores them. Pride leads to self-righteousness, while humility opens the door to grace. The Church cannot be a true instrument of God's love unless it acknowledges its failings, both past and present.

By calling for a Church that seeks forgiveness, Pope Francis challenges believers to embrace humility, recognize their need for grace, and actively pursue reconciliation. While the process of healing may be difficult, it is the only path to restore trust, rebuild credibility, and authentically embody the Gospel message. Through forgiveness, the Church does not simply atone for its past—it finds the strength to move forward, renewed by the very mercy it proclaims.

The Healing Power of Forgiveness: Reflections and Applications for Modern Life

Forgiveness is one of the most profound yet challenging acts a person can undertake. In a world that often glorifies justice through retribution and personal strength through invulnerability, true forgiveness can feel counterintuitive. Society teaches that to forgive is to surrender power, to let an offender escape accountability, or to expose oneself to further harm. Yet, the reality is far more complex. Forgiveness is not about excusing wrongdoing or erasing the past—it is about liberation. It frees the one who forgives from the weight of anger and bitterness, offering the possibility of healing, reconciliation, and inner peace.

The Weight of Unforgiveness: A Silent Prison

Resentment is often compared to carrying a heavy burden. People cling to grudges, believing that remembering past wrongs will shield them from future harm. Yet, instead of offering protection, this burden only deepens the wound. Resentment does not punish the offender; it punishes the one who carries it.

Consider a woman who was betrayed in her marriage. After discovering her spouse's infidelity, she decides never to trust anyone again. Years pass, and though she has moved on externally—establishing a successful career, maintaining friendships, and even forming new relationships—she remains emotionally guarded. Every interaction becomes filtered through the lens of past pain, and without realizing it, she sabotages her happiness. She withholds herself from fully loving or being loved, fearing that to do so would leave her vulnerable to another betrayal. In this case, her refusal to forgive is not an act of justice but a self-imposed imprisonment.

Psychological research backs this reality. Studies show that chronic resentment and anger are linked to higher levels of stress, anxiety, and physical ailments such as high blood pressure and heart disease. The inability to forgive is not only a spiritual burden but also a strain on mental and physical well-being. True healing, then, comes not from clinging to pain but from choosing to release it.

The Struggle to Seek Forgiveness: Admitting Fault in a World That Values Perfection

If offering forgiveness is difficult, seeking it can be even harder. Admitting wrongdoing requires humility, and humility is not always valued in modern culture. In a world obsessed with image and personal success, admitting fault can feel like a weakness. Many people would rather justify their actions, shift blame, or remain silent than acknowledge their mistakes.

This is particularly evident in the workplace. A corporate leader who makes a poor financial decision that negatively impacts employees may hesitate to take responsibility, fearing it will damage their reputation. Rather than admit the mistake, they may cover it up, shift blame, or remain silent. This is particularly evident in the workplace. A corporate leader who makes a poor financial decision that negatively impacts employees may hesitate to take responsibility, fearing it will damage their reputation. Rather than admit the mistake, they may cover it up, shift blame, or remain silent.

The same is true in personal relationships. A father who has been distant from his children may feel deep regret but hesitate to apologize, fearing rejection. His pride tells him it is too late, that admitting failure will make him seem weak. Yet, if he chooses to humble himself and seek forgiveness, he creates the possibility of mending broken bonds. The longer he waits, the wider the divide grows, but with one sincere apology, a lifetime of distance can begin to heal.

Seeking forgiveness is not about erasing the past but about restoring relationships and moving forward with honesty. It is not about losing dignity but about having the courage to acknowledge imperfection.

Forgiveness and Justice: Can They Coexist?

One of the greatest challenges of forgiveness is the question of justice. Many people struggle to forgive those who have caused deep harm—abusers, criminals, or those who show no remorse. How does one forgive without enabling wrongdoing?

Consider the case of a victim of a violent crime. If they choose to forgive their attacker, does that mean the attacker should go free? Not at all. Forgiveness does not negate justice; rather, it transforms the way justice is pursued. True justice is not about revenge but about restoration. A victim who forgives does not condone the crime or absolve the offender from legal consequences. Instead, they choose to free themselves from the emotional grip of hatred. They seek justice not out of vengeance but to prevent further harm.

This is also evident in historical examples. Take the Truth and Reconciliation Commission in South Africa after the end of apartheid. Rather than pursuing mass retribution, the country chose a path of acknowledgment, confession, and forgiveness. Victims and perpetrators were brought together, allowing for the truth to be spoken and wounds to be acknowledged. This did not erase the suffering that had occurred, but it prevented a cycle of endless violence and created the possibility of national healing.

Forgiveness and justice must go hand in hand. To forgive does not mean forgetting or permitting harm to continue—it means choosing a path of healing over destruction.

Faith and Community: The Role of Support in the Act of Forgiveness

Forgiveness is not always something that can be achieved alone. Often, it requires the support of others—a community that fosters healing and provides wisdom. Many people struggle to forgive because they feel isolated in their suffering, believing that no one understands their pain. This sense of isolation can deepen their wounds.

This is why faith communities, support groups, and close friendships are essential in the process of forgiveness. A person who has been deeply hurt may find strength in prayer, seek guidance from a mentor, or find comfort in hearing the stories of others who have walked similar paths. Many religious traditions emphasize the power of communal reconciliation, whether through confession, shared prayers, or acts of service that rebuild trust.

Even outside of religious contexts, the principle remains the same. Support groups for victims, therapy, and open conversations with trusted friends can provide the space needed to process pain and take steps toward forgiveness. No one should have to bear the burden of unforgiveness alone.

Forgiveness as Freedom: Letting Go of the Past to Reclaim the Future

Perhaps the most compelling reason to forgive is the freedom it brings. Many believe that holding onto pain protects them, but in reality, it traps them in the past. Forgiveness is not about erasing memories or pretending something didn't happen—it's about refusing to let the past dictate the future.

Consider a man who was wrongfully accused of a crime and spent years in prison before being exonerated. He has every reason to be bitter, to live in anger at the system that failed him. Yet, when given the choice, he decides to use his experience to advocate for others, to educate, and to build a life that is not defined by injustice but by purpose. In forgiving, he does not excuse what happened to him, but he refuses to let it control his future.

On a smaller scale, this same lesson applies to daily life. A child who was bullied in school may grow into an adult who sees the world through the lens of past wounds, mistrusting others and expecting hostility. But if they choose to forgive, they reclaim their ability to trust, form genuine relationships, and experience joy without fear.

Forgiveness is not just an act of mercy toward others—it is an act of liberation for oneself. It is a decision to no longer be weighed down by resentment and to refuse to let another person's wrongdoing dictate one's happiness.

The Gift of Letting Go

Forgiveness is not about weakness, nor is it about denying justice. It is about choosing peace over bitterness, healing over hurt, and liberation over captivity. It involves acknowledging that while the past cannot be changed, the future remains open.

In the end, to forgive is not to deny that the pain happened but to declare that it no longer holds power. It is to see another human being—not as the sum of their worst actions, but as a person capable of change, just as we hope to be seen ourselves. It is the greatest act of strength, the most profound act of love, and the surest path to freedom.

Reflection Questions for Modern Life: The Challenge and Power of Forgiveness

Forgiveness is one of the most difficult yet liberating acts a person can undertake. It demands humility, self-awareness, and the courage to release resentment while upholding accountability. True forgiveness does not ignore wrongdoing, nor does it justify harm; rather, it is a process of freeing oneself from the burdens of anger, guilt, and regret. These ten reflection questions serve as a guide to examine how forgiveness—or the lack of it—affects daily life, relationships, and personal wellbeing.

1. Am I holding onto past hurts that continue to shape my present?

Many people carry emotional wounds from past betrayals, injustices, or personal failures. Unresolved pain often manifests as bitterness, defensiveness, or an inability to trust others. By reflecting on whether past events are still influencing present relationships and decisions, one can begin to recognize the weight of unforgiveness.

Think of a time when someone hurt you deeply. Does the memory of that event still stir strong emotions? Does it affect the way you interact with others, perhaps making you more guarded or less willing to be vulnerable? Acknowledging lingering pain is the first step toward releasing it.

2. Do I equate forgiveness with weakness?

In a culture that often glorifies strength, forgiveness is sometimes viewed as a sign of weakness or submission. Many believe that to forgive means to condone wrongdoing or to allow themselves to be taken advantage of. However, true forgiveness is not passive; it is an intentional decision to reclaim inner peace.

Consider the lives of historical figures who embodied forgiveness despite immense suffering, such as Nelson Mandela, who chose reconciliation over revenge after decades of imprisonment. Would holding onto anger have made him stronger, or did his ability to forgive enable him to build a new future?

3. Have I sought forgiveness for the wrongs I have committed?

It is often easier to dwell on the wrongs done to us than to acknowledge the ways we may have hurt others. Seeking forgiveness requires humility and a willingness to admit our imperfections. It also takes the courage to accept that some wounds we have inflicted may take time to heal.

Reflect on a time when you wronged someone, whether intentionally or unintentionally. Did you take responsibility? Did you offer a sincere apology, or did pride prevent you from admitting fault? What is preventing you from seeking reconciliation now?

4. Do I forgive myself as readily as I forgive others?

Self-forgiveness is one of the most neglected aspects of emotional healing. Many people hold onto guilt for years, believing they are unworthy of grace. They replay past mistakes in their minds, allowing regret to shape their sense of self-worth.

Think of a mistake you've made that still lingers in your mind. If a friend had made the same mistake, would you hold it against them forever? If not, why do you struggle to extend that same mercy to yourself? Imagine how your life might change if you allowed yourself to move forward, free from the weight of self-condemnation.

5. Am I confusing forgiveness with forgetting?

Some people resist forgiveness, believing it means erasing the past or pretending the pain never existed. In reality, forgiveness isn't about forgetting—it's about choosing to release resentment and reclaim peace. You can forgive while still setting healthy boundaries.

Reflect on a time when you forgave someone. Did forgiveness lead you back into the same relationship, or did it simply free you to release the pain and move forward? How can you embrace forgiveness while still protecting yourself?

6. Does my inability to forgive stem from a desire for control?

Holding onto resentment can sometimes feel like a source of power. When someone has wronged us, keeping them at a distance or clinging to our anger may seem like a way to regain control. Yet, in reality, it often traps us in a cycle of pain.

Think of someone you've struggled to forgive. Does holding onto resentment make you feel stronger, or does it keep you bound to the pain they caused? Could letting go of that resentment help you reclaim your peace?

7. How has holding onto anger affected my well-being?

Medical and psychological studies show that chronic anger and resentment can increase stress and anxiety and even contribute to physical ailments like high blood pressure and heart disease. Unforgiveness doesn't just strain relationships—it also takes a toll on your health.

Reflect on how holding onto past hurt has impacted your emotional or physical well-being. Have you felt tension, restlessness, or even health issues that might be linked to unresolved anger? What would it feel like to release that burden finally?

8. Have I witnessed the power of forgiveness in my own life?

Forgiveness isn't just a concept—it's a transformative experience. At some point, most people have been on the receiving end of forgiveness, whether from a friend, a family member, or even God.

Think of a time when someone forgave you despite the pain you caused them. How did it feel to receive a second chance? How might reflecting on that experience help you extend the same grace to others?

9. How do I respond when I see others struggle with forgiveness?

People often judge those who struggle to forgive, assuming they are bitter or ungrateful. However, true empathy recognizes that forgiveness is a journey, not a single decision. Some wounds take time to heal.

Think of someone in your life who struggles with forgiveness. Do you offer them patience and compassion, or do you pressure them to "just move on"? How can you support them in their journey toward healing?

10. What step can I take today to practice forgiveness?

Forgiveness isn't just an abstract idea—it requires action. It often begins with a small step: writing an unsent letter, praying for someone who has hurt you, or simply acknowledging that forgiveness is possible.

Identify one person, situation, or personal regret that still weighs on your heart. What is one concrete step you can take today to move toward healing? Even if full reconciliation isn't possible, how can you begin to release the resentment within you?

Forgiveness isn't a one-time decision—it's a journey. It requires time, effort, and grace. Some days, it may feel impossible; other days, it may feel free. The key is to stay open to the process, trusting that in letting go of resentment, you gain freedom, peace, and a greater capacity to love.

These questions aren't meant to be answered all at once but revisited throughout life. True healing is rarely instant, yet with each small act of forgiveness, we step closer to a life unburdened by past wounds. The choice is always there: remain imprisoned by anger or walk in freedom.

Chapter 8

A Call to True Compassion: The Parable of the Good Samaritan

Saint Peter's Square - Sunday, 10 July 2016

The Homily

In this homily, Pope Francis reflects on the parable of the Good Samaritan—one of Jesus' most profound teachings in the Gospel of Luke. This parable is more than a lesson in kindness; it is a radical redefinition of love, faith, and the recognition of every person's dignity. The Pope highlights how this passage directly challenges self-centeredness, religious complacency, and the tendency to set limits on whom we choose to love. He emphasizes that true faith isn't measured by words or beliefs alone but by concrete acts of mercy and compassion.

At the heart of this reflection is a question posed by a lawyer in the Gospel: Who is my neighbor? This question implies a desire to define the limits of moral responsibility—to determine who deserves love and who does not. Rather than offering a direct answer, Jesus tells the parable of the Good Samaritan, a story that completely upends conventional thinking. Through this parable, Pope Francis explains how Jesus shifts the focus from identifying neighbors to becoming one. The true question is not about defining who is worthy of love but rather whether we choose to embody love in our daily lives.

The story begins with a man traveling from Jerusalem to Jericho who is attacked by robbers, beaten, and left half-dead on the roadside. A priest passes by, sees him, but keeps walking. A Levite, another religious figure, also notices the injured man yet does nothing to help. Finally, a Samaritan—someone from a group despised by the Jews—stops, tends to the man's wounds, and ensures he receives proper care.

When Jesus finishes the story, he asks the lawyer which of the three men acted as a neighbor. Unable to even utter the word Samaritan due to deep-seated prejudice, the lawyer replies, "The one who had mercy on him." Jesus then commands, "Go and do likewise." This response is crucial because it completely reframes the lawyer's original question. Instead of asking who deserves love, Jesus calls for a love that knows no boundaries.

Pope Francis highlights how this lesson remains relevant today. The temptation to categorize others—to decide who is worthy of compassion and who is not—persists. Many people instinctively show kindness to those who belong to their community, their religion, or their social class but remain indifferent to those outside of these circles. The parable dismantles such divisions, revealing that mercy is not about affiliation or background but about action. Love is not meant to be restricted—it is meant to be lived.

One of the most striking elements of the parable is the failure of the priest and the Levite to show compassion. These were religious men, people expected to embody holiness, yet they refused to help the wounded man. Their actions reveal an empty faith, a spirituality that exists only in ritual but does not translate into love. Pope Francis warns against this same tendency in the modern world. One can be religious yet fail to be truly Christian. It is possible to know doctrine, attend services, and follow traditions while remaining indifferent to suffering. True holiness, however, is not measured by religious observance but by love in action.

The Samaritan—though considered an outsider—is the one who acts with mercy. He does not hesitate. He does not stop to question whether the wounded man shares his people or his faith. He responds. His compassion is not abstract; it is practical, costly, and deeply personal. He binds the man's wounds, takes him to an inn, and ensures he is cared for. This is the kind of love Jesus calls for—a love that moves beyond words, beliefs, and comfort.

Pope Francis urges believers to examine whether their faith bears real fruit. It is not enough to recite prayers or claim righteousness without demonstrating love for those in need. He challenges the faithful to reflect: Are they like the priest and the Levite—focused on religious duties while ignoring the suffering around them? Or are they, like the Samaritan, willing to be inconvenienced for the sake of love?

A recurring theme in Pope Francis' teaching is the call to a faith that is active and tangible. He reminds believers that Christianity is not about abstract concepts but about how love is lived out in daily life. At the Last Judgment, Jesus does not ask people about their theological knowledge or religious affiliation. Instead, he asks, *Did you feed the hungry? Did you welcome the stranger? Did you care for the sick? Did you visit the prisoner?*

Pope Francis makes it clear that faith without action is empty. Love is not just something spoken—it is something demonstrated. The parable of the Good

Samaritan is not a suggestion; it is a command—Jesus' final words: *Go and do likewise,* leave no room for passivity. Every Christian is called to live out this radical mercy, to embody the same compassion that the Samaritan showed, without hesitation and expectation of reward.

Pope Francis strongly warns against the growing culture of indifference. In a world where self-interest often overshadows compassion, it is easy to become detached from the suffering of others. The fast pace of modern life, coupled with the distractions of technology and social media, can make it all too easy to overlook those in need.

The Pope challenges this tendency, urging believers to resist the temptation to "pass by." The Good Samaritan did not help because it was convenient or for recognition—he helped because he saw someone in need. In contrast, many today walk past suffering—ignoring people experiencing homelessness, disregarding refugees, dismissing the elderly, or remaining indifferent to the struggles of those outside their immediate circles.

This challenge extends beyond individuals to society as a whole. Governments and institutions, too, are called to prioritize mercy over profit, people over policies, and human dignity over efficiency. The Pope reminds believers that Christ identifies with the suffering. Every marginalized person, every outcast, every individual in need bears the face of Christ. To ignore them is to ignore Him.

The final message of the homily is one of action. Jesus' words—*Go and do likewise*—are not passive suggestions but direct commands. Christianity is not merely about intellectual agreement but about a life lived in service to others. The Good Samaritan did not wait for an invitation to help. He did not question whether the wounded man was his responsibility. He saw suffering and responded.

Pope Francis calls on every Christian to embrace this mission of mercy. Faith is not meant to be confined to prayers, rituals, or church walls—it must extend into daily life and every encounter with others. The Pope prays that the Virgin Mary, the Mother of Mercy, will guide believers in walking this path. The true path to eternal life is not found in legalism or exclusivity but in self-giving love.

Pope Francis' homily on the Good Samaritan offers a profound reflection on the nature of Christian love. It dismantles any attempt to limit compassion, making it clear that mercy is not bound by nationality, religion, or social status. The question is not who deserves love but whether we choose to love.

In a world where divisions, prejudice, and indifference persist, this message remains as radical as ever. The Pope challenges every believer to make this parable the foundation of their faith—to refuse to categorize people, reject complacency, and respond to suffering with open hearts and hands.

The command of Jesus remains urgent and non-negotiable: *Go and do likewise.*

Homily Analysis: Breaking the Boundaries of Love

The parable of the Good Samaritan is one of Jesus' most powerful teachings, yet its significance extends far beyond a simple lesson on kindness. It is a radical redefinition of love, mercy, and moral responsibility— challenging listeners to reconsider the very foundation of faith. In his homily, Pope Francis unpacks the deeper meaning of this parable, revealing its profound implications for understanding God, humanity, and the nature of true righteousness.

At its core, the parable dismantles the deeply ingrained human tendency to confine love within convenient, self-imposed limits. It exposes the moral blindness that arises when faith is bound by legalism rather than love. Jesus does not merely call his audience to compassion; he compels them to recognize that their understanding of virtue and holiness has been fundamentally flawed. Pope Francis highlights this shift, emphasizing that Jesus does not answer the lawyer's question as expected. The question, "Who is my neighbor?" is turned upside down. Instead of defining who qualifies as a neighbor, Jesus challenges the listener to ask a different question: "Am I willing to be a neighbor to those in need?"

The Priest, the Levite, and the Failure of Religious Formalism

The figures of the priest and the Levite in the parable serve as a stark warning against religious complacency. These men were religious officials, well-versed in the law, and entrusted with the spiritual well-being of the people. Their failure to act is not merely indifference—it is a failure of faith itself. The priest and the Levite likely saw themselves as righteous, yet their righteousness was self-contained, governed by ritual purity rather than the heart of the law: love.

Pope Francis emphasizes that Jesus exposes a fundamental contradiction in their behavior. These men, called to embody holiness, passed by the wounded man without intervening. Their failure was not in committing harm but in withholding the good they had the power to give. This omission is critical because it reveals that sin is not only the presence of evil but also the absence of love. Their refusal to act demonstrates how religion, when detached from compassion, can become an obstacle to genuine faith.

This moment in the parable is profoundly unsettling because it challenges the assumption that Holiness is measured not by external observance alone. The priest and the Levite likely justified their inaction with religious reasoning—perhaps they feared becoming ritually unclean or believed it was not their responsibility. But Jesus' parable makes it clear that religious obligations are meaningless if they do not lead to mercy. Pope Francis presents this as a warning to those who prioritize religious identity over the fundamental call to love. True holiness does not consist of strict adherence to rules but of the willingness to be moved by compassion.

The Samaritan: The Outcast Who Embodies Divine Love

In stark contrast to the religious figures, the Samaritan—an outsider despised by the Jewish people—becomes the embodiment of mercy. This choice is shocking. Samaritans were considered heretics, unclean, and unworthy of inclusion in Jewish society. Yet it is this man, not the priest or the Levite, who fulfills the heart of God's law. The Samaritan does not hesitate, does not weigh the consequences, and does not question whether the man is "deserving" of help—he simply sees suffering and responds.

Pope Francis underscores that Jesus is deliberately provocative in his choice of hero, forcing his audience to confront their own biases and assumptions. The lawyer who asked the question would have been deeply uncomfortable with the answer. By making the Samaritan the example of righteousness, Jesus dismantles the notion that holiness is tied to status, ethnicity, or tradition. Instead, he reveals that true holiness is defined by love—a heart that recognizes the suffering of another and responds without hesitation.

The actions of the Samaritan are detailed and deliberate. He does not merely provide temporary relief; he ensures that the man is taken care of beyond their initial encounter. He binds the man's wounds, takes him to an inn, and even commits to covering any additional expenses. This is not mere charity—it is self-giving love. It is a love that refuses to calculate, does not measure out compassion in portions, but gives fully and without expectation of return.

This portrayal of the Samaritan challenges any notion of a limited or conditional morality. It reveals that love, in its truest form, is boundless. The Samaritan does not love because it is expected or required—he loves because it is the only possible response to suffering. Pope Francis highlights this as the essence of divine love: a love that does not discriminate, does not seek reward, and does not withhold itself based on status or circumstance.

Reversing the Question: The True Test of Righteousness

One of the most striking aspects of the parable is how Jesus shifts the framework of the conversation. The lawyer asks, "Who is my neighbor?"—seeking to define the limits of his moral responsibility. But Jesus does not answer this question directly. Instead, he reframes it entirely, asking, "Which of these three was a neighbor to the man in need?" This marks a fundamental shift in perspective. The issue is no longer about determining who *deserves* love but about whether one is willing to *be* loved.

Pope Francis points out that this reversal is central to the Christian understanding of morality. Love is not a theoretical principle but a concrete, lived reality. It is not about defining boundaries but about crossing them. The parable does not allow for passive belief—it demands action. Jesus is not interested in what people claim to believe but in what they do. The true measure of righteousness is not found in titles, knowledge, or religious identity but in the willingness to love with selflessness and generosity.

This is why the final words of Jesus are so powerful: "Go and do likewise." There is no debate, no conditions—only a command to act. Love is not merely something to be pondered; it is something to be lived. The parable ends without resolution, leaving the lawyer—and every listener—with an unavoidable choice. Will you be a neighbor? Will you cross the boundaries you have created? Will you love as God loves?

The Scandal of Mercy: A Love That Disrupts

One of the most challenging aspects of this parable is that it is disruptive. It does not affirm the existing moral framework of Jesus' audience—it shatters it. Pope Francis emphasizes that Jesus does not simply expand the concept of neighbor; he obliterates any attempt to limit it. There are no boundaries to mercy, no exclusions to love. The priest and the Levite may have seen boundaries—between clean and unclean, between responsibility and non-responsibility—but Jesus reveals that such boundaries are illusions. Love is not about who belongs to one's group but about the willingness to break down every barrier.

This is why the parable remains just as unsettling today as when Jesus first told it. It does not allow for moral complacency; instead, it forces each listener to confront how they, too, have passed by on the other side. It reveals that righteousness is not about status or theology but about the condition of one's heart. It challenges every excuse for withholding love, every justification for inaction, and every attempt to define morality in a way that evades responsibility.

Pope Francis challenges believers to see this parable not as a story about others but as a direct examination of their faith. He emphasizes that the true measure of love is not found in sentiment but in action. True holiness is found in the willingness to love beyond expectation, convenience, and obligation. The Samaritan did not love because he was required to—he loved because mercy compelled him. And it is this mercy that defines the kingdom of God.

The Final Invitation to Radical Love

The parable of the Good Samaritan is not merely a lesson in compassion—it is a declaration of the very essence of divine love. It is a call to a faith that transcends religious identity, a morality unshackled from self-interest, and a love that gives freely, seeking no reward. Pope Francis highlights that Jesus does not invite theological debate—He commands: "Go and do likewise." (*Luke 10:37*)

This is the inescapable invitation of the Gospel: to love as God loves—without calculation, without hesitation, without exclusion. To dismantle every barrier that limits mercy. To recognize suffering and respond. To embody love—not as a concept, but as a lived reality in human encounters. To be, in every moment, a neighbor—not out of obligation, but because love demands nothing less.

Living the Call to Radical Love: The Good Samaritan in Modern Life

The parable of the Good Samaritan is not merely an ancient lesson; it is a direct challenge to how we live today. In an age of deepening division, rampant individualism, and growing indifference, this story compels us to confront difficult questions about our attitudes toward others—especially those beyond our immediate circles of concern. Pope Francis' reflection on this passage underscores the urgency of moving beyond superficial kindness to embrace a deeper, transformative love—one that knows no boundaries and calls for personal sacrifice.

The Samaritan did not merely offer a gesture of goodwill. He took responsibility, altered his plans, and risked his safety to care for a stranger—someone who, in another context, might have been seen as an enemy. This is the challenge Jesus presents to each of us: Are we willing to love when it is inconvenient, when it disrupts our lives, when there is no reward or recognition?

Breaking the Boundaries of Indifference

Modern life conditions people to prioritize efficiency, productivity, and self-interest. The demands of work, family, and financial stability often leave little room for concern beyond one's immediate circle. As a result, indifference to suffering—especially that which does not directly affect us—becomes almost second nature.

For example, homelessness is a crisis in many cities, yet it is often treated as a distant issue. People walk past those sleeping on sidewalks, avoiding eye contact, pretending not to notice. There's a pervasive belief that helping would be too complicated—that someone else, whether the government or a charity, should take responsibility.

Yet, the Good Samaritan did not leave compassion to someone else. He did not assume the next traveler would take responsibility. He saw suffering, stopped, and acted.

Some communities have responded to homelessness with this same radical love. In certain cities, small groups of citizens have taken it upon themselves to build "tiny home" villages, offering not just shelter but stability and a pathway to reintegration into society.

These initiatives are not easy; they demand financial commitment, time, and perseverance. Yet, they embody the essence of the Good Samaritan's love—seeing a need and meeting it, no matter the obstacles.

Love Beyond Obligation: Helping Those Who Cannot Repay

The Good Samaritan helped the wounded man without expecting gratitude or repayment. He cared for him because true compassion does not calculate the cost. In contrast, much of modern charity operates on a transactional basis—people give, but often with an expectation of acknowledgment, recognition, or even financial incentives. True mercy, however, is given freely, without strings attached.

One striking example of selfless love is found in those who care for the elderly, especially those without family. In many cultures, aging individuals who can no longer contribute economically are often seen as burdens. As a result, nursing homes are filled with elderly residents who receive few, if any, visitors. Yet, some volunteers dedicate themselves to spending time with these forgotten individuals—reading to them, bringing small gifts, or simply sitting in silence so they do not feel alone. These volunteers are modern-day Good Samaritans. They step into spaces where love is needed, expecting nothing in return—no social media praise, no financial incentive, no career advancement. They give simply because human dignity demands it.

Overcoming Social Divisions: Who Is My Neighbor Today?

In a world increasingly shaped by identity politics, nationalism, and ideological rigidity, people often focus more on defining who belongs to their group than on recognizing the shared humanity in others. The lawyer in the Gospel sought to set limits on his responsibility by asking, "Who is my neighbor?" But Jesus reframed the question: "Will you be a neighbor?" The focus shifted from determining who is worthy of love to choosing to act with love.

This is especially relevant in how societies respond to immigration and refugee crises. In many places, asylum seekers are met with hostility and viewed as threats rather than human beings in need of compassion. In some countries, some families open their homes to refugees, providing not just shelter but a sense of belonging. A powerful example can be seen in communities where local families "adopt" a refugee family, supporting them as they learn the language, navigate bureaucracy, and integrate into society. These host families do not question whether the refugees "deserve" help; they recognize suffering and respond with compassion.

The same principle applies to racial and religious divisions. In some places, people refuse to engage with those of different beliefs or cultural backgrounds, viewing them as "the other" rather than as neighbors. Yet, some individuals choose a different path—one of bridge-building and understanding. They foster interfaith relationships, create spaces for dialogue, and break down barriers of prejudice. In one city, a group of Muslim and Christian families came together to start a joint food pantry, serving the poor side by side and proving that mercy transcends religious affiliation.

Mercy in the Workplace and Daily Life

Being a neighbor isn't just about responding to dramatic crises—it's also about how we treat others in everyday life. Mercy should extend to our daily interactions, where even small acts of kindness can have a profound impact.

In the workplace, employees may witness colleagues struggling—whether due to excessive workloads, personal challenges, or unfair treatment—but often choose to remain silent because it's easier. Yet, stepping in, offering support, or advocating for someone facing injustice embodies the spirit of the Good Samaritan. Some companies are now prioritizing mental health in the workplace by offering wellness programs, counseling, and flexible work arrangements to ensure employees are treated with dignity and care.

Even within families, this lesson is vital. It is often easier to be kind to strangers than to show patience and mercy to relatives. Family members may hold onto old grudges, stop speaking over past conflicts, or fail to support one another in times of need. The call of the Good Samaritan extends to these relationships as well. It means choosing reconciliation over resentment and offering understanding instead of clinging to past offenses.

The Cost of Love: Are We Willing to Be Inconvenienced?

Perhaps the most challenging lesson in the parable is that love requires sacrifice. The priest and Levite likely had reasonable justifications for passing by—they may have been busy, afraid, or simply indifferent. But love that costs nothing is not the kind of love Jesus calls us to.

One of the most profound examples of selfless love can be seen in those who choose to become foster parents. Welcoming a child into their home—especially one who has endured trauma—is no small task. It upends routines, demands both financial and emotional investment, and offers no assurances of gratitude or success. Yet, those who choose to foster do so because they recognize that love is not about convenience.

Similarly, doctors and nurses who volunteer in conflict zones leave behind comfort and safety to serve in war-torn regions. They risk their well-being to care for strangers, embodying the essence of the Good Samaritan. Instead of staying in secure hospitals, they enter places of great suffering to bring healing.

Go and Do Likewise

Jesus' final command—"Go and do likewise"—is not a suggestion but a directive. It challenges each person to move beyond passive belief into active love. The world does not lack opportunities for mercy; it lacks people willing to take responsibility for others.

Every day presents chances to be a neighbor—helping someone struggling with addiction rather than judging them, standing up against injustice rather than turning a blind eye, and caring for the forgotten rather than assuming someone else will.

The ultimate question is not, "Who is my neighbor?" but, "Am I willing to be a neighbor?" The Good Samaritan teaches that love is not about identifying the "right" people to help but about seeing everyone as worthy of care.

This is the radical love that Jesus calls for—one that is inconvenient, costly, and all-encompassing—a love that does not wait for perfect circumstances but acts whenever and wherever suffering is found; a love that transforms not just the one who receives it but also the one who gives it.

Reflection Questions for Modern Life: The Call to Be a Neighbor

The parable of the Good Samaritan challenges us to reflect on love, mercy, and responsibility. It calls us to move beyond selective compassion and embrace a love that is active, sacrificial, and boundless. These reflection questions invite you to examine your attitudes toward others, the limits of your compassion, and how you can become a true neighbor in today's world.

1. Do I limit my compassion to those I feel comfortable with?

It is easy to show kindness to those we like, who share our values, or who belong to our community. But what about those who challenge us—people from different cultures, faiths, or political views? The Good Samaritan was an outsider, someone presumed to be an enemy, yet he was the one who showed mercy.

Consider moments when you hesitated to help due to personal biases or discomfort. Have you ever avoided engaging with someone simply because they were different? What steps can you take to expand your compassion beyond your comfort zone?

2. Do I prioritize convenience over love?

Love often requires sacrifice, yet modern life prioritizes efficiency and personal comfort. The priest and Levite in the parable likely had good reasons for not stopping—they were busy, afraid, or simply unwilling to be delayed.

Think of a time when you had the chance to help someone but didn't because it was inconvenient. What does this reveal about your priorities? What would it take to embrace love, even when it demands personal inconvenience or disruption?

3. When have I walked past someone in need?

We encounter suffering every day—people struggling emotionally, financially, or physically. Sometimes, like the priest and Levite, we walk past without acknowledging it.

Reflect on a recent moment when you saw someone in distress but didn't get involved. What held you back— fear, indifference, or uncertainty about how to help? What would it take for you to respond differently next time?

4. Do I let judgment prevent me from showing mercy?

Society often teaches us to evaluate people before deciding if they "deserve" help. We judge the homeless, the unemployed, or those struggling with addiction, assuming their circumstances are the result of personal failure.

Have you ever hesitated to help someone because you felt they were responsible for their suffering? What would change if, instead of judgment, you approached every situation with the same mercy that the Good Samaritan showed?

5. Am I willing to take responsibility for the suffering around me?

The Samaritan could have walked away, assuming that someone else would help the injured man. Instead, he took responsibility for the stranger's well-being, committing his time and resources.

Do you see suffering as someone else's problem, or do you take responsibility for the pain around you? In what small but meaningful ways can you help support the well-being of those in your community?

6. Do I help only when it's easy, or do I engage when it's difficult?

Some acts of kindness require little effort, like donating to charity. But the Good Samaritan went further—he tended to the wounded man, carried him, and paid for his care.

When was the last time you helped in a way that required true effort? Are there areas in your life where you should do more, even if it demands more time, energy, or emotional investment?

7. Do I see the face of Christ in the suffering?

Jesus teaches that when we serve the poor, the sick, or the marginalized, we serve Him. Yet, in daily life, it can be hard to see Christ in those who challenge, frustrate, or seem ungrateful.

Think of someone in your life who is difficult to love. How might seeing Christ in them transform your attitude? What would change if you treated every encounter with someone in need as sacred?

8. Do I practice mercy in my own home and workplace?

It is often easier to show kindness to strangers than to extend patience and forgiveness to family, friends, or colleagues. The parable challenges us to be neighbors not only to those on the street but also to those closest to us.

Consider your relationships—are there areas where you withhold kindness? Have you been impatient, resentful, or indifferent toward those at home or work? How can you extend mercy in your daily interactions?

9. Am I willing to forgive those who have wronged me?

The Samaritan had every reason to despise the Jewish man he helped—the Jews had historically mistreated his people. Yet, he set aside resentment and showed mercy.

Is there someone in your life you are struggling to forgive? What is stopping you from extending mercy? How might releasing resentment free you to live more fully in love?

10. How can I be a Good Samaritan today?

The parable is not just a lesson—it is a command to "Go and do likewise." Living as a Good Samaritan is not about grand gestures but about daily choices.

As you reflect, consider a specific action you can take today—checking in on someone struggling, helping a coworker, volunteering in your community, or simply being more present to those in need. What step can you take to embody the radical love of the Good Samaritan?

These questions are not meant to be answered once and forgotten. They invite ongoing self-examination— a continual reassessment of how we love, whom we choose to love, and whether we are truly living as neighbors to those around us.

The story of the Good Samaritan is not just a parable from the past—it is a daily call to break through indifference, love without expectation, and recognize that our neighbor is defined not by race, religion, or status but by shared humanity. The challenge is clear: Will we walk past suffering, or will we stop, act, and love as Christ calls us to?

Chapter 9

The Power of Humility: The Strength in Surrender

Paul VI Audience Hall - Wednesday, 5 February 2020

The Homily

Pope Francis' homily on the first Beatitude, *Blessed are the poor in spirit, for theirs is the kingdom of heaven* (*Matthew 5:3*), presents a profound reflection on the paradox of true happiness found in spiritual poverty. He dismantles the common belief that success, self-sufficiency, and material wealth bring fulfillment, instead emphasizing that true joy and freedom are found in humility, dependence on God, and recognizing one's limitations. The homily challenges the modern pursuit of power, achievement, and self-importance, offering a countercultural path to inner peace, love, and the Kingdom of God.

At the heart of this message is a striking contrast between the values of the world and those of God. Society often insists that to be "someone" in life means having influence, status, and possessions. Success is measured by external accomplishments—job titles, financial security, recognition, and social power.

People are taught to project strength, hide weaknesses, and maintain control at all times. Pope Francis warns that this way of thinking leads to anxiety, competitiveness, and loneliness because it forces people to constantly compare themselves to others, always fearing that they are not enough. It creates an illusion that self-worth is determined by how much one accumulates rather than by the inherent dignity of being a child of God.

However, Jesus turns this mindset upside down, proclaiming that it is not the powerful, the rich, or the self-sufficient who are blessed, but rather those who recognize their poverty—those who understand their need for God and others. To be *poor in spirit* means to acknowledge that, no matter how much one has in life, every human being remains limited, vulnerable, and in need of grace. It is the recognition that, without God, we are incomplete. This Beatitude invites humility—not as a burden, but as a path to liberation. Those who embrace their spiritual poverty are freed from the exhausting need to prove themselves and instead open their hearts to the infinite love of God, the only thing that can truly satisfy the human soul.

Pope Francis explains that poverty of spirit is not something to be attained—it is already part of the human condition. No matter how powerful or self-reliant one may seem, every person is fundamentally fragile. Illness, loss, failure, and time itself serve as constant reminders of human limitations. Yet, rather than accepting this reality with peace, many resist it, clinging to an illusion of invulnerability.

This resistance to humility fosters pride, making people unwilling to seek help, apologize, or admit mistakes. The Pope notes that pride often appears in everyday moments—how difficult it is to say, "I was wrong" or "I need help." In marriages, workplaces, and friendships, pride creates walls that prevent reconciliation and genuine relationships. He humorously notes that saying.

Saying "I'm sorry" is one of the hardest things to do—not because people lack love, but because admitting mistakes challenges the ego. The proud believe they must always be right and cannot bear the thought of appearing weak. Ironically, this illusion of strength makes them weaker, isolating them from others and God.

Pope Francis draws attention to an even deeper aspect of pride—the refusal to acknowledge the need for God's mercy. He warns that many people prefer to maintain a false image of self-sufficiency rather than admit their need for forgiveness. However, carrying the weight of one's sins alone leads to inner exhaustion.

Jesus offers a different path: not one of self-justification but of surrendering to God's love. The Pope beautifully captures the human struggle between pride and grace: "The Lord never tires of forgiving, but we grow tired of asking for forgiveness." This reveals a fundamental truth—God's mercy is limitless, yet human pride often stands in the way of accepting it.

The homily also addresses the fleeting nature of worldly power and possessions. Throughout history, countless empires, rulers, and civilizations have risen to greatness, only to fade away. Wealth and status offer temporary comfort, but they do not endure. The Pope reminds listeners of an old truth: "The shroud has no pockets." No matter how much a person accumulates in life, none of it can be taken beyond death. Power, fame, and possessions will fade, but the Kingdom of God belongs to those who detach from worldly concerns and live with humble trust in Him. He poignantly observes that no one has ever seen a moving truck following a funeral procession—because material wealth ultimately holds no value beyond this life.

Pope Francis emphasizes that true power is not found in control, wealth, or dominance but in love, humility, and self-giving. Jesus, the King of Kings, displayed the greatest power not through force but by humbling Himself, taking the form of a servant, and giving His life for others. Unlike earthly rulers who seek to be served, Christ revealed that true strength lies in serving. This is why the poor in spirit—the humble, the selfless, those

187

who put others first—are truly blessed. Their strength is not found in material security but in unwavering trust in God. The world often sees humility as a weakness, but in reality, it is the greatest source of freedom. The humble are not pressured to prove themselves, nor are they burdened by pride or the need for validation. They are at peace, knowing their worth comes from God alone.

The homily concludes with an invitation to embrace both the poverty of spirit inherent in human nature and the voluntary poverty that frees one from worldly distractions. This Beatitude is not merely a call to renounce material wealth but to cultivate interior freedom—a heart unburdened by pride, greed, or the constant desire for more. Pope Francis challenges believers to rethink their priorities: Do they seek security in wealth and status, or do they place their trust in God? Are they clinging to pride, or are they willing to embrace humility and dependence on grace?

Ultimately, this Beatitude leads to profound joy. When people release their illusion of control and recognize their need for God, they discover a freedom no material possession can offer. They experience the peace of knowing they are loved—not for what they achieve, but simply because they belong to God. This is the Kingdom of Heaven—not just a future promise but a present reality for those who live with humble, trusting hearts. Pope Francis' homily delivers a powerful message: while the world celebrates pride and self-reliance, true happiness is found in the simplicity of a heart open to God.

Homily Analysis: The Paradox of True Greatness

Pope Francis' homily on *Blessed are the poor in spirit, for theirs is the kingdom of heaven* (*Matthew 5:3*) unravels a profound spiritual truth that directly challenges conventional human thinking. It presents a paradox: true greatness and fulfillment are not found in power, wealth, or self-sufficiency but in humility, dependence on God, and the willingness to embrace one's limitations. At the heart of this Beatitude is a radical shift in perspective—one that finds strength in weakness, freedom in surrender, and divine richness in human poverty. It is an invitation to step away from the world's obsession with status and self-reliance and to embrace a way of life that values trust in God over personal ambition.

This Beatitude is foundational because it reshapes our understanding of success, identity, and security. In a society that glorifies achievement, control, and personal strength, Jesus' words offer a radically different measure of greatness—one that embraces human limitation and welcomes divine grace. Those who are poor in spirit are not failures but have discovered the wisdom of relying on God rather than their abilities. Their strength does not come from what they possess or accomplish but from their openness to receiving from God what they cannot provide for themselves.

The Meaning of Poverty in Spirit

The phrase poor in spirit is often misunderstood. At first glance, it may seem to refer only to material poverty, as if Jesus were praising the virtue of lacking wealth. However, Pope Francis clarifies that its true meaning goes much deeper. In biblical language, spirit signifies the essence of a person—the innermost reality of human existence, where one encounters God. To be poor in spirit is not merely a lack of material wealth but a deep recognition of one's radical dependence on God. It is an interior disposition of humility—an acknowledgment that everything—life, abilities, and blessings—comes from God, not from oneself.

This poverty is not something to be acquired artificially; it is already part of the human condition. Every person is ultimately powerless before the vastness of life's realities. No one can control time, prevent suffering, or dictate the course of history. No matter how powerful or successful one may seem, every person is limited and vulnerable. The poor in spirit do not deny this reality but embrace it, allowing their dependence on God to become a source of strength rather than an obstacle.

Pope Francis emphasizes that spiritual poverty is not about glorifying misery or passivity but about acknowledging the truth of one's existence. It is about understanding that, at the core of human life, no one is truly self-sufficient. Even the wealthiest and most powerful individuals face moments of helplessness—

when illness strikes, relationships break down, or death takes a loved one. Those who acknowledge their dependence on God and willingly entrust themselves to Him find peace in these moments, while those who resist this reality experience deep frustration.

The Danger of Self-Sufficiency and Pride

One of the most striking insights from the homily is the contrast Pope Francis draws between those who accept their spiritual poverty and those who resist it through pride and self-sufficiency. Human nature, shaped by worldly values, often equates worth with achievement, status, and control. Society encourages people to build impressive résumés, accumulate wealth, and prove their superiority to feel secure. However, this mindset creates a constant struggle— one in which self-worth is tied to external validation, and failure, weakness, or imperfection are seen as threats.

The *poor in spirit*, in contrast, do not seek to project an illusion of self-sufficiency. They have nothing to prove, no image to maintain. Their strength lies in their openness to God's grace and their willingness to rely on Him rather than their abilities. They are free from the exhausting need to uphold an artificial sense of invulnerability. In contrast, those who resist humility become prisoners of their pride, burdened by the need to maintain control, the fear of failure, and the refusal to acknowledge their need for help.

191

Pope Francis highlights how this manifests in everyday life: pride makes it difficult for people to admit mistakes, ask for forgiveness, or seek help. It creates barriers in relationships, fosters resentment, and isolates individuals from true connection. The inability to say, "I was wrong" or "I need help" is not just a minor personal flaw—it is a symptom of deeper spiritual resistance, a refusal to accept one's limitations. The proud reject the very thing that could free them: the recognition that they do not have to carry everything alone.

Even in religious contexts, people can fall into the trap of spiritual pride. Some believe they must prove themselves worthy before God, accumulating good works as if earning His love. Others judge those they see as less pious, believing themselves superior in faith. This attitude is precisely what Jesus condemns in the Pharisee, who prays, "Thank you, God, that I am not like other men" (*Luke 18:11*).

True spiritual poverty, in contrast, does not rely on one's merits but on God's mercy.

The Kingdom of God and the Illusion of Worldly Power

Pope Francis contrasts the Kingdom of Heaven, promised to the poor in spirit, with the temporary and fragile kingdoms of this world. Throughout history, empires have risen and fallen, leaders have come and gone, and wealth has been accumulated only to be lost. No human achievement lasts forever. Yet, people often place their trust in these fleeting securities, believing that money, power, or status can provide lasting stability. The Pope reminds his audience of a simple truth: the shroud has no pockets. No one takes anything with them beyond death. The kingdoms built on human ambition will fade, while the Kingdom of God remains eternal.

The Beatitude reveals a different kind of power—not the power that dominates or controls, but the power of love, humility, and service. This is the power of God, the power that Christ Himself demonstrated by giving His life for others. Unlike earthly rulers who seek to be served, Jesus came to serve. Unlike worldly kings who seek honor, He embraced humiliation for the sake of love. The poor in spirit share in this divine power by detaching themselves from the illusions of worldly greatness and rooting their security in God's unfailing love.

The Freedom Found in Spiritual Poverty

A central theme in Pope Francis' homily is that true freedom comes from embracing one's spiritual poverty. The world often portrays freedom as the ability to do whatever one wants—being independent, self-reliant, and in control. However, this so-called freedom often leads to anxiety, isolation, and restlessness. The constant need to prove oneself, achieve more, and maintain an image of success becomes a heavy burden.

The *poor in spirit*, on the other hand, experience a different kind of freedom—the freedom of trust. Because they do not seek security in things that fade, they are not enslaved by them. Their happiness does not depend on wealth, reputation, or personal achievements but on their relationship with God. They do not live in constant comparison with others or feel the need to compete for recognition. Their peace remains unshaken by external circumstances because it is rooted in something eternal.

This is why Jesus declares them blessed. Theirs is not a fleeting happiness dependent on good fortune but a deep, unshakable joy that comes from knowing God loves them. The world may see them as weak, but in reality, they possess a strength no earthly power can give.

The Strength in Embracing Spiritual Poverty

The first Beatitude sets the foundation for all the others. It is the starting point of true discipleship because it requires an interior transformation—a willingness to let go of self-sufficiency and trust entirely in God. The poor in spirit are not weak; they possess a strength the world does not understand. Their strength comes from knowing they do not have to rely on themselves alone. Their peace comes from trusting that they are held in the hands of a loving Father.

True greatness is not found in power or possessions but in surrender to the infinite love of God. The

Beatitude of the poor in spirit is not about deprivation but liberation—an invitation to a life unburdened by pride, free from the weight of comparison, and open to the boundless joy of belonging to God's Kingdom.

Embracing Spiritual Poverty in a World of Excess: Living the Lessons in Modern Life

Pope Francis' homily on Blessed are the poor in spirit, for theirs is the kingdom of heaven (Matthew 5:3) challenges modern assumptions about security, happiness, and personal worth. It calls for a profound shift in mindset—one that abandons the illusion of self-sufficiency promoted by the world and instead embraces dependence on God. This teaching is not a call to material poverty in itself but to spiritual poverty that acknowledges human limitations, vulnerability, and the need for divine grace.

Modern society often equates success with independence, control, and self-reliance. People are encouraged to be strong, build their own lives without relying on others, and measure their worth by their achievements. However, this pursuit often leads to anxiety, exhaustion, and deep dissatisfaction. Spiritual poverty, in contrast, invites people to release the illusion of control and find peace in surrendering to God. It offers a different kind of freedom—one not rooted in wealth, power, or status but in the unshakable truth that they are loved by God, regardless of external circumstances.

To fully understand the relevance of this Beatitude in today's world, we must examine how spiritual poverty relates to daily struggles, the pull of materialism, and the emotional burdens that pride and self-reliance create. Through real-life examples, it becomes clear how embracing humility, trust in God, and detachment from materialism leads to a more peaceful and fulfilling life.

The Burden of Self-Sufficiency: Why the Modern World is Exhausted

The world constantly reinforces the idea that a person's worth is tied to self-sufficiency. Society expects individuals to achieve financial independence, maintain a flawless public image, and keep every aspect of life under control. While ambition and responsibility have their place, the illusion of self-sufficiency creates an unbearable burden.

Imagine a young entrepreneur who has dedicated his entire life to building a successful business. He works tirelessly, convinced that his security and happiness depend solely on his. He refuses to ask for help, convinced that doing so would signal weakness. On the surface, he appears successful, but beneath it all, anxiety consumes him. He lives in constant fear—fear of failure, of losing what he has built, of being seen as anything less than perfect. The independence he once sought has become his prison.

Spiritual poverty offers an alternative: instead of clinging to the illusion of self-reliance, it invites an honest acknowledgment of human limitations. It reminds us that we are not meant to carry the weight of the world alone. When we recognize that everything comes from God, we can work diligently—without being paralyzed by the fear of failure. The entrepreneur who learns to trust in God rather than relying solely on his strength will still work hard, but he will do so with peace, knowing that his achievements do not define his worth.

This applies not just to business but to every aspect of life. Many people struggle with the burden of perfectionism, constantly feeling as though they must prove themselves. Parents feel pressured to be perfect for their children, professionals fear appearing incompetent, and students push themselves to extremes to meet unrealistic expectations. The result is a society of individuals who are always striving yet never at peace.

The invitation of spiritual poverty is to let go of relentless striving. It does not mean abandoning goals or responsibilities but rather shifting self-worth from worldly success to God's love. Those who embrace this mindset will still work hard—only now, without the anxiety of proving themselves. Their identity will be rooted not in accomplishments but in their relationship with God.

The False Promise of Wealth and the Freedom of Detachment

In a materialistic world, financial success is often seen as the ultimate goal. Many spend their lives accumulating wealth, believing it will bring happiness, security, and freedom. Yet, time and again, stories emerge of wealthy individuals who, despite having everything, feel empty and unfulfilled.

Consider the case of a man who wins the lottery. At first, it seems like his life has changed for the better. He buys everything he ever wanted—luxury cars, extravagant vacations, a mansion. But as time goes on, he realizes that his relationships have suffered. Old friends treat him differently. New acquaintances see him as a source of money rather than a person. The thrill of spending fades. What once felt exciting now seems meaningless. In the end, he is more isolated than before. The wealth he thought would bring happiness has only left him alone.

Now contrast this with a person who, despite having modest means, lives with contentment. They do not have the newest car or the biggest house, but they have deep relationships, strong faith, and a sense of purpose. They are not consumed by the need for more because they have learned to find joy in what they already have. Their happiness is not dictated by external circumstances but by an inner peace that comes from trusting in God.

Spiritual poverty does not mean rejecting wealth but rejecting dependence on it. It is not about renouncing possessions but about refusing to let them define one's security or identity. Those who embrace this detachment experience true freedom—they are not controlled by money, nor do they live in fear of losing it.

A practical example of this can be seen in people who, despite having little, give generously. They trust that God will provide, and in that trust, they find a joy that wealth alone can never offer. In contrast, those consumed by the need for financial security often live in fear—fear of loss, scarcity, and the unknown. True security is not found in money but in faith.

Pride, Relationships, and the Difficulty of Asking for Help

One of the greatest obstacles to spiritual poverty is pride. Many struggle with asking for help, fearing it will make them appear weak. This is particularly true in personal relationships, where pride can block reconciliation and hinder healing.

Consider a married couple who, after years of tension, stand on the brink of divorce. Both feel hurt, but neither is willing to be the first to apologize. Their pride convinces them that admitting fault would be a sign of weakness. They would rather endure the pain in silence than humble themselves and seek reconciliation. As a result, what could have been healed through a simple act of humility turns into permanent separation.

In contrast, imagine a couple who, despite their struggles, choose humility over pride. When they have disagreements, they are willing to say, "I was wrong, and I'm sorry." They do not see apologies as signs of weakness but as expressions of love. Their relationship is not perfect, but because they embrace spiritual poverty—acknowledging their flaws and need for grace—they experience a deeper unity.

Spiritual poverty teaches that there is no shame in admitting weakness. On the contrary, recognizing one's need for help—whether from God or others—is a source of strength. Jesus Himself modeled this humility, kneeling to wash the feet of His disciples. If He, who was perfect, embraced service and humility, how much more should people be willing to do the same?

Choosing True Freedom Over Illusions of Control

The Beatitude "Blessed are the poor in spirit" is not a call to misery but an invitation to freedom. It reminds us that true happiness is not found in self-sufficiency, wealth, or pride but in wholehearted dependence on God.

Those who embrace spiritual poverty live free from fear, knowing they are never alone. They do not measure their worth by achievements but by their identity in God. Humility does not intimidate them, for they understand that admitting weakness is not failure but an act of trust.

In a world driven by accumulation, competition, and control, this Beatitude presents a radically different way of life. It invites us to release the burdens of self-reliance, redefine success beyond material gain, and discover peace through trusting in God's providence.

The challenge is whether to keep chasing the world's illusions or embrace the true freedom found in spiritual poverty. Those who choose this path soon realize that, rather than losing anything, they gain everything— peace, joy, and security that only God can provide.

Reflection Questions for Modern Life: Living a Life of Freedom and Trust

Embracing spiritual poverty challenges deeply ingrained beliefs about success, self-reliance, and control. It invites individuals to shift their perspective from worldly ambition to a life rooted in humility, trust, and detachment. These reflection questions are meant to encourage self-exploration and transformation, helping to apply this teaching to modern life.

1. Do I define my worth by achievements and external success?

Modern culture equates personal value with accomplishments—career milestones, social status, financial success, and public recognition. As a result, many feel pressured to prove their worth in the eyes of the world, often leading to anxiety and burnout.

Reflect on whether your sense of self-worth depends on external validation. If your titles, awards, and financial success were stripped away, would you still feel valuable? Spiritual poverty offers a different foundation—one that recognizes worth as intrinsic, given by God, not earned through worldly success. How might your life change if you measured your value by your relationship with God rather than by societal standards?

2. Am I able to admit my weaknesses, or do I hide behind pride?

Many people struggle to acknowledge their vulnerabilities, fearing they will be perceived as weak. In personal relationships, workplaces, and even faith communities, there is often pressure to project an image of competence and control.

- Do you struggle to ask for help?
- Are you hesitant to admit mistakes out of fear of how others might perceive you?

True strength does not come from pretending to have everything figured out but from embracing humility.

Reflect on moments when acknowledging a weakness or seeking help could have strengthened your relationships rather than weakened them.

3. How do I react when I experience failure?

Failure can often feel like a personal disaster. When plans fall apart, careers stumble, or personal goals go unfulfilled, it's easy to feel lost. Society equates success with worth—so what happens when success is out of reach or short-lived?

Reflect on how you respond to failure. Does it leave you feeling unworthy, or do you see it as an opportunity for growth? Those who embrace spiritual poverty recognize that their identity is not defined by achievements but by their faith in God's greater plan. How might your perspective change if you saw failure as an invitation to trust rather than a source of shame?

4. Do I seek financial security more than I seek trust in God?

Money offers comfort, stability, and opportunities in life. However, it can also become an idol—something people trust more than God. Some become consumed with accumulating wealth as a safeguard against uncertainty, forgetting that material security is never lasting.

Examine your relationship with money.

- Do you believe that having more will bring you peace?
- Does financial anxiety consume your thoughts?

Reflect on whether your attachment to wealth is driven by fear rather than faith.

- Are you willing to trust that God will provide for your needs, even in times of scarcity?

5. Do I find joy in the present, or am I always chasing the next goal?

Ambition is not inherently bad, but when life becomes a relentless chase for the next milestone, it can breed chronic dissatisfaction. Many people postpone happiness, convincing themselves they will be fulfilled *once they get promoted, buy a house, or retire—yet joy always remains just out of reach.*

Ask yourself: Can I appreciate where I am now, or am I always chasing the future? Those who embrace spiritual poverty find contentment in the present, recognizing that fulfillment comes not from external achievements but from inner peace. What small joys might I be overlooking in daily life because I am too focused on what's next?

6. How do I respond to the suffering of others?

Pope Francis teaches that embracing spiritual poverty means recognizing Christ in the poor, the weak, and the forgotten. Yet, in a world that prioritizes personal advancement, it is easy to overlook the suffering of others.

Consider how you respond when faced with people in need.

- Do you avoid them because it makes you uncomfortable?
- Do you justify inaction by telling yourself their struggles are not your responsibility?

Reflect on how you might practice true compassion— not just by giving from your excess, but by making sacrifices that honor the dignity of every person.

7. Am I too attached to material possessions?

Minimalism has gained popularity, but spiritual poverty goes beyond decluttering—it calls for a deeper examination of one's attachment to material things. Many accumulate more than they need, convinced that possessions provide security, comfort, or even status.

- Do you struggle to let go of material things?
- Are you more focused on acquiring than giving?

Reflect on whether your possessions control you rather than the other way around. Could you give something valuable away today and experience the freedom of detachment?

8. Do I place my identity in my social image?

Social media has fostered a culture where people curate their lives for public display, carefully shaping an image of success, happiness, and control. Yet, this often breeds insecurity and comparison as individuals measure themselves against others' carefully filtered realities.

Ask yourself:

- Do I present an honest version of myself, or do I feel pressure to maintain an illusion?
- Would you be the same person if no one were watching?

Consider what it would mean to live with authenticity rather than striving to impress.

9. How do I handle criticism and correction?

A proud heart resists correction, while a humble heart embraces it. Many struggle to accept feedback, often becoming defensive when their flaws are revealed. Yet, spiritual poverty calls for openness to learning and growth.

Think about your reaction to criticism. Do you immediately reject it, or do you reflect on whether it holds truth?

Those who embrace humility do not see correction as an attack but as an opportunity to become better.

What might change in your life if you approached feedback with a spirit of openness rather than defensiveness?

10. Where do I place my trust—myself or God?

At the heart of spiritual poverty is a willingness to surrender control. Many live under the illusion that they can plan every detail of their lives, yet life remains unpredictable. Clinging to control only breeds fear, stress, and frustration.

Reflect on where you place your trust. Do you believe your happiness depends on controlling outcomes, or are you willing to release your grip and trust that God's plans are greater than your own? Consider what it would mean to truly surrender—to let go of worry and embrace the freedom that comes from trusting in divine providence.

Spiritual poverty is not about deprivation—it is about liberation. It frees people from the need to prove themselves, the exhaustion of maintaining an illusion of control, and the anxiety of clinging to material things. It reveals that true joy is not found in wealth, success, or self-sufficiency but in the peace of trusting that everything rests in God's hands.

These reflection questions are an invitation to examine the attachments, fears, and false securities that prevent true freedom. By embracing spiritual poverty, one uncovers the paradox of the Beatitude: Blessed are the poor in spirit, for theirs is the Kingdom of Heaven. True and lasting happiness is not found by those who strive to build their kingdoms but by those who surrender everything to God.

Chapter 10

The Idols That Blind Us – Recognizing and Removing Modern Idolatry

Paul VI Audience Hall - Wednesday, 1 August 2018

The Homily

The First Commandment of the Decalogue—"You shall have no other gods before me" (*Exodus 20:3*)—is not just an ancient decree for primitive societies that worshiped statues of gold and stone. It is a timeless truth, a commandment that speaks just as urgently to the modern world as it did to the Israelites in the desert. Pope Francis reminds us that idolatry is not a relic of the past or a problem limited to distant cultures; it is an ever-present reality that touches everyone, whether we recognize it or not. It is a subtle temptation that entangles both believers and non-believers, hiding in the things we value, the goals we pursue, and the desires we cling to.

The human heart is restless by nature, constantly searching for something to give it meaning, something to anchor its affections and aspirations. Yet, in this pursuit of fulfillment, we risk placing something other than God at the center of our lives. It is wise, then, to pause and reflect: Who or what do I truly worship? Who holds the highest place in my heart?

When we hear the word idol, we may imagine towering statues in ancient temples or the golden calf that the Israelites worshipped in the wilderness. But Pope Francis reminds us that today's idols are far more subtle and insidious. They do not always take the form of physical objects, nor do they openly declare themselves as rivals to God. Instead, they quietly creep into our lives through power, wealth, beauty, fame, personal ambition, and even success.

The Catechism of the Catholic Church defines idolatry as the act of "divinizing what is not God" (*CCC 2113*). This means that anything—even something good in itself— can become an idol when it takes priority over God and distorts our relationship with Him. A person's idol is whatever they fixate on, whatever they pursue at all costs, whatever they ultimately sacrifice for. Some are consumed by ambition, believing that their worth is tied to their achievements. Others place their trust in financial security, convinced that money alone will provide peace. Still, others obsess over physical appearance, devoting endless hours to perfecting an image that will garner admiration.

These modern idols are even more dangerous than the false gods of antiquity because they often appear virtuous—even necessary. We justify them as essential to our happiness, success, or security. Yet, at their core, they do what all idols have done since the beginning of time: they distract us from God, drain our energy, and enslave our souls.

Pope Francis explains that idolatry follows a predictable three-stage progression. It does not happen overnight, nor is it always obvious. Instead, it gradually takes hold, drawing people in before they even realize they have become captive to their desires.

The first stage of idolatry begins with a vision, a fixation that captivates the heart. The world around us constantly feeds this fixation. Advertising, social media, and cultural trends do not merely sell products—they sell fulfillment. A luxury car, the latest smartphone, a picture-perfect home—these are more than just material possessions; they are marketed as keys to happiness and symbols of a successful life.

At this stage, desire turns into obsession. The object of our longing seems to appear everywhere, convincing us that once we attain it, we will be satisfied. This is the first deception—the illusion that something external, something we can buy or achieve, will finally complete us.

The second stage of idolatry is worship. Idols demand rituals and sacrifices, just as the false gods of ancient times required offerings. In the past, people sacrificed animals or even human lives to their gods. Today, we sacrifice our time, relationships, and well-being at the altar of success, wealth, beauty, and pleasure.

Careers become idols, and in their pursuit, people neglect their families, lose their health, and forget the purpose of life itself. The idol of beauty demands endless devotion—hours spent in front of mirrors, relentless self-criticism, and a never-ending cycle of seeking external validation. The idol of fame requires us to suppress authenticity, shaping ourselves to fit society's expectations rather than living with integrity.

Even wealth, which should be a means to serve others, can become a cruel master.

- How many people have been sacrificed to corporate greed?
- How many jobs have been lost—not because workers were unworthy, but because profits were valued above human dignity?
- How many young people have fallen into drug addiction or self-destructive behavior, deceived by the false promise that pleasure or social status will bring them meaning?

The final and most tragic stage of idolatry is enslavement. What once promised fulfillment now demands everything. People become trapped in an endless pursuit of more—more success, more wealth, more approval—only to realize that none of it truly satisfies.

This is the greatest lie of idolatry: it promises happiness but leaves us exhausted and empty. It begins with an illusion of fulfillment and ends with a life spent chasing a mirage—always seeking but never finding.

Unlike idols, God does not take life—He gives it. Idols rob us of our joy, but God restores us. Idols make us obsess over the future, but God teaches us to live in the present.

Pope Francis urges us to reflect deeply: How many idols do I have? Which one dominates my heart? Recognizing our idols is the first step toward freedom and grace.

Idolatry is not just a spiritual problem—it is a barrier to love. When an idol takes center stage in our lives, everything else suffers—our families, our relationships, our faith.

- How many marriages have been broken by an obsession with status or success?
- How many friendships have been abandoned because one was too consumed by self-interest?

Love requires freedom, but idols enslave us. The more we are attached to something that is not God, the less capable we are of truly loving others.

So, what must we do? Identify our idols. Remove them. Throw them out of the window.

This is not just a metaphorical suggestion—it is a real and urgent call to action. If success has become an idol, we must reorient our priorities. If social media validation has taken over our lives, we must step away from the need for approval. If financial security consumes our thoughts, we must rediscover what it means to trust in God truly.

Pope Francis does not mince words: idols blind us, rob us, and enslave us. They offer counterfeit joy while stripping away the life God intends for us.

There is a way out. When we remove idols from our hearts, we become free to love, free to live, and free to find joy in God alone. Only He can satisfy the deepest longings of the human heart. Only He can offer true peace, true fulfillment, and true life.

So today, ask yourself: What is my idol? Find it, name it, and throw it out. True happiness is waiting on the other side.

Homily Analysis: The Modern Reality of Idolatry

Pope Francis' homily on idolatry is not just a theological reflection on an ancient commandment but a direct challenge to modern society. Many people assume that idolatry is a relic of the past, something that belonged to an age when people bowed before statues of gold and stone. The Pope warns that idolatry is still very much alive today, though it has taken on more subtle and insidious forms. The problem of idolatry has not disappeared; it has merely evolved, becoming more deceptive and harder to recognize.

Modern idols are not statues in temples but the ambitions, desires, and pursuits that quietly take over our lives. Wealth, power, success, beauty, fame, and social validation have become the new golden calves. These things, in themselves, are not necessarily bad. However, when they become the center of our existence—demanding our time, energy, and devotion above all else—they turn into false gods. Unlike the idols of the past, today's idols do not openly present themselves as rivals to God. Instead, they appear as ordinary aspects of life, often even as virtues—hard work, self-improvement, and financial security. But when these things become absolute priorities, when they consume us and take precedence over faith, love, and morality, they enslave rather than fulfill.

The Pope's message is clear: humanity has always been tempted by idolatry, but today's idols are more dangerous than ever because they do not seem like idols. They disguise themselves as essential to a successful life, making it difficult to recognize when ambition has crossed the line into worship.

This is why Pope Francis urges us to examine our hearts, identify the idols we serve, and break free from their grip.

The Human Need to Worship

At the core of Pope Francis' homily is the idea that human beings are made to worship. This is not simply a religious statement but an observation of human nature itself. Every person, regardless of faith or background, seeks something to give life meaning and direction. Worship is not optional; it is an intrinsic part of who we are. The question is not whether we will worship but what or whom we will worship.

Throughout history, humans have created gods to fill this need. In biblical times, idol worship was explicit—people built altars to deities they believed could grant them fertility, protection, wealth, or power. They performed rituals, made sacrifices, and sought favor from gods they could see and touch. Today, idolatry is far more subtle, yet its essence remains unchanged. Instead of offering sacrifices at stone altars, people devote their time, effort, and energy to pursuing financial success, social status, physical perfection, or public recognition. Just like the idols of the past, these modern gods demand service, obedience, and, ultimately, sacrifice.

The Three Stages of Idolatry:

The Idol Captivates the Vision

Pope Francis explains that idolatry begins in the mind and heart long before it manifests in action. It starts with a vision—something that captivates our imagination and convinces us that we need it in order to be happy. This is how idolatry subtly takes hold, shaping our desires before we even realize it.

In today's world, this process is carefully designed by advertising, social media, and cultural influences. Society constantly bombards us with messages about what we should desire, what we should aspire to, and what will supposedly bring us happiness. A luxurious house is not just a home; it is a status symbol. A high-paying job is not just employment; it is a mark of success. A well-toned body is not just about health; it reflects one's worth in the eyes of others.

The real danger is that these messages are so pervasive they shape our thinking without us even realizing it. We begin to measure our worth by external achievements, believing that unless we attain certain goals, we are incomplete. This is the first trap of idolatry: the illusion that happiness is always just out of reach, waiting to be acquired.

The Idol Demands Worship and Sacrifice

Once an idol takes hold of the heart, it begins to demand devotion. In ancient times, people made offerings to their gods, believing that sacrifices would earn their favor. Today, sacrifices still exist, but they have taken a different form. Instead of burning incense at a temple, people sacrifice their time, relationships, and inner peace to satisfy the demands of modern idols.

Pope Francis highlights some of the most common forms of modern idolatry. The idol of career success requires long hours at the office, often at the expense of family, faith, and personal well-being. The idol of beauty demands relentless self-criticism, strict diets, and, in extreme cases, surgical alterations to fit an unrealistic standard. The idol of wealth deceives people into believing that financial security will bring them peace, yet no amount of money ever seems enough. The idol of social validation forces people to construct a public image that may not reflect their true selves, leading to anxiety, insecurity, and exhaustion.

What makes these idols so deceptive is that they initially promise something good— stability, admiration, achievement. Over time, they take more than they give. They convince us that if we sacrifice enough, we will finally be happy. Yet the more we sacrifice, the more they demand.

The Idol Becomes a Master

The final stage of idolatry is enslavement. What begins as the pursuit of happiness becomes an unbreakable cycle. The idol that once promised fulfillment now controls every decision, every thought, every moment of life.

Pope Francis warns that this is where idolatry becomes truly destructive. The businessman who once worked hard to provide for his family now neglects them for the sake of his career. A person who initially pursued fitness for health becomes obsessed with their appearance, never satisfied with what they see in the mirror. The social media influencer who once created content out of passion now lives for likes, comments, and approval.

At this point, the idol no longer serves the person; the person serves the idol.

- What was once freedom became slavery. What should bring peace leads to anxiety?
- What promises fulfillment results in emptiness?

The Consequences of Idolatry: Why It Destroys Love

One of the most devastating effects of idolatry, Pope Francis explains, is that it blinds us to love. Love requires presence, self-giving, and sacrifice—but in the form of freely giving oneself for the good of another. Idolatry, by contrast, demands sacrifice for the sake of the idol, turning everything inward.

A person consumed by idolatry sees others not as people to love but as obstacles or tools. The parent obsessed with career success may justify their absence from home as "providing for the family," while their children long for their presence. The person addicted to wealth may prioritize profits over people, reducing human relationships to transactions. The person seeking fame may surround themselves with admirers but feel profoundly alone.

Idolatry ultimately makes people incapable of genuine love because love requires detachment from self, while idols demand absolute self-centeredness.

Breaking Free: The Path to True Worship

Pope Francis does not propose a gradual approach to escaping idolatry. He does not advocate for moderation or balance. His message is simple and urgent: Identify your idols. Remove them. Cast them away without hesitation.

This is not metaphorical advice—it is a direct call to action. Idols do not release their grip easily. To break free, one must make intentional choices. If money has become an idol, practice generosity. If vanity holds power, cultivate inner beauty. If work consumes your life, establish boundaries and prioritize relationships.

True worship does not enslave—it liberates. Unlike idols, which always demand more, God offers rest. Unlike idols, which consume, God renews. Unlike idols, which leave people empty, God fills the heart with lasting peace.

Pope Francis ends with a challenge: Who or what do you worship? What dictates your time, energy, and desires? What do you fear losing the most?

Idolatry is a prison, but God offers the key. The only question is: Will we take it?

Breaking the Chains of Modern Idolatry: Living with True Freedom

The world we live in is deliberately shaped to cultivate idolatry. From the moment we wake, we are bombarded with advertisements, social media updates, and societal expectations that dictate what we should desire, strive for, and consider a successful life. We are conditioned to believe that our achievements, possessions, and appearance measure our worth. Whether it is the pressure to climb the corporate ladder, the obsession with physical perfection, or the relentless pursuit of financial security, modern life is structured in a way that constantly feeds false gods—idols that promise fulfillment but never deliver.

Despite this, people are more anxious, restless, and unsatisfied than ever. The rates of stress, depression, and burnout continue to rise. Social media, which was meant to connect us, has left many feeling more isolated. Wealth has not brought peace; instead, it has created a world of endless comparison and dissatisfaction. We accumulate, we strive, we consume—yet we remain unfulfilled.

Pope Francis reminds us that idolatry is not a thing of the past. It is woven into the very fabric of modern life.

The key question we must ask ourselves is: How do we break free?

The Idol of Success: When Work Becomes Worship

Success is one of the most glorified idols in today's world. Hard work and ambition are often exalted as ultimate virtues, leading many to equate a person's worth with career achievements, wealth, and social standing. Society conditions us to believe that the more we accomplish, the more valuable we become.

While ambition itself is not inherently wrong, work can swiftly become an idol when it defines our identity. Many sacrifice their health, relationships, and even moral integrity in pursuit of career success. Workplaces reward those who dedicate every waking moment to their jobs, praising employees who work late into the night, answering emails on vacation, and sacrifice their personal lives for professional recognition.

Success is a moving target. A promotion sparks the desire for another, and a salary increase soon feels insufficient. Someone once content with their job title grows restless, seeking the next level of prestige. The problem with the idol of success is that it never allows rest.

Breaking free from this idol requires a radical shift in mindset. Work should serve our lives, not consume them. Rather than viewing career advancement as the ultimate goal, we must ask:

- Does my work bring meaning?

221

- Does it align with my values?
- Does it allow me to be present for my loved ones?

If work is robbing us of peace, perhaps it is time to reassess that for which we are truly striving.

The Idol of Wealth: The Illusion of Financial Security

Money is essential for survival, but when the pursuit of wealth becomes the ultimate goal, it turns into a false god. Many devote their lives to accumulating more— more savings, more investments, more luxury— believing that financial security will finally bring them peace.

Yet, the wealthiest people in the world are often the most anxious. Those with millions in the bank still fear losing everything. Billionaires continue to work tirelessly—not out of necessity, but out of fear of scarcity. The pursuit of financial security does not bring lasting peace; instead, it only deepens the desire for more.

This is the great deception of wealth: it convinces us that "just a little more" will bring contentment. But the truth is, contentment has nothing to do with how much money we have. A person earning a modest salary who lives generously and gratefully is far richer in spirit than a multimillionaire who is constantly worried about protecting their assets.

True financial freedom is not found in wealth accumulation but in our relationship with money. If money dictates our decisions, controls our emotions, or leads us to hoard rather than share, it has become an idol. Generosity is the antidote to financial idolatry— when we give freely, we break money's hold over us.

The Idol of Beauty and Social Validation

Modern society is obsessed with appearances. Social media has turned self-image into a constant performance, where people carefully curate their lives to gain approval. The rise of plastic surgery, diet culture, and influencer lifestyles has created a generation that equates self-worth with physical attractiveness and social validation.

No matter how much effort someone puts into maintaining their appearance, the standards of beauty are always changing. A person may achieve their "ideal" weight, but soon another fitness trend arises. They may buy the trendiest clothes, but fashion constantly evolves. They may alter their face with cosmetic procedures, but the aging process continues.

Social media amplifies insecurity by flooding us with filtered, unrealistic portrayals of perfection. Many invest hours editing photos, applying filters, and curating idealized versions of their lives, seeking validation. Yet, this pursuit creates a cycle of Dependence on social media validation creates an endless cycle—each "like" offers a fleeting sense of worth, yet it never truly satisfies. Breaking free from this idol requires a shift in focus. Our value is not defined by appearance or follower count but by our character, actions, and relationships. True confidence comes from knowing we are loved for who we are, not for how we appear.

The Idol of Pleasure and Distraction

Many people seek refuge in entertainment, distractions, and instant gratification to avoid life's discomforts. Streaming services, video games, social media, and even substance use offer fleeting relief from stress, boredom, or emotional pain.

While entertainment itself isn't inherently harmful, it becomes an idol when it replaces genuine engagement with life. Those who spend hours scrolling through their phones, binge-watching television, or chasing fleeting pleasures often find themselves feeling empty once the distraction fades. The pursuit of pleasure, without deeper meaning, leads to an unfulfilled life.

Breaking free from this idol requires a return to presence. Instead of passively consuming entertainment, we must ask: How can I use my time in ways that enrich my life and the lives of others? This might mean pursuing hobbies that bring creativity and joy, engaging in deep conversations, spending time in nature, or learning to be still and reflective.

Escaping the Cycle: The Path to True Worship

Idolatry is, at its core, a matter of misplaced priorities. There is nothing wrong with seeking success, financial stability, physical health, or enjoyment. The problem arises when these pursuits take center stage, defining our worth and dictating our decisions.

Breaking free from modern idolatry requires a deliberate shift in perspective. Instead of chasing temporary fulfillment, we must pursue what is lasting— love, faith, relationships, and purpose. This means redefining what success looks like, loosening our grip on financial security, embracing our authentic selves rather than curated images, and finding joy in real experiences rather than digital distractions.

God does not ask us to abandon our dreams and ambitions. He asks that we place Him first so that everything else falls into its proper place. He does not take away joy—He restores true joy. Unlike idols, which always demand more, God gives abundantly without enslaving us.

Pope Francis challenges us to reflect: Who or what do I worship? What dictates my time, energy, and desires? What do I fear losing the most? The answers to these questions reveal where idolatry has taken root in our lives. But the good news is that freedom is always within reach.

God offers us the key.

The only question is: Will we take it?

Reflection Questions: Applying the Homily on Idolatry to Modern Life

1. What is the first thing I think about when I wake up and the last thing I think about before I sleep?

Our minds naturally drift toward what we value most. If our thoughts are consumed by work, money, status, or appearance, we may have unknowingly made them into idols.

2. What do I spend most of my time, energy, and resources on?

Time is one of our greatest gifts. Where we invest, it often reveals what we worship. Reflect on whether your daily habits align with what truly matters in life.

3. Do I feel like I am constantly chasing something—success, wealth, beauty, or approval—without ever feeling satisfied?

Idols often create a sense of restlessness, making us believe that just a little more will finally bring peace. Consider whether you are caught in an endless cycle of striving.

4. Have I ever sacrificed relationships, integrity, or faith in pursuit of success or financial gain?

True success should never come at the expense of our deepest values. Take a moment to reflect—have any of your ambitions compromised your moral character or strained your relationships?

5. Do I define my worth by external achievements, possessions, or social validation?

Many people determine their self-worth by their career, income, appearance, or online presence. Take a moment to reflect—have you allowed these factors to define your value?

6. How do I react when I lose control over something I value deeply?

When an idol is threatened—whether it's money, career status, or reputation—we often feel anxious, angry, or desperate. Reflect on whether your peace depends too much on external circumstances.

7. Do I use distractions—social media, entertainment, or pleasure—to escape from discomfort or deeper reflection?

Sometimes, idolatry manifests as avoidance. Reflect on whether you rely on distractions to fill a void that should be addressed with deeper meaning and purpose.

8. Am I truly present in my relationships, or am I often mentally preoccupied with other pursuits?

Love requires presence. If our minds are always consumed with personal ambitions, we may be neglecting the people who matter most. Reflect on whether you are fully engaged in your relationships.

9. How do I view money and material possessions? Do I see them as tools for good, or do I hoard them out of fear?

Money can be either a blessing or a trap. Take a moment to reflect—does your approach to finances reflect generosity and trust in God, or does it reveal an unhealthy attachment to wealth?

10. Do I practice generosity, or do I hold tightly to what I have?

If I had to give up one thing that has taken too much space in my heart, what would it be?

Identifying the idol in your life is the first step toward freedom. Reflect on what you may need to release in order to live with greater peace, love, and purpose.

Use these questions as an opportunity for honest self-reflection. What areas of life need realignment? What steps can be taken today to break free from modern idols and live with true freedom?

Chapter 11

The Courage to Invest: Using Our God-Given Talents

Vatican Basilica, 33th Sunday of Ordinary Time, 15 November 2020

The Homily

In his homily, Pope Francis reflects on the parable of the talents, drawing profound spiritual lessons to guide believers through life's different stages. He structures his message around the parable's beginning, middle, and end, using each phase to illustrate the journey of faith and service.

The parable begins with the master entrusting his wealth to his servants, giving them talents of great value. Pope Francis highlights how this initial act reflects God's generosity toward humanity. Everything starts with grace, not human effort. The gifts we receive—life, talents, and virtues—are not given randomly but with divine purpose. God sees each person as unique, precious, and irreplaceable, created in His image.

However, humans often fail to recognize their blessings, focusing instead on what they lack. The Pope warns against the destructive power of the phrase "If only"—if only I had more success, more money, fewer problems. This mindset blinds people to the talents they already possess. Rather than fixating on what is lacking, believers are called to trust in God's providence, knowing that He gives according to each person's ability and expects them to use their gifts wisely.

At the core of the parable is the work of the servants, which Pope Francis interprets as a call to service. Life gains meaning through service, and those who do not live to serve ultimately "serve for little in this life." The Pope emphasizes that true service requires taking risks. In the parable, the faithful servants invest their talents, embracing uncertainty and stepping beyond their comfort zones. This willingness to take risks is essential because faithfulness is never passive.

He warns against a defensive, rule-following Christianity that seeks only to avoid mistakes rather than actively doing good. The third servant in the parable, who buries his talent out of fear, represents a faith that is stagnant and unproductive. His failure lies not in wrongdoing but in doing nothing at all. Pope Francis describes this as a "mummification of the soul"—a refusal to engage, to give, or to take risks for the sake of love. Faith, he insists, is not about clinging to what we have but about giving freely, just as God does.

The Pope explains that true faithfulness to God requires courage—the courage to surrender one's plans and embrace service, even when it disrupts personal comfort. Some Christians choose to remain within safe boundaries, hesitant to step out in faith. Faith without action becomes lifeless. The Gospel calls for a bold response, not mere compliance with rules.

The parable highlights the fate of the unfaithful servant, who is rebuked for his inaction. The Pope draws attention to the master's harsh words—calling the servant "wicked"—to show that failing to use God's gifts is itself a sin. God expects believers to live generously and invest their talents in love and service. Holding back out of fear or selfishness leads to spiritual stagnation.

Pope Francis connects the lesson of the parable to the role of the poor in Christian life. He interprets the master's command to invest talents as a call to care for the marginalized. People with low incomes, he says, are the "bankers" who offer eternal returns. Serving the poor is not just an act of charity; it is an investment in heaven.

He warns against the poverty of love, which he sees as the most dangerous form of spiritual emptiness. The

Gospel cannot be fully understood without the poor, for Jesus himself lived in poverty, giving everything for others. The book of *Proverbs* praises the woman who "Opens her hand to the poor" (Proverbs 31:20), serving as a model for all believers. Pope Francis urges Christians to replace the consumerist mindset of "What can I buy?" with the more Christ-like question: "What can I give?"

The homily concludes with a reflection on the final judgment presented in the parable. In the end, those who hoarded their gifts will find themselves impoverished, while those who gave freely will receive true wealth—eternal life. The illusion of power, success, and material wealth will fade, leaving only the love that was shared. Pope Francis quotes Saint John Chrysostom, who describes death as the moment when the "theater" of the world is abandoned, and people are judged solely by their deeds.

He offers the example of Father Roberto Malgesini, a priest who dedicated his life to serving the poor. He did not seek recognition or theorize about faith; he saw Jesus in the poor and served them with love. His life, centered on prayer and charity, stands as a witness to the Gospel in action.

Pope Francis concludes by calling all believers to be Christians not just in words but in actions—to use their talents courageously and to live lives of service and love. The true measure of a Christian life is not personal achievement but the fruit it bears for others. May this be the path all believers follow.

Homily Analysis: The Paradox of Risk and Reward

Pope Francis' homily on the Parable of the Talents (*Matthew 25: 14-30*) offers a profound theological reflection that moves beyond a simplistic reading of the passage as a lesson on productivity. Instead, he frames it as a challenge to rethink faithfulness, responsibility, and the relationship between risk and reward in the Christian life. The homily presents a vision of discipleship that is active, bold, and deeply engaged with God's gifts. It warns against passivity and fear-driven faith, instead advocating for a spirituality rooted in trust, courage, and service.

Divine Generosity as the Starting Point

The parable opens with the master entrusting his wealth to his servants, each receiving a different amount based on their abilities. Pope Francis highlights a crucial detail that is often overlooked: the master's overwhelming generosity. A single talent was equivalent to twenty years' wages—an immense fortune. This is not a minor responsibility but a profound trust, symbolizing the abundance of God's grace.

By emphasizing that everything begins with God's generosity rather than human merit, Pope Francis reinforces a foundational Christian truth: grace is given freely, not earned. This challenges the meritocratic mindset, which sees gifts and success as rewards for effort or inherent worth. In contrast, the homily emphasizes that God gives not according to what we deserve but according to His divine wisdom and love.

This framing shifts the focus of the parable. The servants are not merely tested on their abilities; they are entrusted with something sacred. The real question, then, is not about their skill in multiplying talents but about their response to divine trust.

Fear vs. Fruitfulness: The Core Tension of the Parable

Pope Francis highlights the fundamental difference between the first two servants, who invest and multiply their talents, and the third servant, who hides his talent out of fear. This contrast reveals a deeper theological theme: faithfulness is not about maintaining the status quo but about engaging with God's gifts in a way that brings forth fruit.

The Pope challenges a passive, rule-bound approach to Christianity that equates faithfulness with merely avoiding mistakes. He criticizes those who play it safe in their spiritual lives, seeking to preserve what they have rather than expanding it through love and service. The third servant's failure lies not in an active sin but in a failure to act at all. His fear of losing what he was given prevents him from doing anything with it.

This presents a paradox: the servant who tries to safeguard his gift ultimately loses it, while those who take risks are rewarded. The message is clear—faith requires action. Faithfulness is not about cautious preservation but about courageous engagement.

The Risk of Love: A Radical Redefinition of Faithfulness

One of the most striking aspects of Pope Francis' homily is his radical redefinition of faithfulness. He moves beyond conventional notions of obedience and righteousness, suggesting that faithfulness to God is fundamentally tied to risk and love.

Traditionally, faithfulness is often understood as consistency, reliability, and adherence to moral and spiritual obligations. However, the Pope argues that true fidelity to God requires stepping into uncertainty, embracing discomfort, and taking risks for the sake of love. The faithful servants in the parable were not merely diligent; they were bold. They understood that what they had been given was meant to be used, not stored away.

This insight challenges an overly cautious spirituality that prioritizes self-protection over service. Pope Francis warns against a faith that remains in defensive mode, where people are more concerned with avoiding errors than with actively living out their calling. He likens such an attitude to a form of spiritual mummification, where people become so afraid of making mistakes that they render themselves spiritually lifeless.

This carries profound implications for understanding discipleship. Following Christ is not about playing it safe—it is about stepping out in trust, even when risks are involved. Just as the first two servants took a chance by investing their talents, Christians are likewise called to invest themselves fully in the mission of love and service.

The Servant's Fear: A Symbol of Distrust

The third servant, who buries his talent, represents an attitude of spiritual stagnation and distrust in God. Pope Francis highlights the servant's justification: "I was afraid." This fear does not arise from reverence but from a misunderstanding of the master's character. The servant perceives the master as harsh and demanding rather than generous and trusting.

This misperception is crucial. If the master represents God, then the servant's failure is not merely a refusal to act but a failure to truly understand God's nature. His actions expose a lack of trust in divine goodness. Instead of responding to grace with gratitude and boldness, he allows his distorted view of God to paralyze him.

This reflects a broader spiritual truth: our actions are shaped by how we perceive God. Those who see God as loving and abundant are willing to take risks in faith, while those who see Him as harsh and unforgiving become fearful and withdrawn.

The parable, then, is not just about talents—it is about how we relate to God's generosity.

The Eternal Economy: The Logic of Divine Investment

Pope Francis draws a parallel between the master's expectation of investment and the Christian call to serve others. He suggests that the most meaningful way to invest our talents is by giving to the poor. This reflects Jesus' consistent teaching that whatever we do for the least among us, we do for Him.

This interpretation introduces another paradox: in the economy of the world, giving things away makes one poorer; in the economy of God, giving is the only way to gain true wealth. The more one invests in love, service, and generosity, the richer one becomes spiritually. This echoes Christ's words: "Store up for yourselves treasures in heaven" (*Matthew 6:20*).

The Pope emphasizes that the poor are not just recipients of charity but the key to understanding the Gospel. Jesus Himself became poor, emptying Himself. To understand Christ, one must be willing to engage with and serve those in need. The true measure of wealth, then, is not what one has accumulated but what one has given away.

The Final Judgment: Love as the Ultimate Standard

At the end of the parable, the servants are judged based on what they did with their gifts. The first two are rewarded, while the third is cast out. Pope Francis connects this to the final judgment, where the only thing that will matter is love. Success, power, and wealth will fade, but love will endure.

This poses a sobering challenge: What will remain of our lives when all worldly measures of success are stripped away? The parable suggests that the only thing of eternal value is the fruit we bear through service. Those who cling to their gifts for themselves will ultimately lose them, while those who give freely will receive even more.

Pope Francis concludes with a call to take this lesson to heart. He warns against indifference and self-absorption, urging instead a life of active, risk-taking love. To be truly Christian is to bear fruit—not just in words, but in action.

The Courage to Live Fully

This homily ultimately calls for a transformation of perspective. Rather than viewing faithfulness as passive obedience, Pope Francis redefines it as active, courageous engagement with God's gifts. True faith demands stepping beyond fear, embracing risk, and using one's talents in service to others.

The paradox of the Gospel is that security comes not from holding back but from giving freely. The one who buries his talent in an attempt to protect it ultimately loses everything, while those who risk everything in love gain eternal life.

Pope Francis leaves his audience with a powerful challenge: Will you play it safe, or will you take the risk of love?

Living Lessons in Risk, Reward, and the Fear of Wasted Potential

Modern life is a continuous balancing act between risk and security. Whether in career choices, financial decisions, creative pursuits, or personal relationships, individuals must choose between stepping forward boldly or playing it safe. Society reinforces a mindset of self-preservation—protect your assets, safeguarding your reputation, and avoid failure. While caution has its place, an overemphasis on security can lead to stagnation, where the greatest loss is not a visible failure but a waste of potential.

Contemporary culture is dominated by the fear of failure. People are conditioned to believe that making mistakes is worse than doing nothing at all. Yet history proves otherwise. Those who have shaped the world— scientists, artists, entrepreneurs—took significant risks. If they had allowed fear to dictate their actions, much of human progress would not exist.

Take Elon Musk, for example. His decision to launch Tesla and SpaceX was filled with risk, pushing both companies to the brink of bankruptcy in their early years. Had he played it safe and stayed within traditional industries, Tesla would not have led the electric vehicle revolution, nor would SpaceX have redefined space exploration. Musk's success did not stem from avoiding failure—it came from embracing it as a steppingstone to progress.

The most overlooked failure in life is not a visible loss but wasted potential. A gifted musician who never records a song, a brilliant thinker who never writes down their ideas, or a compassionate person who never extends a helping hand—all represent missed opportunities. Inaction is the true thief of progress.

The Paralysis of Playing It Safe

Risk aversion is deeply ingrained in modern decision-making. This is evident in career choices, where many opt for "safe" jobs that offer stability but little personal fulfillment. The fear of instability keeps people stuck in jobs they dislike, enduring years of dissatisfaction. While financial security is important, an unfulfilling career can be just as damaging in the long run, leading to stress, unhappiness, and regret.

Consider Jeff Bezos. Before founding Amazon, he had a stable, high-paying job on Wall Street. He could have remained there comfortably, avoiding the uncertainty of starting an online bookstore at a time when e-commerce was in its infancy. However, he leaped, recognizing that not trying was a greater risk than failure itself. Today, Amazon is one of the most successful companies in history—not because Bezos played it safe, but because he was willing to act on his vision despite the unknowns.

This same principle applies to businesses as well. Kodak and Blockbuster were once industry leaders, but their reluctance to innovate led to their downfall. Kodak had early access to digital photography technology but hesitated to embrace it, fearing it would undermine their film business. Blockbuster had the chance to acquire Netflix in its early days but dismissed the idea, believing physical rentals would always be dominant. Their refusal to take risks led them to irrelevance, while those who embraced change thrived.

On a personal level, relationships suffer when people hesitate to take emotional risks. Fear of rejection or vulnerability causes many to hold back from expressing love, addressing conflicts, or making meaningful connections. Friendships drift apart, family bonds weaken, and romantic opportunities fade—not because of external barriers but because of an unwillingness to step forward. Successful relationships are not built on avoidance but on courageous engagement.

A powerful example is Brené Brown's research on vulnerability. She discovered that the most fulfilling relationships and personal growth come to those who allow themselves to be vulnerable—who risk rejection and discomfort for the sake of genuine connection. In contrast, those who build emotional walls for self-protection often find themselves isolated and unfulfilled.

The Misconception of Security

Modern society offers endless ways to create an illusion of security—financial planning, insurance policies, social media personas—but nothing guarantees real stability. The COVID-19 pandemic exposed this harsh reality. Industries collapsed overnight, long-established companies vanished, and millions faced unforeseen uncertainties. Those who clung to traditional notions of security were left unprepared, while those who adapted swiftly and took decisive action discovered new opportunities.

A prime example of adaptation is the restaurant industry. During the pandemic, businesses that relied solely on in-person dining struggled, while those that swiftly pivoted to delivery, curbside pickup, and online sales not only survived but thrived.

Companies like DoorDash and Uber Eats experienced exponential growth because they embraced bold adaptation rather than passive waiting.

Instead of chasing an illusion of control, individuals can cultivate a different kind of security: the security of adaptability, resilience, and bold action. This means shifting from a mindset of risk avoidance to one of strategic risk-taking.

Consider two professionals facing job loss. One sees it as the end of their career, dwelling on what they have lost. The other sees it as an opportunity to pivot—learning new skills, exploring different industries, and even considering entrepreneurship. Though still facing uncertainty, the latter finds a way forward by investing in possibilities rather than burying their potential.

Investing in Growth Instead of Hoarding Resources

The modern world often equates success with the accumulation—of wealth, achievements, and possessions. However, true fulfillment often comes from what is given rather than what is hoarded. Those who hold back their talents—whether in creativity, knowledge, or generosity—may avoid criticism or failure, but they also deny themselves and the world something valuable.

Consider philanthropy. Billionaires like Warren Buffett and MacKenzie Scott have committed vast portions of their wealth to charitable causes, recognizing that idle money serves no purpose. Their investments in education, healthcare, and social welfare have transformed millions of lives. The same principle applies beyond finances: unused knowledge, unexpressed kindness, and untapped creativity serve no one.

Even on a smaller scale, the principle remains the same. A teacher who passionately shares knowledge instead of merely going through the motions can transform students' lives. A doctor who invests extra time in patient care rather than treating medicine as a transaction leaves a lasting impact. A parent who takes time to nurture a child's curiosity rather than prioritizing convenience fosters a lifelong love of learning. What is unused stagnates; what is shared multiplies.

Breaking Free from Fear: A New Perspective on Risk

Redefining risk is essential for overcoming fear-driven decision-making. While risk is often seen as dangerous, avoiding it carries its perils—missed opportunities, stagnant lives, and unrealized dreams. Instead of treating risk as something to fear, we should recognize it as a necessary catalyst for growth and purpose.

One of the best examples of this mindset shift comes from Sara Blakely, the founder of Spanx. When she started her business, she had no experience in fashion, no industry connections, and very little capital. However, instead of fearing failure, she embraced it. She deliberately sought out rejection, viewing it as a necessary step toward success. Today, Spanx is a billion-dollar company, and Blakely credits her success to her willingness to fail rather than her fear of trying.

Similarly, before becoming a global media icon, Oprah Winfrey was fired from her first television job. Rather than letting this setback define her, she took the risk of exploring a new format—one that emphasized authenticity and depth.

Her bold approach not only revived her career but also reshaped the landscape of television and media.

In everyday life, this means taking steps forward even when uncertainty remains— applying for that job despite the fear of rejection, starting that creative project even if success isn't guaranteed, and initiating difficult but necessary conversations in relationships.

The only true failure is refusing to try.

Reflection Questions for Modern Life: Risk, Growth, and Living with Purpose

In a world that often prioritizes security overgrowth, many people find themselves trapped in routines that offer comfort but lack fulfillment. Fear of failure, criticism, or instability can prevent individuals from stepping into their true potential.

This chapter offers ten reflection questions to help readers explore how risk, action, and faith in their abilities can shape their lives. These questions are designed to challenge perspectives, uncover untapped potential, and inspire meaningful action.

1. What is one talent, skill, or idea I have been hesitant to pursue, and why?

Many people have hidden talents or unspoken dreams that remain dormant due to fear of failure or rejection. Some hesitate to write a book, start a business, or pursue a new career path because they doubt their chances of success. Others suppress their creativity out of fear of criticism.

Reflecting on this question involves distinguishing between genuine limitations and self-imposed fear.

- What possibilities could unfold if that talent or idea were explored rather than buried?
- What small steps could be taken today to start using it?

2. Where in my life am I playing it safe when I should be taking a bold step forward?

Many people fall into predictable patterns, avoiding change because it feels risky. They stay in jobs they dislike, maintain relationships out of habit rather than genuine connection, or hold back from speaking up even when they have something meaningful to contribute.

This question invites reflection:

- Is my current path leading to growth, or am I merely maintaining the status quo?
- If I took a step forward—whether in my career, personal life, or creative pursuits, what's the worst that could happen?
- More importantly, what's the best thing that could happen?

3. How do I define success: by what I accumulate or by what I contribute?

Modern society often equates success with personal gain—wealth, recognition, and power. Yet, fulfillment often comes not from accumulation but from impact.

Those who share their knowledge, help others, or invest in meaningful relationships often feel a deeper sense of purpose.

This reflection asks:

- If I shifted my definition of success from "What do I own?" to "How have I contributed?" how would that change my decisions?
- What areas of my life would look different if my focus was on creating value rather than collecting rewards?

4. What is a past failure that actually led to personal growth or opened new opportunities?

Many people view failure as an endpoint rather than a steppingstone. Yet history is full of examples of setbacks leading to breakthroughs—entrepreneurs who failed before building successful businesses, artists whose early work was rejected, and individuals who turned adversity into strength.

Reflecting on this question involves revisiting moments of failure with a new perspective.

- What lessons did I learn?
- How did that experience shape me?

- Would I have reached certain milestones if I hadn't first faced obstacles?

5. Do I spend more time preparing for stability or preparing for adaptability?

People often focus on securing stability, saving money, avoiding risks, and maintaining routine—without realizing that true success requires adaptability. The world is unpredictable, and those who thrive aren't the ones who resist change but those who embrace it.

This question challenges individuals to evaluate their mindset:

- Am I trying to control my environment, or am I preparing myself to navigate change effectively?
- If unexpected circumstances forced a career or lifestyle shift, would I be ready?
- What skills or perspectives could I develop to adapt rather than struggle?

6. How often do I make decisions based on fear rather than on potential?

Fear often disguises itself as logic, responsibility, or caution, leading people to believe they are making the "safe" choice when, in reality, they are avoiding uncertainty.

Someone might not apply for a promotion out of fear of rejection, and others may abandon a creative pursuit because they fear judgment.

This reflection asks:

- Am I choosing my path based on what excites and challenges me, or am I choosing based on what feels safest?
- If fear was removed from the equation, what decision would I make instead?

7. Who in my life is modeling courage, and what can I learn from them?

Courage is contagious. People who take risks, embrace challenges, and push past obstacles often inspire others to do the same. Whether it's an entrepreneur, an activist, or a friend who pursues their dreams without hesitation, these individuals can serve as guides.

Reflecting on this question means identifying individuals, whether from real life or history—who have embraced risk, resilience, and growth.

- What qualities do they possess that I admire?
- How can I apply similar principles to my journey?

8. How am I using my gifts to serve others rather than just myself?

Many people focus on personal success without realizing that true fulfillment comes from sharing what we have with others. A talented writer who never shares their work, an expert who never mentors others or a leader who only prioritizes self-interest all waste opportunities to make a difference.

This reflection challenges individuals to ask:

- Am I holding onto my talents, or am I using them to uplift others?
- Whether through mentorship, creativity, or acts of kindness, what is one step I can take today to use my gifts for a greater purpose?

9. If I knew my time was limited, what risk would I finally take?

People often postpone meaningful action, assuming there will always be time "later." When faced with the reality of limited time, priorities shift. Dreams that once seemed too risky suddenly become urgent.

This question serves as a reality check:

- If I had five years left, what would I do differently?
- What project would I start?
- What words would I say to the people who matter?
- What am I waiting for that should be acted upon today?

10. What is one small, meaningful risk I can take this week to invest in my growth?

Reflection is valuable, but action is what creates transformation. Growth does not come from thinking about risk—it comes from taking risks.

This question challenges individuals to take immediate, tangible steps.

- Can I apply for a job, publish my writing, start an important conversation, or enroll in a course?
- What action can I take today to move from hesitation to progress?

The modern world provides countless reasons to play it safe, favoring predictability over possibility and avoiding failure rather than pursuing success. Yet, history's most impactful figures and those who lead the most fulfilling lives recognize that risk is not the enemy—stagnation is.

Success, growth, and purpose are not found in hesitation but in the courage to move forward despite uncertainty. Reflection is the first step toward change, but true transformation begins when reflection turns into action.

The question that remains is simple: Will you bury your potential, or will you invest in the life you were meant to live?

Chapter 12

The Holy Spirit and the Unity of Marriage

Saint Peter's Square - Wednesday, 23 October 2024

The Homily

In this homily, Pope Francis examines the role of the Holy Spirit in Christian life, particularly within the sacrament of marriage. Drawing on the theological insights of Saint Augustine, he highlights how the Holy Spirit, as the bond of love within the Trinity, also fosters unity between husband and wife. Through this reflection, he emphasizes that Christian marriage is more than a human contract—it is a divine covenant upheld by the Spirit's presence and guidance.

The homily opens with a reflection on the Holy Spirit's role within the Trinity. Drawing from Saint Augustine's teaching, Pope Francis describes God as love itself: the Father as the one who loves, the Son as the one who is loved, and the Holy Spirit as the bond of love that unites them. This dynamic reveals that God is not solitary but a perfect communion of persons. Some theologians even suggest calling the Holy.

Spirit is not the "third-person singular" of the Trinity, but the "first-person plural," as He represents the Divine, We—the unity between the Father and the Son.

This understanding of the Holy Spirit as the source of unity extends beyond the Trinity to human relationships, especially within the Church and the family. Just as the Spirit unites the persons of the Trinity, He also brings individuals together in communion, forming the Church as one body. Pope Francis argues that this same divine force of communion is essential in marriage.

Marriage, instituted by God, is more than a mere partnership—it reflects His divine nature. In creating humanity in His image, God formed them male and female (*Genesis 1:27*), establishing marriage as the first and most fundamental expression of divine communion. Just as the Holy Spirit binds the Father and the Son in love, He is also the one who enables husbands and wives to live out their vocation of self-giving love.

Pope Francis highlights the beauty of marital union by emphasizing how spouses transition from being two distinct individuals—"I" and "you"—to forming a unified "we" before the world. This unity is especially evident in the way parents speak to their children, using phrases such as "your mother and I" or "your father and I," which subtly yet powerfully reinforce their oneness within the family. He notes that children deeply need this unity, and when it is broken—through separation or lack of love—they are the ones who suffer the most.

Acknowledging that unity in marriage is not always easy, Pope Francis stresses that true self-giving love requires divine assistance. Left to human strength alone, love often deteriorates into a routine, habit, or even conflict. However, where the Holy Spirit enters, the capacity for true self-giving is renewed.

The Holy Spirit, as the gift exchanged between the Father and the Son, is also the source of joy within the Trinity. Some early Church Fathers even used marital imagery—such as the kiss and the embrace—to describe the Spirit's role in uniting the Father and the Son. Similarly, the Spirit's presence in a marriage transforms the ordinary and mundane into something extraordinary.

Pope Francis compares this transformation to the miracle at Cana, where Jesus turned water into wine. He explains that the Holy Spirit continues to work this miracle in marriages today, renewing and revitalizing relationships that may have grown dull or strained.

When spouses turn to the Spirit in prayer, He renews their love, making it joyful and lifegiving once more.

Marriage, the Pope reminds us, was designed by the Creator to be built on rock, not on sand. In today's world, it may seem easier to approach relationships with a temporary or superficial mindset. However, the consequences of weak foundations are evident in the growing number of broken families. Pope Francis emphasizes that children often bear the greatest burden when marriages fail, facing pain and instability due to the absence of unity between their parents.

Citing Jesus' parable of the wise and foolish builders (*Matthew 7:24-27*), Pope Francis warns that marriages built on shallow foundations—such as convenience, attraction, or social expectations—are fragile. True, lasting marriages require a solid foundation of faith and divine support.

In many parts of the world, couples preparing for marriage receive legal, psychological, and moral guidance. While these are important, Pope Francis suggests that spiritual preparation is equally essential. Without the Holy Spirit as the foundation, even the best human advice can fall short. He argues that marriage preparation should include a focus on how the Holy Spirit creates and sustains unity between spouses.

Pope Francis recalls an Italian proverb: "Never place a finger between husband and wife," meaning that no one should interfere in a marriage. However, he adds that there is one exception—the finger of God, referring to the Holy Spirit, whose presence strengthens and sustains the marital bond. Just as the Spirit strengthens and sanctifies the Church, He also fortifies the bond between husband and wife, making their union not just human but divine.

Pope Francis ends with an invitation to all married couples: turn to the Holy Spirit. Those who rely solely on their strength often find themselves struggling, but those who invite the Spirit into their relationship will experience renewed joy and unity. Marriage is not meant to be an endurance test but a reflection of the love that exists within the Trinity—a love made possible by the Holy Spirit's presence.

For a marriage to flourish, it must be grounded in faith, nurtured through prayer, and receptive to the work of the Holy Spirit. In this way, couples not only grow closer to one another but also become active participants in the divine mystery of God's love, reflecting the very communion of the Trinity.

Homily Analysis: Depth of the Holy Spirit in Marriage

Pope Francis' homily presents marriage not merely as a social or legal institution but as a sacramental reflection of the divine communion within the Trinity. Drawing on Saint Augustine's theology of the Holy Spirit, he describes marriage as a participation in God's own life, with the Holy Spirit as the active force of unity, love, and renewal. His homily is deeply rooted in Trinitarian theology, emphasizing the Holy Spirit's essential role not only in sustaining divine love but also in sustaining human relationships.

This theological perspective moves beyond a functional view of marriage as a practical arrangement and instead situates it within the cosmic order of divine love. It affirms that marriage is not something humans invented for companionship or social stability; rather, it is an institution woven into the very fabric of creation. Understanding marriage in this way radically transforms how it should be approached, emphasizing its divine foundation, its enduring nature, and the necessity of grace in sustaining it.

The Holy Spirit as the Essence of Unity in the Trinity and Marriage

One of the most profound insights of this homily is how Pope Francis parallels the unity of the Trinity with the unity of marriage. As Augustine explains, the Holy Spirit is not just one of the three persons of the Trinity but the very love that binds the Father and the Son. In this sense, the Holy Spirit is not just a distinct person within the Trinity but the very act of love itself—the living bond of divine unity.

This theological framework enables Pope Francis to emphasize that marriage is more than the union of two individuals—it is a participation in a unity that reflects divine communion. When a husband and wife come together, their love is not merely a human effort, but a sacramental reality infused with the Holy Spirit.

This has profound implications for how we understand what sustains marriage. If the Holy Spirit is the very force that unites the Trinity, then He is also the one who sustains the bond of marriage. Just as the Father and the Son are eternally united through the Spirit, so too are husband and wife called to remain united through His presence.

By referring to the Holy Spirit as the "first-person plural" rather than the "third-person singular," Pope Francis reinforces this relational aspect of God. The Spirit does not merely accompany love; He creates and sustains it. This truth extends to the theology of marriage, where the Spirit actively transforms two individuals into a unified "we."

This understanding deepens the sacramental nature of marriage. It is not just a legal or emotional bond; it is a divine participation in the unity of the Trinity. The couple does not simply exist side by side; their unity is a living reflection of the divine We.

Marriage as the First and Most Elementary Reflection of Divine Love

The Pope further roots this understanding of marriage in *Genesis 1:27*, where God creates humanity in His image—male and female. This reference underscores that marriage is not an afterthought in God's plan, nor merely a human adaptation for survival or

258

companionship. Instead, it is the earliest and most fundamental expression of divine love in creation.

This means that marriage is not just a human arrangement but a divine design. The

Pope's homily thus challenges modern, secular understandings of marriage that reduce it to a social contract, an emotional commitment, or a legal agreement. Instead, he presents it as something deeply ontological—that is, marriage is woven into the very nature of human existence as a reflection of God's love.

Furthermore, this perspective highlights that marriage is fundamentally about self-giving. Just as the Trinity exists in an eternal exchange of love, marriage is meant to be a continuous cycle of mutual self-gift. This theological insight challenges the individualistic mindset often found in modern relationships, where self-fulfillment is prioritized over self-sacrifice.

This also explains why the Pope emphasizes the transition from "I" and "you" to "we" in marriage. This shift is more than just a change in language—it is a transformation of identity. In marriage, husband and wife do not lose their individuality; rather, their identities are elevated and deepened through their new unity.

The Holy Spirit as the Giver of Joy and Renewal in Marriage

Pope Francis moves beyond simply describing the Holy Spirit as the bond of unity— he also highlights Him as the giver of joy in marriage. The theological significance of this cannot be overstated. The Pope draws on early Church Fathers who describe the Spirit as the very joy that exists between the Father and the Son, a joy that is not fleeting but eternal and sustaining.

This insight is particularly crucial when considering the reality of marriage in everyday life. Marriage, for many, begins with romantic enthusiasm and excitement, but over time, it can be worn down by routine, stress, and conflict. What Pope Francis suggests here is that true joy in marriage does not come from human emotions alone—it is something that the Holy Spirit must constantly renew.

By using marital imagery to describe the Spirit—such as "the kiss" and "the embrace" of divine love—the Pope highlights that the Spirit is neither distant nor abstract. Instead, He is intimately present in the love between husband and wife. This understanding redefines how we perceive the renewal of love in marriage. It is not merely about rekindling passion or finding new activities to do together; it is about invoking the Spirit's presence to renew the joy of being united.

The comparison to the miracle at Cana, where Jesus turns water into wine, further reinforces this point. Just as Christ transformed the ordinary into the extraordinary, the Holy Spirit transforms routine into joy in marriage. Yet, as with the miracle at Cana, this transformation requires an invitation. Just as Mary asked Jesus to intervene, spouses must also invite the Holy Spirit into their marriage.

The Fragility of Marriage Without a Spiritual Foundation

While affirming marriage's divine foundation, Pope Francis also acknowledges its vulnerability. He references Jesus' parable of the wise and foolish builders (*Matthew 7:24-27*) to illustrate the contrast between marriages built on rock—a firm foundation of faith—and those built on sand, where external pressures and self-interest ultimately lead to collapse.

This comparison reveals an important theological point: marriage is not immune to challenges simply because it is sacramental. Like any covenant relationship, it must be continually strengthened by divine grace. The Spirit does not force unity or love upon a couple; He must be invited to act. Without this openness to grace, even the strongest marriages can become vulnerable.

The Pope's emphasis on children as the primary victims of broken marriages highlights the communal nature of marriage. Just as disunity weakens the Church, the family also suffers deeply when marital unity collapses. This highlights the moral and spiritual responsibility of marriage— not just between spouses, but as a foundation for the well-being of future generations.

Marriage as a Covenant Sustained by the Spirit

Pope Francis' homily provides a theologically rich vision of marriage that is rooted in the Trinity and sustained by the Holy Spirit. By framing marriage as a participation in divine communion, he elevates it beyond a human institution and reaffirms its sacramental reality.

The Holy Spirit is not a passive presence in marriage but an active force of unity, joy, and renewal. Without Him, marriage risks becoming fragile, routine, or merely functional. With Him, it becomes a living reflection of God's love.

Ultimately, this homily challenges the modern world's individualistic and contractual view of marriage. It calls for a return to a spiritual understanding, where marriage is not about maintaining happiness but about mirroring divine communion. The presence of the Holy Spirit ensures that marriage is not merely about enduring commitment but about constant renewal, growth, and transformation.

Love and Unity: Living the Lessons on the Power of the Spirit in Marriage

Modern relationships exist in a world of shifting social values, rising divorce rates, and a growing emphasis on individual fulfillment over-commitment. Love is often seen as fleeting—an emotional experience that lasts only as long as it remains gratifying. The notion of love as a covenant—an enduring commitment that transcends personal satisfaction—is increasingly challenged by cultural narratives that equate love with convenience rather than perseverance. Yet, the relationships that stand the test of time are not simply those built on passion, financial security, or shared interests but those anchored in something greater than the individuals themselves.

The foundation of a meaningful relationship is not merely an emotional connection, shared goals, or mutual attraction. Rather, it is something deeper—a force that binds two people together through hardship, monotony, and the inevitable imperfections of human nature. Many relationships fail not because love disappears but because the individuals involved stop investing in the deeper elements that sustain it. The real challenge is not falling in love but staying united despite the struggles that arise over time.

The Fragility of Love Without a Foundation

In today's world, many relationships rest on unstable foundations. While physical attraction, financial security, and personal convenience may influence love, they are not enough to sustain it. When love depends on circumstances, it becomes fragile—prone to collapse the moment those circumstances shift.

Consider the pattern that often unfolds in high-profile celebrity marriages. From the outside, these relationships seem to have everything—beauty, wealth, success—yet many of them end in spectacular failure. The reason is rarely a lack of initial passion or attraction. Rather, it's the absence of a deeper foundation beyond fleeting enjoyment. When challenges arise, personal ambitions diverge, or excitement wanes, nothing remains to hold the relationship together. The foundation is too weak to withstand life's inevitable storms.

This is not just a phenomenon among celebrities. Many relationships crumble when the initial excitement wears off, when financial difficulties arise, or when one or both partners feel emotionally unfulfilled. Often, the issue isn't that love never existed but that it was built on a fragile foundation, unable to sustain itself through hardship. When love is reduced to a mere exchange of benefits, "What am I getting from this relationship?"—it loses its essence of true unity. Instead, it becomes a transaction; the moment one party feels they aren't receiving enough, they begin to withdraw.

In contrast, relationships that endure are those built on something deeper than circumstance. A couple who remains together through decades of hardship, raising children, overcoming illnesses, and facing financial struggles is a testament to a love that has been tested and strengthened. Their unity is not the result of luck or an absence of difficulty but a conscious decision to stand together even when it is not easy.

The Role of Commitment in a Disposable Culture

One of the greatest threats to love in modern times is the disposable mentality—the idea that when something stops working perfectly, it should be replaced rather than repaired. This mindset dominates many aspects of life, from technology to careers and, unfortunately, even to human relationships.

The rise of dating apps and the illusion of limitless romantic options have reinforced this mindset. Many people enter relationships with the belief that if one partner does not fully meet their expectations, they can move on to someone else. This constant search for a better option erodes the idea of commitment, making it easy to abandon relationships at the first sign of difficulty.

In contrast, relationships that last are built on a different perspective—one where love is understood not as a fleeting emotion but as a daily decision to invest in another person. This does not mean staying in toxic or abusive relationships, but it does mean recognizing that love requires effort, patience, and forgiveness.

Consider a couple who have been married for fifty years. When asked about the secret to their longevity, they do not say they never fought or that they were always happy.

Instead, they say they chose to stay. They chose to communicate rather than walk away. They chose forgiveness over resentment. They chose to adapt to life's changes together, not apart.

This kind of love is not passive. It is not a matter of simply enduring a relationship. It is an active investment in the well-being of the other person and the union itself. It requires letting go of ego, practicing self-sacrifice, and developing a long-term vision rather than seeking immediate satisfaction.

The Power of Self-Giving Love

One of the main reasons relationships falters is the mindset of getting rather than giving. Many enter relationships expecting their partner to fulfill them— providing happiness, emotional support, validation, and companionship. While these elements are important, relationships thrive when both individuals prioritize giving over receiving.

The difference between these two mindsets is profound. A relationship where each person constantly asks, *"What am I getting out of this?"* is fragile. The moment one partner feels their needs are unmet, resentment builds, and love turns into negotiation. In a relationship where both people ask, *"What can I do to support and uplift the other?"* love is constantly renewed through action.

An extraordinary example of this is found in relationships where one partner becomes ill or incapacitated. Countless stories exist of husbands and wives who devote years to caring for a spouse with Alzheimer's, cancer, or a disability. These individuals remain not because it is easy but because they understand that love is about giving, not just receiving. Their commitment reflects a deeper understanding of love—one that goes beyond attraction, beyond personal benefit, into true self-giving.

This is the kind of love that endures. It isn't based on a constant evaluation of whether the relationship fulfills every desire at every moment. Instead, it is rooted in the understanding that love flourishes when nurtured, given freely, and honored as something sacred rather than transactional.

The Need for Renewal in Love

Even the strongest relationships require effort to endure. Overtime, routine, responsibilities, and external pressures can drain the energy and excitement that once defined them. Love, like anything precious, must be nurtured, renewed, and protected.

Many couples reach a point where they feel distant—not because they no longer love each other, but because they have stopped actively choosing to cultivate their love. Just as a fire needs oxygen to continue burning, love needs intentional renewal to remain strong.

In lasting relationships, renewal happens in small yet significant ways—expressing gratitude, making time for meaningful conversations, supporting each other's dreams, and rediscovering shared joys. These simple actions form the foundation that sustains love through every stage of life.

The Strength Found in a Shared Purpose

Many of the strongest relationships are those where both individuals share a sense of purpose beyond themselves. This could be a shared faith, a commitment to family, or a mission to make a meaningful impact on the world. When couples are united by something greater than personal happiness, they are more likely to stay strong even in the face of hardship.

A powerful example of this can be seen in couples who dedicate their lives to a common cause—whether it is serving in humanitarian efforts, raising children with a shared vision, or supporting each other's professional or creative pursuits. Their relationship is strengthened because they are not only together for themselves but for something beyond themselves.

This idea extends beyond romantic relationships. Friendships, communities, and even professional partnerships flourish when built on a shared mission. Those who unite in pursuit of a common goal strengthen their bonds through their collective vision.

Love That Endures

The modern world often portrays love as fleeting—an emotion that ebbs and flows, a connection that lasts only as long as it remains convenient. But true love runs deeper. It is rooted in self-giving, commitment, and the ongoing choice to nurture and strengthen the bond between two people.

The relationships that endure are not those that are perfect or free from struggle but those where both individuals are willing to invest in each other, adapt to life's changes, and stand together in every season. Love does not survive on passivity, it thrives when it is actively cultivated, protected, and cherished.

Reflection Questions on Love, Unity, and Commitment in Modern Life

In a world where relationships are often viewed as fleeting and disposable, many struggle to understand what truly sustains love over time. The rise of individualism, digital distractions, and the belief that relationships should be effortless have led many to give up on love at the first sign of difficulty. Yet, the strongest relationships aren't those without struggle but those where both partners choose to invest, adapt, and grow together.

1. How do I define love, and is my definition helping or hurting my relationships?

Many people believe love should always feel effortless, that if struggles arise, something must be wrong. Love is often portrayed as an emotion that should never require work. Is this definition too narrow?

Reflecting on this question means asking whether love is seen as something to be experienced passively or as something to be actively nurtured.

- If the expectation is that love should always be easy, does that mindset make it harder to navigate difficult seasons in a relationship?
- What if love, rather than being a constant feeling, is actually a series of intentional choices?

2. Am I more focused on what I receive in relationships than on what I give?

Modern culture prioritizes personal happiness, often at the cost of commitment and self-sacrifice. Many enter relationships expecting love, validation, and emotional support but rarely consider what they give in return.

This reflection invites the reader to examine whether they approach love with a transactional mindset.

- Are relationships measured by how well they fulfill personal needs?
- Or is love seen as a space to give freely without constantly weighing what is received in return?
- How might relationships transform if the focus shifted from receiving to offering kindness, patience, and presence?

3. Do I run from discomfort, or do I allow challenges to deepen my love?

Difficulties in relationships are inevitable. Many, when faced with struggles, assume that something is fundamentally broken. But what if challenges were opportunities for growth rather than signs of failure?

This question invites reflection on how conflict is handled.

- When disagreements arise, is the instinct to withdraw, shut down, or walk away?
- Or is there a willingness to engage, listen, and seek resolution?

The strongest relationships aren't free from hardship; they are the ones where both partners choose to face challenges together rather than apart.

4. Have I taken love for granted?

The longer a relationship lasts, the easier it becomes to take it for granted. Those who were once cherished may start to feel like background figures, their efforts unnoticed and unappreciated. Love doesn't always fade because it disappears, but because it is no longer recognized.

This reflection encourages the reader to consider whether they are expressing appreciation for the people they love.

- When was the last time they expressed gratitude for a partner's support, a friend's loyalty, or a family member's kindness?
- Are daily acts of love viewed as mere routines or as gifts to be cherished?

Taking a moment to recognize love in its many forms—both big and small—can reignite a sense of gratitude and connection.

5. How much time and energy do I invest in strengthening my relationships?

Love, like any valuable pursuit, requires intentional effort. Yet, many people assume that relationships will maintain themselves without conscious investment. Time passes, priorities shift, and what was once strong may weaken through neglect.

The reader is encouraged to assess their level of investment in relationships.

- Are meaningful conversations a priority, or do routine and surface-level interactions replace them?
- Are efforts being made to create new shared experiences, or is love merely running on autopilot?
- If a relationship feels stagnant, what intentional steps can be taken to restore energy and depth?

6. Do I fear vulnerability, and is it preventing me from having a deeper connection?

Many people find it difficult to open up fully in relationships. Fear of judgment, rejection, or appearing weak leads them to build walls instead of bridges. Yet, love without vulnerability remains shallow—true intimacy requires courage.

This reflection invites the reader to consider whether they are holding back parts of themselves.

- Is the fear of being truly seen preventing a deeper emotional connection?
- Are difficult emotions being suppressed instead of expressed?
- What might happen if vulnerability was embraced as a pathway to stronger, more meaningful relationships?

7. Do external distractions take priority over the people I love?

In an era of digital connectivity, real human connection often suffers. Many people spend more time engaging with screens than with their loved ones, checking their phones during conversations, or prioritizing work over personal time.

This reflection asks the reader to evaluate their attention.

- Are loved ones getting the same level of focus and presence as other commitments?
- When spending time with a partner, friend, or family member, is attention fully given, or is it divided between social media, emails, and other distractions?

Small changes—such as setting aside phones during meals or scheduling dedicated quality time—can make a significant difference in restoring intimacy.

8. Do I share a vision for the future with my loved ones?

Strong relationships are often rooted in a shared sense of purpose. Whether it is a romantic partnership, a friendship, or a family bond, relationships thrive when there is alignment in values, dreams, and long-term goals.

The reader is encouraged to reflect on whether they and their loved ones are moving in the same direction.

- Are they building something meaningful together or drifting apart without realizing it?
- If a sense of unity is missing, what conversations could help create a stronger, more connected vision for the future?

9. Am I showing love in a way that the other person understands?

People express and receive love in different ways. Some value words of affirmation, while others prioritize quality time, acts of service, physical touch, or gifts. A common reason relationships struggle is that love is not expressed in a way that the other person recognizes.

This reflection encourages the reader to consider whether they are loving others in the way they prefer or in the way their loved ones truly need.

- Is love being expressed in a way that is genuinely felt and understood by the other person?

Taking the time to recognize and adapt to these differences can strengthen emotional bonds and deepen connections.

10. What is one meaningful action I can take today to deepen a relationship?

Reflection is valuable, but without action, it remains intellectual rather than transformative. Love is sustained not by grand gestures alone but through small, consistent acts of care.

This final question challenges the reader to take a tangible step toward nurturing a relationship today. It could be a heartfelt conversation, a simple expression of gratitude, an apology, or dedicating uninterrupted time to someone who matters. Love grows when it is actively expressed, and the strongest relationships are built by individuals who consistently choose to invest in each other.

The modern world often portrays love as something effortless or temporary, fading when it is no longer convenient. But real love—the kind that lasts—is not passive. It is a choice, a practice, and a continuous commitment.

The relationships that endure are not the ones without struggles but the ones where both people recognize that love is worth investing in, renewing, and protecting. Reflection is the first step, but real transformation happens when thought leads to action.

The question that remains is simple: Will love be something passively experienced, or will it be something actively built and sustained?

Chapter 13

Family: The First School of Love and the Path to Holiness

Saint Peter's Square - Saturday, 25 June 2022

The Homily

Pope Francis' homily at the Tenth World Meeting of Families was a powerful reflection on the beauty, mission, and challenges of family life. Speaking to families gathered in Rome and across the world, he expressed deep gratitude for their witness to faith, love, and perseverance. He likened their participation to a great offertory procession, presenting before God the joys, struggles, and hopes of family life. This gathering was not just an event but a living sign of the Church, a vast "constellation" of experiences from different cultures and backgrounds, united by the desire to strengthen family bonds in light of the Gospel.

At the heart of his message, Pope Francis explored the theme of freedom, one of the most cherished values in modern society. Many today view freedom as the ability to act without limits, live without restrictions, and shape one's destiny without external influence. Yet, Pope Francis pointed out that this false notion of freedom often leads to isolation, selfishness, and disillusionment. True freedom, he explained, is not about pursuing personal desires at any cost but about being set free from selfishness so that we may love and serve others.

Quoting Saint Paul's words—"For freedom Christ has set us free" (*Galatians 5:1*)—the pope emphasized that freedom is not something we create for ourselves; it is a gift from God. Jesus liberated humanity from the slavery of sin, not so that people could live for themselves, but so they could become "slaves to one another through love" (*Galatians 5:13*). This paradox of freedom—finding true liberation through self-giving— lies at the heart of family life. Married couples, in choosing to build a family, make a radical and courageous decision: to place love above personal comfort, serve one another rather than live as isolated individuals, and embrace family life as a vocation rather than a burden. The pope reaffirmed that the family is the first place where love is learned and practiced.

However, Pope Francis acknowledged that this ideal is not always easy to live out. Families today face many challenges—economic difficulties, societal pressures, and cultural shifts that threaten the very foundation of family life. In particular, he warned against the toxins of individualism, selfishness, and the culture of waste, which distort the meaning of love and lead to broken relationships. The family, he emphasized, must resist these pressures and remain a place of welcome, service, and deep connection—where no one is discarded or forgotten. The essence of family life is not about seeking personal fulfillment alone but about building a community of love that endures through both joyful and difficult times.

Drawing from the *Old Testament* reading on Elijah and Elisha, (*1 Kings 19: 19-21*) Pope Francis reflected on the relationship between generations and the importance of passing on faith and wisdom from parents to children. Elijah, at a moment of crisis and uncertainty, is commanded by God to anoint Elisha as his successor. This moment symbolizes a transfer of mission and responsibility—Elijah throws his mantle over Elisha, signifying that the prophetic calling will continue beyond his lifetime. This passing of the torch mirrors the role of parents in guiding their children toward their callings, helping them discern their mission in life, and trusting in God's plan for them.

The Pope acknowledged that, in today's world, relationships between generations are often strained. Many parents fear for their children's future, worrying they will struggle to find their way amid the complexities of modern society. Some, out of fear, become overprotective, trying to shield their children from all hardships. Others become discouraged, doubting whether they can raise children well in a world that often seems chaotic and uncertain. Pope Francis reminded parents that God is not anxious or overprotective—He does not prevent young people from facing challenges, but He entrusts them with great missions. Parents, he said, should help their children embrace life's challenges with courage rather than attempting to remove every obstacle for them.

Reflecting on the Gospel passage, Pope Francis compared Jesus' journey to Jerusalem to the journey of marriage and family life. Jesus, knowing He would face rejection, suffering, and death, set His face toward Jerusalem with unwavering determination and faith. He did not turn back or seek an easier path, even when faced with hostility. In the same way, families must embrace their vocation with courage, knowing that there will be difficulties but trusting that God goes before them. Marriage, like discipleship, is an unpredictable journey—filled with joys, hardships, and unexpected turns. The pope encouraged families to move forward with faith, even when challenges arise, and to never let discouragement or nostalgia hold them back.

A striking moment in the homily came when Pope Francis addressed young adults hesitant to marry, a growing concern in many societies. With humor, he remarked that some young men remain at home well into adulthood, relying on their mothers for everything. He playfully suggested that mothers should "stop ironing their sons' shirts" and encourage them to leave the nest, embracing the vocation of marriage and family life with confidence. Marriage, he emphasized, requires courage—not because it limits freedom, but because it is a beautiful, lifelong commitment to love and responsibility.

To couples facing difficulties, Pope Francis urged them not to give up too easily. Every family experiences crises, moments of pain, and seasons of doubt. But love does not simply disappear—it must be rekindled, rediscovered, and renewed. He encouraged spouses to look beyond their struggles and remember the spark that first brought them together. Marriage is not about perfection but about perseverance, about choosing to love even when emotions wane, or challenges arise.

Pope Francis concluded by reminding families that they are not alone. The Church itself is a family—born from the Holy Family of Nazareth and sustained by the countless families that form its body. The Church walks with them, prays for them, and supports them in their vocation. The mission of the family is not just to survive but to thrive as a beacon of love, service, and hope.

The final words of encouragement were a call to move forward with faith and joy, trusting that God's love will sustain every family through its journey. Families are a sign to the world that love is real, commitment is possible, and holiness is found in simple, everyday moments of life. Love, when shared and given freely, grows stronger, purer, and more transformative.

With this message, Pope Francis left families with a profound reminder: their love is not just for themselves but for the world. By choosing to live out their vocation with courage and generosity, they become living witnesses to God's love, shaping the Church and society in ways that will endure for generations.

Homily Analysis: The Family as a Divine Vocation

Pope Francis' homily offers a profound meditation on the nature of family as a vocation, the essence of true freedom, the intergenerational transmission of faith, and the call to persevere in love and discipleship. His words are not just pastoral encouragement but a deeply theological exposition of the mission of the family within the Church and God's greater plan for humanity.

The homily reflects key themes in Catholic theology— family as a domestic Church, marriage as a sacramental vocation, and love as a reflection of divine self-gift. Pope Francis does not present an idealized or romanticized view of family life. Instead, he acknowledges the challenges, crises, and struggles that accompany marriage and parenthood. However, he reframes these struggles not as obstacles to happiness but as integral to the Christian path of sanctification and discipleship.

The Family as an Offering: A Sacramental Vision of Marriage

One of the central images in the homily is the family as an offering to God—a living sacrifice presented to Him in love. Pope Francis compares the families gathered to a great offertory procession, bringing before God their joys, hopes, struggles, and wounds.

This imagery evokes the Catholic understanding of sacrificial love, particularly in the context of marriage. In Catholic theology, marriage is not merely a legal or emotional bond—it is a sacramental reality, a covenant that mirrors Christ's love for the Church. Just as Christ offered Himself for the salvation of humanity, spouses, too, are called to offer themselves fully and unreservedly to each other and their children.

Theologically, this reflects the Eucharistic nature of Christian love. In the Eucharist, Christ's body is broken, and His blood is poured out for the sake of others. In the same way, family life demands self-giving, sacrifice, and service. Spouses are called to die to themselves—to their ambitions, selfish inclinations, and individualistic desires—so they may live fully in communion with one another and with God.

This vision challenges modern notions of marriage, which often reduce it to mutual convenience, compatibility, or personal fulfillment. Pope Francis reminds us that true love is not about self-interest but about total self-giving. A family that sees itself as an offering to God does not measure success by material wealth, personal achievements, or external status but by the depth of love it cultivates the faith it nurtures, and the holiness it fosters.

Freedom in Christ: A Radical Reinterpretation of Autonomy

One of the most theologically profound aspects of the homily is Pope Francis' discussion of freedom, rooted in the teachings of Saint Paul. Modern society exalts personal autonomy, self-determination, and the ability to live without constraints as the highest expression of freedom. However, Saint Paul presents a radically different vision: "For freedom, Christ has set us free" (*Galatians 5:1*).

Pope Francis builds upon this Pauline theology, emphasizing that true freedom is not the ability to do whatever one desires but the ability to love without restraint. Christ's death and resurrection liberated humanity not for selfish indulgence but for self-giving service.

This understanding of freedom is particularly significant within the context of marriage and family. Many today view marriages as a restriction on personal freedom, a commitment that limits individual choice and independence. Yet, Pope Francis, following Saint Paul, argues that freedom is not found in isolation but in communion. True love does not enslave; it liberates. A husband and wife who commit to one another in marriage are not losing their freedom; they are exercising the highest form of freedom—the freedom to give themselves entirely and unconditionally to another.

This challenges contemporary notions of commitment and self-fulfillment. In a culture that often prioritizes personal happiness over lifelong fidelity, Pope Francis affirms that love is not about what we gain but about what we give. The paradox of Christian freedom is that one finds oneself not by seeking self-fulfillment but by offering oneself in love.

Passing the Mantle: The Family as the First School of Faith

Pope Francis grounds his reflection on the transmission of faith in the biblical story of Elijah and Elisha. This theologically rich narrative underscores the continuity of God's mission across generations.

When Elijah places his mantle over Elisha, he entrusts him with a divine calling. This act symbolizes that God's work does not end with one generation but must be carried forward. Pope Francis extends this biblical imagery to parenthood, emphasizing that parents have a sacred duty to pass on their faith to their children.

In Catholic tradition, the family is called the "domestic Church," meaning that faith is first experienced, taught, and lived within the home. Parents are not just providers of material security; they are spiritual shepherds responsible for guiding their children toward a deeper relationship with God.

However, the Pope acknowledges the challenges modern families face in transmitting faith. Many parents worry about their children's future, uncertain if they will be able to navigate a world shaped by moral relativism, secularism, and competing ideologies. Some parents respond by overprotecting their children, shielding them from hardship, while others become discouraged, wondering whether their efforts will have any lasting impact.

Here, Pope Francis offers a theological response to parental anxiety. He reminds parents that God does not shield His children from challenges. Rather, He entrusts them with great missions, confident in their ability to embrace life with courage and faith. Just as Elijah had to trust Elisha to carry on the prophetic mission, parents must entrust their children to God's providence, teaching them not just what to believe but how to seek God for themselves.

This perspective shifts parenting from control to trust, from fear to faith. It encourages parents to lead by example, not only by teaching doctrine but by living lives of holiness and joyful witness.

Marriage as a Journey: Following Christ to Jerusalem

A striking moment in the homily is Pope Francis' reflection on Jesus' journey to Jerusalem, which he compares to the journey of marriage and family life.

Jesus knew He was walking toward suffering, rejection, and sacrifice, yet He did not turn away. Likewise, marriage is not a path of comfort and certainty but a commitment to a journey together through both joy and hardship.

Pope Francis cautions against the temptation to 'look back'—to cling to nostalgia or regret rather than embracing the present mission of family life. Just as Jesus resolutely set His face toward Jerusalem, spouses must set their hearts on the mission of love, even when it requires sacrifice.

This reflects the Catholic understanding of marriage as a vocation—not merely a relationship of convenience but a lifelong commitment to holiness. It reminds couples that their highest calling is not to seek happiness alone but to walk together toward Christ.

The Family as a Witness to God's Love

Pope Francis concludes his homily with a profound ecclesiological reflection: the Church itself is a family born from the Holy Family of Nazareth. Families are not alone in their struggles; they are supported by the Church, strengthened by grace, and called to be a visible sign of God's love in the world.

Ultimately, this homily is a theological manifesto on the sacredness of family life. It is a call to embrace love as a vocation, to transmit faith with courage, and to persevere in the face of trials. By grounding marriage and family in self-giving love, trust in God's plan, and the journey of discipleship, Pope Francis presents a vision of the family that is not merely a human institution but a divine reality—a reflection of God's love for humanity.

Reflections and Applications: Living the Vocation of Family in the Modern World

Family life is often romanticized as a source of joy, love, and fulfillment, yet in reality, it is also a journey that requires sacrifice, patience, and perseverance. Many today struggle to see the value of lifelong commitment, fearing that marriage and children will limit their ambitions. Others find themselves overwhelmed by the pressures of raising a family in a fast-paced world that constantly demands more— more productivity at work, more social success, more financial security. In an era that celebrates **self-sufficiency**, family calls for **interdependence**. In a culture that values **personal success**, family demands **self-giving love**. These tensions create challenges that every family must navigate. Still, those who do so with faith, resilience, and intentionality will discover that family is not just a duty or obligation—it is a profound path to meaning and fulfillment.

Freedom and Commitment: Finding True Fulfillment

Modern culture often portrays freedom and commitment as opposites. Young people are encouraged to prioritize their dreams before considering marriage. Careers, travel, and financial stability are viewed as prerequisites for family life, leading many to delay serious relationships indefinitely. While planning for the future is important, many people eventually find that endless personal pursuits leave them feeling unfulfilled.

Take, for example, a corporate executive in his late 40s who has spent decades climbing the corporate ladder. He enjoys financial security, travels frequently, and leads an exciting social life. Yet, as he watches friends and colleagues build families, he begins to question whether he has sacrificed meaningful relationships for temporary achievements. His success feels empty without people to share it with. On the other hand, consider a married couple who made financial sacrifices early on so that they could spend more time raising their children. They may have fewer luxuries, but they have built something lasting—a home filled with love, shared memories, and meaningful relationships.

The belief that freedom means having no obligations is one of the greatest misunderstandings of modern life. True freedom is not about avoiding commitments; it is about choosing those that give life meaning. A person who spends their life avoiding responsibility may feel unrestricted, but they will likely end up feeling isolated. Meanwhile, those who embrace the responsibility of family may face difficulties, but they will also experience a depth of love and purpose that independence alone can never provide.

One of the most profound truths about family life is that it teaches us to prioritize others. In a world that constantly asks, "What's in it for me?" family forces us to ask, "What can I do for the people I love?"

A young mother who wakes up at 3:00 a.m. to care for her crying baby is not acting out of obligation alone; she is learning to love in the most selfless way possible. A husband who takes care of his wife when she is ill, putting aside his own needs to ensure her comfort, is choosing love over convenience. A teenage boy who stays home to help his younger siblings with their homework rather than going out with friends is beginning to understand what it means to sacrifice for others.

None of these acts are extraordinary, yet they form the foundation of a meaningful life. People who serve only when it is convenient will never understand the full depth of love. However, those who learn to serve when it is difficult, inconvenient, and unnoticed will build relationships far stronger than those based on personal benefit alone.

Passing On Values Across Generations

One of the greatest challenges for families today is bridging the generational gap, particularly when it comes to passing on values. Parents want their children to be kind, responsible, and morally grounded, yet they often struggle to instill these values in a world filled with conflicting influences.

A father who tells his children to be honest but cheats on his taxes should not be surprised when they begin lying to him. A mother who tells her children that family comes first but constantly prioritizes her career over family time will likely raise children who do the same. Children may not always listen to what their parents say, but they will always see how they live.

Consider a family where the parents actively involve their children in acts of charity. Instead of merely telling them to be generous, they bring them along to help distribute food at a shelter. Over time, these experiences shape the children's understanding of compassion, humility, and gratitude. In contrast, a child who grows up in a home where material success is the highest priority may internalize the idea that status and wealth matter more than relationships and integrity.

Raising children with strong values does not happen overnight. It is not a single conversation or a set of rules—it is the sum of thousands of small moments where parents show, rather than tell, what truly matters.

Many parents become anxious when their children begin questioning the values they were raised with. A teenager who stops attending church, a young adult who challenges the family's beliefs, or a child who makes poor choices can make parents feel as though they have failed. However, true wisdom recognizes that faith, morality, and maturity all take time to develop.

Consider a mother whose teenage son has drifted away from faith. She fears that he will abandon it entirely, yet she chooses not to force him back into religious practice. Instead, she continues living her faith authentically—praying, serving others, and maintaining a deep sense of peace and love in the home. Years later, after experiencing personal hardships, the son returns to faith not because he was forced but because he remembers the quiet strength of his mother's example.

Trusting that children will find their way requires patience. Values are not something that can be programmed into a person; they are seeds that need time to grow.

Parents who continue to love, guide, and model the life they hope for their children—despite resistance—often see the fruits of their efforts later in life.

Persevering in Love: Overcoming Difficult Seasons

Many modern relationships fall apart not because of one dramatic event but because of small acts of neglect that accumulate over time. Spouses become too busy to spend quality time together, allowing distance to grow between them. Parents become too distracted to engage deeply with their children. Over time, love does not disappear—it fades from lack of attention.

A couple that once shared everything slowly drifts apart when they stop communicating beyond the logistics of daily life. A parent who spends more time on their phone than with their child creates an emotional distance that will only grow with time. Love, like any living thing, requires constant care.

Every relationship faces difficult seasons. A married couple may endure financial struggles, illness, or emotional distance. Parents may face rebellion from their children. In these moments, it is easy to believe that love has run its course, but in reality, these challenges present an opportunity to rediscover what first brought the family together.

A husband and wife struggling in their marriage can choose to focus on the reasons they fell in love rather than on the frustrations they feel today. A parent with a difficult teenager can strive to understand their struggles rather than simply reacting in frustration. Choosing to stay, to fight for love, and to rebuild what has been lost is the difference between relationships that endure and those that fail.

The Family as a Witness to the World

Families that live with love, perseverance, and faith become a light in the world. A strong family not only benefits the individuals within it but also has a ripple effect on society.

A child raised in a home where love is unconditional will grow into an adult who shares that love in their workplace, community, and friendships. A couple who model respect and selflessness teach their children to do the same. A family that remains strong despite hardships shows others that commitment is not a burden but a source of strength.

The modern world is filled with distractions, superficial relationships, and fleeting happiness. Yet those who invest in the family—who love deeply, sacrifice willingly, and persevere through hardship—discover that true fulfillment is not found in independence but in belonging. Family is not always easy, but for those who embrace it fully, there is no greater source of joy, strength, and purpose.

Reflection Questions for Modern Life: Strengthening Family Bonds in an Age of Disconnection

In today's world, where technology dominates communication, careers demand long hours, and personal ambitions often overshadow communal responsibilities, family life can become strained and distant. Many people find themselves so focused on external success that they neglect the relationships that matter most.

The pressures of modern life make it easy to take family for granted, assuming that love will always endure even without nurture. However, deep connections, mutual understanding, and a lasting sense of belonging do not happen automatically—they require intention, effort, and reflection.

1. Do I Make Time for My Family, or Do They Only Get What's Left Over?

The modern world glorifies busyness, equating productivity with worth. Many people devote their energy to work, social obligations, and personal ambitions, leaving their families with only what remains. Over time, this creates emotional distance. A father who consistently works late may believe he is providing for his children, but if he is never emotionally present, they may feel neglected. A spouse constantly distracted by their phone or preoccupied with external worries may unknowingly weaken their bond with their partner.

This question invites reflection on whether family time is a priority or an afterthought. It requires asking:

- Am I fully present when I spend time with my family, or am I distracted?

- Do I intentionally create time for meaningful conversations, shared experiences, and moments of connection?
- If I continue on my current path, will my family relationships grow stronger or weaken over time?

2. Do I Show My Love in Ways That My Family Recognizes and Appreciates?

Love is often given with the best intentions but not always received as intended. A parent may express love by providing financial stability while their child longs for words of encouragement. A husband may assume his acts of service demonstrate affection, while his wife craves quality time together.

Each person experiences love differently, and relationships thrive when individuals take the time to understand how their loved ones receive love. This question asks:

- Do I assume my family knows I love them, or do I actively show it in ways that matter to them?
- Have I taken the time to understand how my spouse, children, or parents feel most valued and appreciated?
- If I were to ask my loved ones what makes them feel loved, would their answer match my assumptions?

3. Do I Handle Family Conflicts with Humility and a Desire for Resolution?

No family is without disagreements. However, the way conflicts are handled determines whether relationships deepen in trust or fracture over time. Some people react to conflict with anger, creating further distance. Others avoid difficult conversations, allowing resentment to fester. Many believe they must always be right, prioritizing their ego over the well-being of the relationship.

This reflection challenges individuals to consider how they approach tension in family life. It is important to ask:

- Do I listen to understand, or do I argue to win?
- Am I willing to apologize when I am wrong, or does pride get in the way?
- When conflicts arise, do I seek solutions that strengthen the relationship, or am I more focused on defending myself?

True resolution comes not from proving a point but from valuing the relationship over the argument.

4. Am I Setting the Example I Want My Children to Follow?

Children learn far more from what they see than from what they are told. A parent who preaches honesty but tells small lies for convenience teaches their child that truth is optional. A father who emphasizes respect yet speaks harshly to his spouse models a contradiction. Parents often expect their children to uphold values they do not fully practice.

This question challenges individuals to reflect on whether their daily actions align with the values they hope to instill in the next generation. It prompts self-examination:

- Am I modeling kindness, patience, and integrity, or do I expect my children to uphold values that I neglect?
- Do my words and actions match, or do they send conflicting messages?
- If my child grew up to be just like me, would I be proud of the person they become?

5. Do I Take My Loved Ones for Granted?

It is easy to assume that family will always be there. However, relationships weaken when appreciation is not regularly expressed. Many people only realize how much someone meant to them after that person is gone. Spouses drift apart because they stop expressing gratitude. Parents and children grow distant because affection and acknowledgment become rare.

This reflection encourages individuals to ask:

- Do I actively express appreciation for my spouse, children, parents, and siblings, or do I assume they already know how much they mean to me?

- When was the last time I sincerely thanked my loved ones for the role they played in my life?
- If today were my last day, have I said everything I would want my loved ones to know?

Gratitude strengthens bonds, and taking the time to express appreciation can profoundly impact relationships.

6. Am I Present in the Moments That Matter?

Modern distractions—phones, television, and endless responsibilities—can make it difficult to engage with loved ones fully. Many people spend time around their family but not truly with them. A spouse who is physically present yet emotionally distant creates an invisible wall in the relationship. A child who grows up with parents who are always 'too busy' may learn to seek validation elsewhere.

This reflection invites self-examination:

- When my loved ones speak to me, am I fully listening, or am I distracted?
- Do I prioritize meaningful conversations and shared experiences, or do I multitask even during important moments?
- How often do I set aside work, screens, and external stress to be fully present with my family?

7. Do I Let Small Resentments Build Up Instead of Addressing Them?

Unspoken frustrations can erode even the strongest relationships. Many family conflicts do not stem from a single major issue but from years of small, unresolved disappointments. A spouse who feels unappreciated yet never voices it may eventually grow distant. A sibling who harbors resentment over past misunderstandings may gradually disconnect.

This reflection encourages honesty:

- Am I holding onto unresolved frustrations instead of addressing them?
- Do I communicate openly with my loved ones, or do I allow small annoyances to build into resentment?
- Would my relationships be stronger if I addressed conflicts with honesty and kindness rather than avoiding them?

8. Am I Teaching My Family to Be Selfless, or Am I Encouraging a Culture of Entitlement?

In an age of convenience, family members can easily become accustomed to receiving without giving. Many children grow up expecting their needs to be met without learning the value of hard work, generosity, or service. Adults, too, may fall into the habit of expecting love and effort from others while neglecting to reciprocate.

This question invites individuals to ask:

- Am I fostering a spirit of gratitude and responsibility in my family?
- Do I encourage my children to contribute, to be generous, and to appreciate what they have?
- Do I personally practice generosity, or do I take more than I give?

Families who thrive are those where every member contributes to the well-being of the whole.

9. Do I Prioritize Long-Term Relationships Over Temporary Distractions?

Many people invest time and energy into things that will not last—careers, material possessions, social status—while neglecting the relationships that will matter in the long run.

This reflection invites individuals to consider:

- Am I investing enough effort into the relationships that will outlast life's fleeting successes?
- If I stay on my current path, will I look back with fulfillment or regret?

10. What Is One Simple Action I Can Take Today to Strengthen My Family?

Reflection is valuable, but action creates change; small, intentional efforts—whether a kind word, an act of service, or a moment of connection—can profoundly impact family life.

This final question challenges individuals to reflect:

- What is one small action I can take today to express love, appreciation, or commitment to my family?
- How can I make my presence more meaningful, my words more uplifting, and my actions more intentional?

Family relationships are not built on grand gestures but on daily choices. Those who consistently nurture, appreciate, and strengthen their family bonds will discover that love, given freely and intentionally, creates a lasting legacy for generations.

Chapter 14

The Forgotten Children: A Call to Protect the Innocent

Audience Hall - Wednesday, 8 January 2025

The Homily

In this homily, Pope Francis highlights the plight of children, especially those who are exploited, abused, or neglected. While modern society advances at a staggering pace—with innovations like artificial intelligence and aspirations to colonize Mars—it continues to neglect one of the most fundamental injustices: the suffering of children. The Pope challenges the world's priorities, asking how humanity can reach for the stars while ignoring those who suffer in society's shadows. He argues that civilization's progress is meaningless if it does not uplift the most vulnerable—children deprived of their dignity, childhood, and future.

To emphasize the value of children, Pope Francis highlights Sacred Scripture, where the word 'son' appears nearly five thousand times in the *Old Testament*. This frequent reference underscores how central children are to God's plan for humanity. The *Psalms* affirm that children are a divine gift, a source of joy, and a reward from the Lord. Yet, Scripture does not shy away from portraying the suffering of children throughout history. The cries of starving infants and the devastation of young lives torn apart by war are not just ancient tragedies—they reflect the ongoing injustices faced by children today.

The Pope recalls the heartbreaking words from the Book of *Lamentations 4:4*: "The tongue of the infant cleaves to the roof of its mouth in thirst; children beg for bread, but no one gives them a piece." These haunting lines remind us that hunger and deprivation are not new realities but persistent scars on human history. He also references the prophet Nahum's lament over the destruction of cities like Thebes and Nineveh, where children were brutally killed. These passages, written centuries ago, still speak to the atrocities committed against children in the present— whether through war, famine, human trafficking, or systemic neglect. (*Nahum 3:8-10*)

Even in the life of Christ, the suffering of children is evident. From His birth, Jesus was a target of cruelty. King Herod's massacre of Bethlehem's infants serves as a grim reminder that power, driven by fear and greed, often seeks to silence the innocent. The Holy Family was forced to flee into Egypt, making Jesus a refugee in His infancy—a reality still experienced by countless children today who are displaced by war, poverty, and persecution.

Despite these early hardships, Jesus was raised in a modest, humble home in Nazareth. The Gospels describe Him as a child who 'grew and became strong, filled with wisdom, and the favor of God was upon Him.' (*Luke 2:40*) His childhood was not defined by privilege but by simplicity, as He learned a trade under Joseph's guidance. However, when He entered His public ministry, Jesus did something revolutionary for His time. He elevated the status of children, recognizing them as examples of faith rather than treating them as passive members of society.

The Pope recalls the moment when mothers brought their children to Jesus for a blessing, only for the disciples to turn them away. Jesus rebuked them, declaring that the Kingdom of God belongs to those who are like children. He then issued a grave warning: anyone who harms a child will face severe consequences.

"It would be better for him to have a great millstone hung around his neck and to be drowned in the depths of the sea," Jesus said, making it clear that the protection of children is not optional—it is a divine mandate. (*Matthew 18:6*)

Pope Francis then turns to the harsh realities of child exploitation today. Millions of children are forced into labor, deprived of education, play, and the hope of a better future. For them, the joy of childhood is an unknown experience. A child who does not smile, who does not dream, is a child whose potential is being stolen.

Pope Francis condemns economic systems that value profit over human dignity, reducing children to mere commodities for cheap labor. In factories, fields, and domestic servitude, countless children endure long hours of work for meager wages, robbed of the opportunity to learn, grow, and thrive in a nurturing environment. This is not just an issue of poverty—it is an issue of justice. When children are treated as disposable, the world loses its greatest source of hope and love.

Beyond labor exploitation, Pope Francis sheds light on the many other forms of suffering endured by children today—those who are trafficked, abused, forced into armed conflicts, or abandoned. He calls on society to recognize the gravity of these injustices and to reject indifference.

Pope Francis reminds us that, as Christians, we bear the responsibility of protecting children. To follow Christ is to ensure that no child is neglected, mistreated, or deprived of their fundamental rights. Jesus Himself set the example—welcoming children, defending their dignity, and revealing that their faith, joy, and innocence are gifts to the world.

Pope Francis calls on every person to reject indifference and take action. We cannot simply turn away when we see suffering. The duty to protect children extends beyond our own families—it includes children on the streets, those in war zones, those suffering from neglect in wealthy countries, and those forced to grow up too quickly because of economic exploitation.

Pope Francis concludes his homily with a prayerful plea: May the Lord open our hearts to tenderness so that every child may grow in age, wisdom, and grace, receiving and giving love as God intended. This is more than a moral duty—it is a reflection of our deepest identity as children of God. The way we treat children reveals the depth of our faith, the sincerity of our love, and the future of our world.

Homily Analysis: The Moral Imperative to Protect Children

Pope Francis' homily on children is not simply an appeal for social justice; it is a deeply theological reflection on the dignity, innocence, and sacredness of childhood. Pope Francis' message unfolds in several key layers, grounding the protection of children in biblical teaching, highlighting their spiritual significance in the Christian faith, and emphasizing the moral urgency of safeguarding them from harm. He presents children as both a divine gift and a living image of vulnerability and trust—qualities that all believers are called to emulate.

Children as a Gift from God: A Scriptural Perspective

From the beginning, Pope Francis anchors his reflection in the biblical witness to childhood. The sheer frequency with which Scripture references children— nearly five thousand times in the *Old Testament*— underscores their centrality in God's plan for humanity. The psalmist proclaims, 'Children are a gift from the Lord' (*Psalms 127:3*), affirming that their presence is a blessing, not a burden. This biblical perspective challenges any view that diminishes their worth— rejecting the notion that children are merely dependents or lesser beings in comparison to adults.

The Pope does not shy away from acknowledging the other side of Scripture's depiction of childhood—the suffering of children throughout human history. From the cries of starving infants in the Book of *Lamentations* to the violent deaths of children in the conquests of Thebes and Nineveh, as recorded by the prophet Nahum, the *Bible* is painfully honest about the injustices that befall children. This duality—children as both divine gifts and victims of cruelty—forms the heart of the Pope's theological argument. While God intends for children to be cherished, human sin repeatedly subjects them to suffering.

The Vulnerability of Christ: Jesus as a Child and a Refugee

The suffering of children is not an abstract concept within Christianity, as even Jesus, the Son of God, experienced it firsthand. The Pope recalls how Christ's infancy was marked by hardship—threatened from birth by the violence of King Herod, who sought to destroy Him out of fear and jealousy.

This forced the Holy Family to flee to Egypt, making Jesus a refugee before He had even spoken His first words.

The significance of this is profound. If Christ Himself experienced the vulnerability of childhood—facing hunger, displacement, and the threat of death—it reveals that God intimately identifies with the weakest and most defenseless members of society. The

Incarnation does not bypass suffering; it enters fully into it. In presenting Jesus' infancy in this way, Pope Francis reminds the faithful that Christ is not a distant God removed from human pain. He was born into it, lived through it, and ultimately transformed it through His sacrifice.

This reality carries profound theological implications. If God, in the person of Jesus, was once a child, then every child reflects the divine. To harm a child is to reject Christ Himself. To protect, nurture, and love children is to honor the very heart of God's incarnation.

Children as a Model for the Kingdom of God

One of the most striking aspects of Jesus' ministry was His radical treatment of children. In a culture where they were often overlooked and considered insignificant, Jesus did the opposite—He placed them at the very center. The Pope highlights the moment when Jesus, defying social norms, welcomed children after His disciples tried to turn them away. "Let the children come to me and do not prevent them," Jesus said, declaring that "the kingdom of God belongs to such as these" (*Luke 18:16-17*).

The radical nature of this statement cannot be overstated. Jesus was not merely affirming the innocence of children; He was elevating them as the very model of faith. The qualities that define childhood—trust, openness, dependence, and humility—are the same attributes required to enter the kingdom of heaven.

This redefinition of greatness—where the least in society becomes the greatest in

God's eyes—echo throughout Jesus' teachings. The Pope recalls another moment when Jesus took a child, placed him among the disciples, and declared, "Unless you turn and become like children, you will not enter the kingdom of heaven" (*Matthew 18:3*). This is a powerful call to conversion. To follow Christ is not to seek power or prestige but to reclaim the childlike qualities of faith, purity, and dependence on God.

The Pope does not offer this teaching as mere sentimentality about childhood but as a direct challenge to the disciples—and to all believers. If children embody the ideal posture before God, then mistreating or neglecting them is not just a social failing but a profound spiritual betrayal.

The Severe Warning Against Harming Children

One of the most striking aspects of Jesus' teaching about children is His warning against those who would cause them harm. Pope Francis recalls Jesus' words: "Whoever causes one of these little ones to sin, it would be better for him to have a great millstone hung around his neck and to be drowned in the depths of the sea" (*Matthew 18:6*). This is among the most severe condemnations issued by Jesus in the Gospels.

The severity of this warning underscores the profound consequences of harming or leading a child astray. Whether through abuse, neglect, exploitation, or moral corruption, any act that wounds a child's innocence carries deep spiritual weight. The Pope presents this not merely as a moral obligation but as a divine mandate.

This passage reinforces the idea that children are not merely recipients of care but moral agents whose faith and formation are profoundly significant. Leading a child into sin—whether through exposure to violence, neglect, or failure to provide moral guidance—is a grave responsibility that cannot be ignored.

The Church's Mission to Defend the Innocent

Given these strong biblical foundations, Pope Francis makes it clear that protecting children is not merely an act of charity—it is a fundamental duty of the Church. Christians cannot ignore the suffering of children, nor can they remain passive in the face of exploitation and abandonment.

The Church's mission, modeled after Christ's ministry, is to protect and uplift the most vulnerable actively. This responsibility goes beyond safeguarding children; it calls for creating an environment where they can truly flourish—where they are loved, nurtured, and empowered to develop their God-given gifts.

The Pope's homily presents this mission as an essential aspect of Christian discipleship. To follow Christ is to defend the dignity of every child, ensuring that none are deprived of love, care, or protection.

The Divine Judgment on Those Who Exploit Children

Pope Francis concludes his reflection with a sobering reminder: those who exploit or harm children will one day answer to God. The exploitation of children—whether through forced labor, abuse, neglect, or systemic injustice—is not just a crime against humanity; it is an offense against God Himself.

Throughout history, societies have often treated children as an afterthought, prioritizing economic, political, and technological advancements over their well-being. Pope Francis warns against this mindset, reminding the world that true progress is meaningless if it comes at the expense of the innocent.

He calls upon every believer to reject indifference, urging people to be attentive to the plight of children in their communities and around the world. The measure of a just society is not found in its wealth or power but in how it treats its most vulnerable members.

Children, Innocence, and Responsibility: A Call to Protect and Nurture the Future

Children are the most vulnerable members of society, yet they are often overlooked, neglected, or even exploited. In a world that prides itself on technological advancements, economic growth, and scientific progress, the fundamental duty of protecting and nurturing children is often ignored. While humanity makes great strides in artificial intelligence, space exploration, and global finance, millions of children still suffer from poverty, child labor, online exploitation, and neglect. The true measure of a society is not its wealth or technological progress but how it cares for its most vulnerable members.

This chapter explores how modern society fails to protect its children and the urgent need for individuals, communities, and governments to take responsibility.

It examines the economic, digital, and emotional challenges that children face today and provides a call to action for a world that often prioritizes profit, power, and convenience over the well-being of its youngest members.

Children in a World That Prioritizes Profit Over Protection

Economic systems driven by efficiency, productivity, and profit often contribute to the exploitation of children. Many industries, particularly in developing nations, depend on child labor, treating children as a cheap and disposable workforce. In the relentless pursuit of lower production costs, corporations frequently overlook the inhumane conditions under which their products are made, ignoring the harsh reality that their profits come at the cost of children's futures.

The global garment industry provides a clear example of this injustice. In many countries, children as young as five or six are forced to work long hours in textile factories, sewing clothes under harsh and often unsafe conditions. These children work for a fraction of an adult's wage, inhaling toxic chemicals and operating dangerous machinery instead of receiving an education. The very clothes worn by people worldwide may have been stitched by hands that should have been holding books and pencils in a classroom.

Similarly, the chocolate industry has long been tainted by child labor. In West Africa, thousands of children toil on cocoa plantations, enduring grueling tasks such as carrying heavy loads and wielding machetes to harvest cocoa pods. Many of these children are trafficked or forced into labor, deprived of education, and subjected to abusive working conditions. While consumers enjoy chocolate bars in grocery stores, the hidden cost of this treat is the suffering of children who remain trapped in exploitative labor.

The problem is not limited to developing countries. Even in wealthy nations, economic systems fail children in different ways. In low-income communities, child poverty remains widespread, leaving many without access to proper nutrition, healthcare, or education. In some cases, economic inequality pushes children into labor to help support their families, robbing them of the carefree childhood they deserve.

The responsibility to address this crisis does not fall solely on governments. Individuals must become conscious consumers, making ethical purchasing decisions and supporting brands that uphold fair labor practices. Businesses, too, must take responsibility by ensuring their supply chains are free from child exploitation. Governments must enforce labor laws that prioritize human dignity over corporate profits.

The Digital World and the Exploitation of Children

While technology has created many opportunities for education and communication, it has also exposed children to new dangers. The rise of the internet has made children more vulnerable than ever to cyberbullying, online predators, and digital addiction. The online world, though filled with possibilities, is also a space where children can be manipulated, exploited, and harmed.

Social media has become a dominant force in children's lives, shaping their self-image and emotional well-being. Platforms like TikTok, Instagram, and YouTube promote unrealistic beauty standards, social comparison, and peer pressure that can lead to anxiety, depression, and low self-esteem. Many children today measure their worth by the number of likes, comments, or followers they receive, creating a generation that is increasingly disconnected from real-life interactions.

The internet has also become a breeding ground for child exploitation. Human traffickers and online predators use social media, gaming platforms, and messaging apps to target vulnerable children. Many of these predators disguise themselves as peers, gradually manipulating and deceiving children into dangerous situations. In some cases, children are coerced into sharing personal information, photos, or videos, which are then used against them.

Addressing these dangers requires a collective effort. Parents must actively monitor their children's online activities, educate them about digital safety, and set clear boundaries to shield them from harmful content. Schools should integrate digital literacy into their curricula, equipping children with the skills to navigate the internet safely. Governments and technology companies must implement stronger safeguards to prevent online exploitation, holding platforms accountable for the safety of their users.

Neglected and Abandoned Children: A Crisis in Every Society

One of the greatest tragedies of modern life is the countless children who grow up without love, guidance, or care. Neglect and abandonment are not always visible; they do not always take the form of physical desertion. In many cases, children suffer emotional neglect, growing up in households where they are ignored, overlooked, or treated as burdens rather than cherished members of the family.

Many children today grow up in fractured families where financial instability, domestic violence, or addiction foster environments of fear rather than security. Some are placed in foster care due to abuse or neglect, shuffling between homes, and never knowing the stability of a permanent family. Others are left to navigate the world alone, raising themselves emotionally because their parents are too distracted by work, social media, or personal ambitions to provide the attention and love they need.

In some wealthier societies, emotional abandonment takes a different form. Children may be given material comforts but lack meaningful parental engagement. In an age dominated by smartphones and social media, many parents are physically present but emotionally absent, choosing to engage with their screens rather than with their children. This absence creates a silent but profound wound in children, leading to feelings of isolation, insecurity, and unworthiness.

The responsibility to address this crisis lies not only with parents but with society as a whole. Communities must ensure that families in crisis receive support rather than judgment. Schools and churches should create environments where children feel valued and safe. Every person has a role to play in making sure no child grows up feeling unloved.

Recognizing Christ in the Most Vulnerable

At the heart of this discussion lies a simple yet profound truth: children are sacred. They are not merely future adults but full human beings in their own right, deserving of dignity, love, and protection. To mistreat a child is to violate the very foundation of human morality.

Recognizing Christ in children means seeing their suffering and responding with action. It means advocating for policies that protect them, making ethical consumer choices, and being present for the children in our own lives. It means ensuring that no child grows up feeling unseen or unloved.

A society is ultimately judged by how it treats its most vulnerable members. In a world that equates success with economic output, technological advancements, and social status, the true measure of progress should be how well it protects and nurtures its children. There is no higher calling than to ensure that every child is given the chance to grow, dream, and flourish in an environment of love and security.

Reflection Questions on the Dignity and Rights of Children

Children are the most vulnerable members of society, yet they are often overlooked, neglected, or even exploited. Pope Francis' message is a powerful reminder that children are not just future adults; they are individuals with dignity, potential, and the right to be loved and protected. This chapter offers ten reflection questions to help readers evaluate their attitudes, responsibilities, and roles in safeguarding children's well-being. These questions are designed to challenge both personal and societal perspectives while inspiring meaningful action.

1. Do I Truly See Children as a Gift from God?

It is easy to take children for granted, viewing them as obligations rather than as blessings. In a fast-paced world, many parents, caregivers, and communities fail to appreciate the sacredness of childhood. A child's laughter, curiosity, and innocence are reflections of divine love, yet modern culture often sees children as burdens rather than treasures.

Reflecting on this question requires asking whether children in our lives—our own or those in our communities—are treated with love, patience, and respect. Do we engage with them meaningfully, or are they sidelined while we prioritize work, personal ambitions, or social distractions? Recognizing children as gifts means cherishing their presence and ensuring they feel valued, protected, and nurtured.

2. How Do I Contribute to the Well-Being of the Children in My Life?

Children are shaped not only by their parents but also by the broader community. Teachers, neighbors, extended family members, and even strangers all contribute to their development. This question invites us to reflect on the impact of our influence.

- Are we patient when children make mistakes, understanding that learning is a process?
- Do we take time to guide and encourage them, or do we leave them to navigate life's challenges alone?

Even small actions—offering encouragement, spending time with them, or simply showing kindness—can have a profound impact. Ensuring that children feel safe and supported is not just the responsibility of parents but of society as a whole.

3. Have I Been Indifferent to the Suffering of Children Around the World?

In an era of global news and social media, stories of child exploitation, poverty, and abuse are ever-present. Yet, many people feel detached from these realities, assuming that responsibility falls solely on governments, charities, or international organizations.

This reflection challenges us to consider whether we have turned a blind eye to the suffering of children in conflict zones, sweatshops, refugee camps, or abusive households. Have we chosen to ignore their plight because it feels distant? Recognizing the suffering of children should not lead to despair but to action, whether through advocacy, charitable support, or simply raising awareness.

4. Am I Supporting Ethical Practices That Protect Children?

Many industries profit from child labor, human trafficking, and exploitation. From clothing brands that use child labor in factories to chocolate companies that rely on child workers in cocoa fields, consumer choices often contribute to these injustices.

This question challenges readers to consider their purchasing habits.

- Do we research the companies we buy from?
- Do we support fair-trade products that ensure children are not being exploited?

Ethical consumption is a tangible way to stand against child labor and support businesses that uphold human dignity.

5. How Do I Ensure That Children Have Access to Education?

Education is one of the most powerful tools for breaking the cycle of poverty and exploitation. Yet, millions of children worldwide are denied access to quality education due to financial hardship, war, or systemic neglect.

Reflecting on this question involves considering how we support educational opportunities for children.

- Do we contribute to initiatives that provide schooling for underprivileged children?
- Do we encourage children in our communities to value education?

Even simple actions—such as tutoring, donating books, or mentoring—can make a significant difference in a child's future.

6. Do I Take the Safety of Children Seriously?

Children are vulnerable to many forms of abuse—physical, emotional, and digital. Sadly, countless cases go unnoticed because society too often hesitates to intervene in so-called "private matters."

This reflection asks whether we are attentive to signs of neglect or abuse.

- Do we actively advocate for stronger protections for children in our communities?
- Are we proactive in safeguarding their digital well-being, educating them about online dangers, and setting responsible boundaries?

Protecting children requires vigilance, awareness, and the courage to intervene when something feels wrong.

7. Have I Shown Compassion to Children Who Are Marginalized or Neglected?

Many children grow up without parental love due to abandonment, foster care, or orphanhood. Others are marginalized due to disabilities, illness, or social stigma.

This question invites reflection on how we treat children who are different or disadvantaged.

- Do we look away from homeless children begging on the streets?
- Do we make an effort to include children with special needs in social and community activities?

A truly compassionate society ensures that no child is left behind.

8. Do I Make Time for the Children in My Life?

Modern life is full of distractions—work, social media, entertainment, and endless responsibilities. As a result, many adults unintentionally neglect children's emotional needs, being physically present yet emotionally absent.

This reflection encourages readers to examine their priorities.

- Do we spend quality time with our children, nieces, nephews, or young family members?
- Do we listen to their thoughts, dreams, and fears?

Children need to feel heard and valued, not just provided for materially.

9. Do I Encourage a Culture of Love, Faith, and Moral Values in Children?

Children learn not only from what they are taught but also from what they observe. When they witness kindness, generosity, and faith practiced in their homes and communities, they are more likely to embrace and carry those values into adulthood.

This reflection challenges adults to consider the example they set.

- Do we demonstrate compassion, honesty, and integrity?

- Do we encourage faith and spirituality in young people, helping them develop a sense of purpose and morality?

Cultivating a loving and faith-filled environment shapes children's understanding of the world and their place in it.

10. How Can I Be an Advocate for the Rights of Children?

Recognizing the injustices children face is not enough—action must follow. Advocacy takes many forms, such as speaking out against child labor, supporting child welfare programs, volunteering at shelters, or donating to organizations that protect children's rights.

This question challenges readers to move beyond reflection and take meaningful action.

- What practical steps can we take to defend and uplift children in need?

Whether through small acts of kindness or larger advocacy efforts, everyone has a role in ensuring that children are treated with dignity and care.

The Pope's message serves as a powerful reminder that children are sacred gifts who must be loved, protected, and nurtured. A society cannot call itself advanced while its children suffer from neglect, exploitation, and injustice. Each of us has the power to help create a world where children grow in safety, dignity, and hope.

Reflecting on these questions is only the beginning. The real challenge is to act—to be a voice for the voiceless, to protect those who are vulnerable, and to ensure that no child is ever treated as anything less than a beloved and valued member of the human family.

Chapter 15

The Mystery of Death: The Hope of the Resurrection

Paul VI Audience Hall - Wednesday, 1 August 2018

The Homily

In this homily, Pope Francis reflects on the Christian perspective on death, drawing inspiration from Saint Joseph, who has long been venerated as the patron of a good death. The Pope explains that this devotion arises from the belief that Saint Joseph passed away in the loving presence of Jesus and Mary. Although no historical record of Joseph's death exists, Christian tradition envisions him dying peacefully, surrounded by those dearest to him. This image of a death filled with

327

love and faith stands in contrast to the way modern society often views death—as something to be feared, ignored, or delayed at all costs.

Pope Francis acknowledges that discussions about death are often avoided in contemporary culture. Many people live as if death is distant or irrelevant, yet the Pope reminds us that it is ever-present. The COVID-19 pandemic made this reality painfully clear, as countless individual lost loved ones suddenly, often without the chance to say goodbye. He recounts the moving story of a nurse who helped a dying woman connect with her family via mobile phone, allowing her to say farewell.

This example highlights the deep human need for connection in our final moments and the importance of being present for those who are nearing death. The Pope warns against the unconscious illusion of immortality—the tendency to chase wealth, success, and material possessions as if they will last forever. He echoes the well-known saying, "The shroud has no pockets," reminding us that no one can carry their riches beyond the grave.

At the heart of the homily is the Christian response to death, which is not denial or avoidance but faith in the resurrection. Pope Francis quotes Saint Paul's words in the First Letter to the *Corinthians*: "If Christ has not been raised, then our preaching is in vain, and your faith is in vain." He asserts that the resurrection of Christ is the light that illuminates the darkness of death, transforming it from a terrifying unknown into a passage toward eternal life. This belief, he insists, should shape the way we live. If we accept that death is inevitable, we should focus on what truly matters: love, kindness, reconciliation, and generosity. The Pope challenges his listeners to ask themselves:

- What is the purpose of accumulating wealth if, in the end, we cannot take it with us?
- Why cling to grudges when we all must one day face death?

The Pope urges us to seek peace with others, forgive freely, and live each day with gratitude and purpose.

Pope Francis then addresses the ethical questions surrounding death, particularly the growing acceptance of euthanasia and assisted suicide in some parts of the world. He warns against the mentality that treats life as disposable, emphasizing that life is a right, but death should never be seen as something to be administered. He stresses the importance of accompanying the dying with care and dignity rather than seeking to hasten their passing. The Pope firmly advocates for palliative care, which seeks to ease suffering without intentionally ending life. He also expresses deep concern for the elderly, condemning the neglect and denial of proper medical treatment simply because they are viewed as burdens on society. He describes this as a form of social injustice, reminding the faithful that the elderly are treasures of wisdom and should be cherished, not discarded.

The homily concludes with a reflection on the mercy of God in our final moments.

Pope Francis reminds the faithful that in the Hail Mary, we pray, "Holy Mary, Mother of God, pray for us sinners, now and at the hour of our death." This simple yet profound prayer shows that Christians have always sought the intercession of the Blessed Virgin Mary at the moment of death, trusting in her to guide them safely into the presence of God. He invites everyone to join in prayer for those who are dying, as well as for those who are mourning the loss of loved ones. The Pope's final words serve as a reminder that while death remains a mystery, it is not the end. For those who place their faith in Christ, death is a doorway to eternal life—a moment of encounter with the God who has conquered the grave.

Homily Analysis: Embracing Death with Faith, Dignity, and Compassion

The Fear of Death in Contemporary Society: A Culture of Denial

In his homily, Pope Francis addresses the modern world's growing discomfort with the reality of death. In contemporary society, death is often seen as an inconvenience—hidden away in hospitals and nursing homes, sanitized by medical advancements, and softened by euphemisms. Rather than being accepted as a natural part of life, death is often seen as a failure—something to be avoided at all costs. The Pope challenges this denial, reminding us that no amount of wealth, power, or medical technology can prevent the inevitable.

The COVID-19 pandemic forced death back into public consciousness, making it impossible to ignore. Many people witnessed the heartbreaking reality of dying alone, unable to say farewell to loved ones. Pope Francis highlights the heartbreaking stories of those who longed for human connection in their final moments. He praises simple acts of compassion—such as a nurse using a mobile phone to grant a dying patient one last conversation with their family. These stories serve as reminders that, despite all efforts to prolong life, death remains a deeply personal and communal experience that demands dignity, presence, and care.

The Pope warns against a culture that pushes death to the margins. Instead of pretending it does not exist, he calls for a renewed understanding of mortality—one that embraces death with faith, recognizing it as a transition rather than an end. In his homily, the Pope urges people to reflect on difficult but essential questions:

- Are we truly prepared for death?
- Have we made peace with our mortality?
- How do we accompany others in their final moments?

The Christian Response to Death: Resurrection as the Foundation of Hope

At the heart of Pope Francis' message is the Christian understanding of death. While secular culture often views death as the ultimate loss, the Christian faith proclaims it as a passage into eternal life. Drawing from Saint Paul's writings, the Pope emphasizes that belief in Christ's resurrection is central to Christianity. If Christ has not been raised, as Paul warns, then faith is in vain.

This theological truth reshapes how Christians should approach death. Rather than being paralyzed by fear, believers are called to trust in the promise of resurrection. Death is not an unknown abyss but a doorway to something greater. This faith does not erase grief and sorrow; instead, it gives the strength to face death with courage.

However, the Pope does not passively present this hope. He challenges Christians to live in a manner that reflects their faith in resurrection. If we truly believe that death is not the end, then our lives should reflect a focus on what is eternal rather than temporary. This means valuing relationships over possessions, choosing reconciliation over resentment, and prioritizing love over material gain.

His famous remark, "I have never seen a hearse followed by a moving van," humorously but profoundly underscores this point. Accumulating wealth, chasing status, or holding onto grudges is meaningless when faced with death. What truly matters is how we have loved, how we have lived, and how we have prepared for eternity.

The Ethics of Death: Euthanasia, Assisted Suicide, and the Treatment of the Elderly

One of the most urgent moral concerns raised by Pope Francis is society's approach to the elderly, the sick, and the dying. He strongly condemns what he describes as a growing trend of viewing the elderly as disposable. In many parts of the world, aging populations are often viewed as burdens—financially, socially, and medically. Some healthcare systems prioritize younger, more "productive" individuals, leaving the elderly with limited options for care.

The Pope warns that this mindset is not only unethical but profoundly inhumane. He condemns a society that seeks to "accelerate" the death of the elderly by withholding essential treatment or neglecting their needs. He describes this as a hidden but very real form of euthanasia—one that does not necessarily involve direct action but rather a slow and passive disregard for those who can no longer contribute economically.

In contrast, he emphasizes the importance of palliative care, which focuses on providing comfort and dignity to the dying rather than hastening their death. He insists that life is always a right, while death is something to be accepted naturally, not administered artificially. His words serve as a strong rejection of euthanasia and assisted suicide, both of which have become increasingly accepted in some societies under the guise of personal choice.

The Pope's ethical stance is grounded in the belief that every human being possesses inherent dignity, regardless of age, health, or economic productivity. He reminds us that the elderly are not burdens but bearers of wisdom and history. Rather than isolating them, we should honor and care for them, ensuring they feel valued and loved.

This message is particularly relevant in light of the increasing legalization of assisted suicide in various countries. Pope Francis' warning serves as a challenge to reconsider the moral implications of allowing society to decide when a life is "no longer worth living." Instead of offering death as a solution, he calls for a renewed commitment to compassion, presence, and ethical care for the dying.

The Call to Reconciliation: Preparing for Death with a Peaceful Heart

A particularly moving aspect of the homily is the Pope's emphasis on the importance of reconciliation before death. He urges people not to wait until their final moments to seek forgiveness or mend broken relationships. Death has a way of putting life into perspective—resentments that once seemed significant suddenly feel trivial when faced with mortality.

Pope Francis urges people to release anger, pride, and division. He invites them to reflect: What is the point of holding onto grudges when, in the end, we all share the same fate? He calls for a life of peace—peace with oneself, peace with others, and peace with God.

This message is especially relevant in a world where conflicts—both personal and global—persist. Family divisions, workplace rivalries, political hostilities, and social tensions all contribute to a culture of resentment and unforgiveness. The Pope reminds us that death will come for all, and when it does, it is far better to meet it with a heart that is reconciled rather than one weighed down by anger and regrets.

This is an invitation to reflect on our relationships:

- Have we forgiven those who hurt us?
- Have we asked for forgiveness from those we have wronged?
- Have we expressed love to those who matter most?

The Pope's words encourage a proactive approach to reconciliation, urging us to resolve conflicts now rather than wait until it is too late.

Mary and Saint Joseph: Models of a Good Death

Pope Francis concludes his homily by invoking the intercession of Mary and Saint Joseph. In Catholic tradition, Saint Joseph is honored as the patron of a good death, as he is believed to have passed away in the presence of Jesus and Mary. His death was not marked by fear but by faith, love, and the comforting presence of those dearest to him.

This image stands in stark contrast to the way many people die today—alone in hospitals, separated from family, or in fear of what lies ahead. The Pope calls for a renewed understanding of death as an experience of divine mercy. Just as Mary and Jesus accompanied Joseph, so too should we accompany the dying with compassion and faith.

The tradition of praying for a good death, as seen in the Hail Mary's plea, "pray for us sinners, now and at the hour of our death," highlights the importance of spiritual preparation. The Pope's words encourage believers to cultivate a life of faith so that when death does come, they can face it with the same trust and surrender as Saint Joseph.

A Call to Live Well in the Face of Death

Pope Francis' homily is more than a meditation on death—it is a call to live differently. He challenges a world that refuses to face death's reality and urges people to embrace it with faith, hope, and dignity. His words offer a profound countercultural message: rather than fearing death, we should use it as a guide to live more meaningfully.

By shifting focus from material accumulation to love, from fear to faith, and from division to reconciliation, he presents a vision of life that is truly prepared for death.

His homily is a powerful reminder that the best way to die well is to live well—by prioritizing relationships, embracing faith, and ensuring that, when the time comes, we meet death not with fear but with peace.

Death, Dignity, and Faith in Modern Life

Death is the great equalizer—an inevitable reality that no wealth, power, or status can evade. Yet modern society does everything possible to ignore, sanitize, or push it into the background. In his homily, Pope Francis challenges this avoidance, urging us to face death with faith, dignity, and wisdom. Rather than seeing death as something to fear or avoid, he encourages us to reflect on its meaning and use that awareness to shape how we live.

Facing Mortality with Honesty and Courage: A Society in Denial

The modern world is built on the illusion of permanence. Society celebrates youth, innovation, and progress, but it rarely makes space for discussions about aging and death. Anti-aging treatments, technological advancements, and the pursuit of medical breakthroughs create the sense that death is something we can delay indefinitely, if not defeat altogether.

However, moments of crisis—such as the COVID-19 pandemic—shatter this illusion. The pandemic was a stark reminder that life is fragile, that circumstances can change in an instant, and that death remains beyond human control. Many families were unprepared to say goodbye to their loved ones, and many individuals faced their mortality for the first time in a truly visceral way.

Yet, despite this reminder, there is still a tendency to push the thought of death aside. People avoid discussions about end-of-life care, delay writing wills, and neglect spiritual preparation. Ignoring death does not make it any less real. Reflecting on mortality is not about living in fear; rather, it is about living with greater intention and wisdom.

A man diagnosed with terminal cancer initially falls into despair, but he soon realizes that he has been given a unique gift—clarity. Aware that his time is limited, he no longer wastes energy on trivial concerns but instead focuses on what truly matters. He mends broken relationships, cherishes time with loved ones, and deepens his faith. His impending death does not paralyze him—it frees him.

The challenge for all of us is to adopt this mindset *before* a crisis forces us to do so. Why wait until time is running out to live fully?

Valuing People Over Possessions: The Empty Promises of Consumerism

One of the most powerful reminders in Pope Francis' homily is that no one takes material wealth with them when they die. No amount of money, property, or possessions can follow us beyond the grave. This is a truth that is easy to acknowledge intellectually but difficult to live by in a world obsessed with consumerism.

Modern culture relentlessly reinforces the idea that our worth is defined by what we own. Advertisements promise happiness through the latest gadgets, luxury brands, and bigger homes. Social media intensifies comparisons, making people feel as though they are falling behind unless they are constantly upgrading their lifestyle. Many sacrifice relationships, personal well-being, and even ethical principles in the pursuit of wealth.

When death comes, none of these matter. What matters is how we love, how we treat others and the legacy of kindness we leave behind.

A wealthy businessman devotes his life to chasing financial success, convinced that money will bring lasting happiness. Yet, on his deathbed, he realizes he has neglected his family and is left without meaningful relationships. Meanwhile, another person who lived but gave generously is surrounded by loved ones in their final moments. Who truly lived a richer life?

This reflection challenges us to reassess our priorities.

- Are we so consumed by financial success that we neglect our relationships?
- Are we investing in people rather than possessions?

If we truly embraced the reality of death, we would focus less on material accumulation and more on love, generosity, and community.

Reconciling Before It's Too Late: Letting Go of Grudges

Many people carry resentment for years, refusing to forgive or seek reconciliation. Pope Francis urges us to ask: What is the point of holding onto anger when we will all face death one day?

Modern life is rife with conflict—family disputes, workplace tensions, and political divisions. Social media amplifies outrage, making it easier to attack than to understand. Yet, in the face of death, these conflicts lose all meaning. What will truly matter is whether we live with love and forgiveness.

Two brothers have not spoken in years due to a misunderstanding. When one becomes critically ill, the other finally visits, realizing how much time was lost to resentment. They reconcile—but how much richer life would have been if they had done so sooner?

This reflection calls us to let go of pride and take the first step toward healing broken relationships. Reconciliation should not be postponed until a crisis forces it upon us.

The Treatment of the Elderly: A Test of Our Humanity

Pope Francis condemns the neglect of the elderly in modern society. In many places, seniors are isolated, placed in care homes, and forgotten or denied medical treatment because they are no longer seen as "productive." Some health systems subtly prioritize the young over the old, creating a culture where aging is viewed as a burden.

This is a test of our humanity. How we treat the elderly reflects what we truly value. If we discard those who can no longer contribute economically, we fail to recognize their inherent worth as human beings.

In some cultures, the elderly are honored and respected, living within multigenerational homes where their wisdom is valued. In contrast, in other parts of the world, loneliness and depression among seniors are at an all-time high. Which approach reflects true human dignity?

This reflection challenges us to reconsider how we care for our elders.

- Do we visit them?
- Do we listen to their stories?
- Do we ensure they feel valued?

Preparing Spiritually for Death: The Role of Faith

Many people prepare for retirement but not for death. They plan financially for the future but neglect to prepare spiritually for the inevitable. Pope Francis reminds us that faith should be at the center of our lives, not just an afterthought when we are facing the end.

A person who has cultivated a deep faith throughout life faces death with peace, trusting in God's promises. Another, who ignored spiritual matters, faces death with fear and uncertainty. The difference is profound.

Are we preparing not just for financial security but for our spiritual journey into eternity?

Living with Purpose in the Face of Death

Pope Francis' homily is not just about death—it is about how we live. By facing mortality with faith, valuing people over possessions, seeking reconciliation, caring for the elderly, defending human dignity, and preparing spiritually, we reshape our perspective on life itself.

Death is inevitable, but fear is not. When we live with purpose, love, and faith, we can face our final moments with peace, knowing that we have lived well.

The question remains:

- Are we truly ready—not just to die, but to live in a way that makes death a transition rather than an end?

This is the challenge Pope Francis presents to us: Do not wait until it is too late to change. Love deeply. Forgive freely. Serve others. Prepare for eternity. Only then can we truly say we have lived.

Reflection Questions on Living with Purpose: Embracing Life in the Face of Death

1. If I were to die tomorrow, what would I regret the most?

Modern life is fast paced, often leaving little room for reflection. Many people become consumed by career ambitions, material pursuits, or social pressures, only to realize too late that they have neglected what truly matters. If today were your last day, what would you wish you had done differently?

- Would you regret not telling someone you love them?
- Would you wish you had spent more time with family instead of chasing promotions?
- Would you wish you had given more to others instead of accumulating wealth?

Reflecting on these questions helps reframe daily decisions to align with what holds meaning.

2. Have I made peace with the people in my life?

Holding onto grudges, anger, and unresolved conflicts can poison relationships. In an age of social media outrage and political division, many people prioritize winning arguments over maintaining relationships. But at the end of life, none of these disputes will matter.

Is there someone you need to reconcile with? Are there old wounds that need healing? Imagine facing death with unresolved bitterness—would it have been worth it? Seeking peace now rather than later allows us to live and die without regrets.

3. Am I prioritizing people over possessions?

Consumer culture tells us that happiness comes from acquiring more—better cars, bigger houses, and the latest technology. Yet, when death approaches, material wealth loses all meaning. What truly endures is the love and relationships we have nurtured.

Do you measure success by what you own or by the depth of your relationships?

- Are you sacrificing family time in pursuit of financial gain?
- Do you prioritize accumulating possessions over helping those in need?

Taking a moment to reflect on these questions can help realign your priorities toward a more fulfilling and meaningful life.

4. How do I treat the elderly in my family and community?

Society often relegates the elderly to the margins, viewing them as burdens rather than as reservoirs of wisdom and experience. Too many seniors spend their final years in solitude, longing for visits that never come.

- Do you make time for elderly family members?
- Do you engage in meaningful conversations with them, seeking their wisdom?
- Are you advocating for better care for the aging population?

How we treat the elderly is a reflection of our values.

5. What is my attitude toward suffering?

Modern medicine and technology strive to eliminate suffering, but suffering is an unavoidable part of life. The temptation to escape it through assisted suicide or euthanasia is growing, but Pope Francis warns against treating death as a solution to suffering.

- Do you see suffering as meaningless, or do you believe it can have a purpose?

- When facing challenges, do you seek deeper meaning, or do you try to avoid pain at all costs?

Reflecting on suffering can help cultivate resilience and a deeper trust in God's plan.

6. Am I preparing spiritually for death, or am I avoiding the topic?

Many people plan for retirement but not for death. They focus on financial security but neglect spiritual preparation. Death is not just an end—it is a transition.

- Are you regularly engaging in prayer, confession, and spiritual reflection?
- Are you deepening your relationship with God, or are you delaying faith until a crisis forces you to confront it?
- What legacy of faith will you leave behind?

Taking time now to prepare spiritually allows for a peaceful, grace-filled death.

7. How do I spend my time, and does it reflect my values?

Many people waste time on distractions—mindless scrolling through social media, binge-watching TV, or obsessing over things that won't matter in the long run. Time is the one resource we can never get back.

- Are you spending your time in alignment with your deepest values?

- Are you investing in relationships, service, and personal growth or allowing trivial concerns to drain your energy?

Being mindful of how you use your time ensures that life is lived with intention rather than passively.

8. What legacy am I leaving behind?

Everyone leaves a legacy, whether they realize it or not. Some people leave behind wealth, but others leave behind love, wisdom, and acts of kindness.

- What kind of person do you want to be remembered as?
- Will people say that you were generous, kind, and faithful?
- Or will they remember a life consumed by personal ambition?

Reflecting on this question helps shape a life worth remembering.

9. Do I see death as an end or as a transition to eternal life?

Many people fear death because they see it as the end. But faith teaches that death is not an annihilation; it is a passage into eternal life.

- How do you view death?

- Do you live in fear of it, or do you trust in God's promise of resurrection?
- Are you nurturing your faith so that when death comes, you are ready to embrace it with hope rather than fear?

Strengthening faith in eternal life transforms how we live today.

10. If I had one final message to share with the world, what would it be?

Imagine you had one last chance to speak to your loved ones, to share your wisdom, your faith, and your love. What would you say?

- Would you encourage them to live with compassion?
- Would you remind them to trust in God?
- Would you express gratitude for the life you've been given?

Writing down a final message now—before facing death—helps clarify what truly matters and can serve as a guiding principle for how to live each day.

These reflection questions are not intended to be morbid but to awaken us to the beauty of life. Embracing the reality of death allows us to live with greater purpose, deeper love, and stronger faith.

Pope Francis' homily challenges us not just to prepare for death but to live in a way that makes death a transition rather than an end. By valuing people over possessions, reconciling with those we have wronged, caring for the elderly, preparing spiritually, and prioritizing faith, we can ensure that when our time comes, we will face death not with fear but with peace.

The real question is: How will you live today so that when death comes, you will have no regrets?

Chapter 16

Final Thoughts: Embracing the Journey of a Life Rooted in Faith, Love, and Trust

Finding Meaning in Our Struggles

Life is a series of highs and lows, victories and defeats, joys and sorrows. Many of us experience seasons of life where we feel abandoned, haunted by regret, burdened by fractured relationships, and blinded by fear. In these moments, it's natural to question the purpose of suffering, wonder why hardships arise, and feel overwhelmed by the weight we carry.

Yet, if there is one resounding truth found in the teachings of Christ and echoed in these pages, it is this: suffering is not meaningless. Every struggle, heartbreak, and challenge hold the power to shape us, refine us, and draw us closer to God. The trials we face are not meant to break us but to strengthen our faith until it becomes unshakable.

Consider the stories of the saints, the disciples, and even Christ Himself. None of them lived lives free of suffering. Yet, they embraced their struggles with faith, using them as a means of drawing nearer to God. When viewed through the lens of faith, suffering is not an end; it is a passageway to transformation. It teaches us patience, deepens our compassion, and reminds us of our dependence on God's grace.

The question, then, is not *if* we will face hardship but *how* we will respond to it.

- Will we allow suffering to harden our hearts, filling us with anger and despair?
- Or will we let it refine us, teaching us perseverance, wisdom, and faith?

Every difficulty we face is an opportunity—an invitation to grow in faith and to trust that God is working, even in silence.

Choosing Faith Over Fear

One of the greatest struggles in the human experience is the tension between faith and fear. Fear is often the first response to uncertainty, failure, and loss. It is the voice that tells us we are alone, that we are not enough, that we cannot trust God's plan. It paralyzes us, keeping us from taking risks, from loving deeply, and from surrendering control.

Faith tells a different story. Faith reminds us that we are never alone, that God's love is greater than our failures, and that true peace is not found in avoiding pain but in trusting God through it. Faith calls us to step forward even when the road is unclear, to believe in God's goodness even when we cannot see the outcome, and to surrender our anxieties to the One who holds all things in His hands. Think of Peter walking on water toward Jesus. As long as his eyes were fixed on Christ, he did the impossible. But the moment he let fear take over, he began to sink.

The same is true for us. When we fixate on our problems, our fears, and our weaknesses, we lose sight of God's power. When we choose faith and keep our eyes on Christ, we discover a strength we never knew we had.

This is the choice we face daily:

- Will we let fear control our lives, or will we walk in faith, trusting that God is with us every step of the way?

The Power of Love and Forgiveness

If there is one lesson that stands above all others, it is this: love and forgiveness have the power to heal, restore, and transform. Love is not just a feeling; it is a decision, an action, a commitment. It is what binds families together, what mends broken relationships, and what gives meaning to our existence.

Love is also costly. It requires vulnerability. It asks us to put others before ourselves. It calls us to forgive, even when it is difficult.

Forgiveness, in particular, is one of the hardest yet most freeing choices we can make. In a world that encourages revenge, nurtures grudges, and defines people by their worst moments, Christ offers a different path. He calls us to release bitterness, let go of resentment, and extend the same mercy we have received.

This is not to say that forgiveness is easy. It is a process, often requiring time and healing, but it is always worth it. Forgiveness does not mean excusing wrongdoing or forgetting the pain inflicted. Instead, it is a choice to no longer be held captive by the hurt. It is choosing freedom over bitterness.

Think of the story of the Prodigal Son (*Luke 15:11-32*). The father does not hold onto resentment or demand repayment. He welcomes his son home with open arms. That is the love of God—a love that does not keep score, which does not withhold grace, but that embraces and restores.

- How different would our relationships look if we chose to love and forgive in this way?

Living with Purpose and Hope

As we move forward from this book, the most important question remains:

- How will we live?
- Will the lessons we have encountered remain words on a page, or will they take root in our hearts?

Each of us has a purpose. We are not here by accident. Our experiences—both joyful and painful—shape us into who we were meant to be.

No matter where you've been, what mistakes you've made, or what burdens you carry, there is always hope. Each new day offers a chance to love more deeply, trust more fully, and live with greater faith.

Consider the many people who came before us— saints, prophets, and ordinary believers who, despite their struggles, chose to live with faith and love. Their stories remind us that holiness is not reserved for a select few but is available to all who seek it.

God continually calls us forward, inviting us into a deeper relationship with Him. The question are:

- Will we answer?

- Will we cling to old fears, regrets, and wounds, or will we step into the life He has prepared for us?

Final Thoughts

This is not the end. It is an invitation to begin again—to embrace a life of faith, to love boldly, to trust completely. It is an invitation to recognize the sacred in the ordinary, to see every challenge as an opportunity for growth, and to walk forward with the confidence that God is with us.

The journey of faith is not always easy. There will be struggles, moments of doubt, and times when the path ahead seems unclear. We are not alone. God walks with us. He strengthens us when we are weak, comforts us when we are broken, and calls us forward when we are afraid.

So, step forward—not in fear, but in faith. Move ahead with confidence, knowing your story is still being written and that, with God, the best is yet to come.

_About the Author

Daryl Lim is a writer, speaker, and business owner with a deep passion for faith, leadership, and personal transformation. He served as a catechist for a decade, guiding young Catholics in their spiritual formation and deepening his understanding of Scripture and Church teachings. Beyond his ministry, Daryl has built a successful career as an entrepreneur, bringing the same values of integrity, resilience, and service into his business ventures. His experiences in both faith and business have given him a unique perspective on navigating life's challenges with wisdom and purpose. Inspired by the teachings of Pope Francis, Daryl chose to focus on his homilies and messages due to the Pope's emphasis on mercy, compassion, and faith in action. Pope Francis' call for a more inclusive and loving Church, his advocacy for social justice, and his ability to connect faith with real-world challenges resonated deeply with Daryl's own experiences.

Through *The Light of Faith*, he seeks to make these teachings more accessible and relatable, helping readers find clarity, strength, and a deeper relationship with God in the complexities of daily life. He currently resides in Singapore, where he continues to explore the intersection of faith, leadership, and business.

Daryl can be reached at thelightoffaithbook@gmail.com

THE LIGHT OF FAITH

Dear Reader,

Thank you for taking the time to read my book on the Homily and the Pope. I hope you found it insightful, enriching, and perhaps even thought-provoking. My goal was to explore this important topic in a way that deepens understanding and inspires reflection.

If you enjoyed the book (or even if you have constructive feedback), I would truly appreciate it if you could take a moment to leave an honest review on Amazon. Your thoughts not only help other readers discover the book but also support authors in continuing to share their work.

Once again, I sincerely appreciate your time and support. Thank you for being a part of this journey with me!

With gratitude,

Daryl

Daryl Lim

www.ingramcontent.com/pod-product-compliance
Lightning Source LLC
Chambersburg PA
CBHW072337090426
42741CB00012B/2820